ABOLITION
FOR THE PEOPLE

ABOL
FOR THE

THE MOVEMENT FOR A FUTURE

KAEPERNICK
PUBLISHING

ITION
PEOPLE

WITHOUT POLICING & PRISONS

Edited by

Colin Kaepernick

ABOUT THE COVER

The cover art for Abolition for the People *was produced in collaboration with Emory Douglas, the revolutionary artist and former Black Panther Party Minister of Culture. An adaptation of Douglas's iconic 1969 "Paper Boy" print and his 2018 "Paper Girl" illustration, this artwork depicts a youthful, confident, and courageous Black feminine-presenting person announcing the call for abolition.*

This representational choice reflects our uncompromising commitment to honoring the centrality of Black women, trans, and gender non-conforming folx as leaders and luminaries of the abolition movement. It furthermore pays homage to the work of Emory Douglas and the Black Panther Party's historic demand for "an immediate end to POLICE BRUTALITY and the MURDER of Black people."

Revolutionary art has the power to bridge the past and the present. It has the power to move us to build a future that is safer, healthier, and truly free.

—The Editors, Kaepernick Publishing

COVER IMAGE DESCRIPTION

The cover art for Abolition for the People *is an illustration of a young, confident, and courageous Black feminine-presenting person announcing the call for abolition. The figure is superimposed against a background of alternating yellow and cream sun rays radiating from behind them. They are holding a full-length newspaper in one hand that reads "Abolish the Police!" "Close the Prisons!" and a folded newspaper in the other that reads "Over 30 Voices for the People." They are wearing a turquoise shirt emblazoned with black flower silhouettes, a cowrie shell in their hair, hoop earrings, and mauve lipstick that matches their nail polish. They are wearing a peace sign pin on their shirt and are holding a cell phone with a pink case in the same hand as the folded paper.*

Contents

Prisons & Carcerality

Fuck Reform

Abolition Now

A Journey to Safer Futures

By Colin Kaepernick,
Connie Wun, *and* Christopher Petrella

W elcome! We're appreciative that *Abolition for the People* has found its way to you and we're humbled that you've chosen to join us on this collective learning journey. We've made every effort to ensure that the book before you is useful and that it inspires you to take action to build a world without and beyond police and prisons.

Abolition for the People draws on historical analysis, empirical data, and the firsthand accounts of survivors of interpersonal and state-sanctioned white-supremacist, anti-Black, and hetero-patriarchal violence in the form of the carceral state to make a straightforward argument: Neither prisons nor police keep people safe, nor do they create the conditions necessary for communities to thrive. *Abolition for the People* further argues that efforts to reform police and prisons have nearly always enhanced their power, reach, and legitimacy. Simply stated, police and prisons—including the anti-Black ideologies that have created and sustained them—are death-making machines that run counter to harm reduction and the possibility of authentic human flourishing.

Our hope is that *Abolition for the People* will support and amplify collective efforts, as contributor Mariame Kaba writes, to "build a society where it is possible to address harm without relying on structural forms of oppression or the violent systems that increase it."

Conceived as a comprehensive introduction to abolitionist concepts, principles, practices, histories, and ways of relating to one another and the world, *Abolition for the People* builds on decades of organizing and writing against police and prisons. As contributor Naomi Murakawa notes, "Abolitionist lineages run deep." From the proto-abolitionist Journey of Reconciliation and "We Charge Genocide," to the Black Panthers, the Young Lords, and queer liberation movements to the Prison Moratorium Project, Critical Resistance and INCITE!, to BYP100, Dream Defenders, and the National Council for Incarcerated and Formerly Incarcerated Women and Girls, Black, Indigenous, and people of color organizers—often underresourced and underprotected—have been courageously working with conviction to create safer futures without and beyond prisons and policing.

While you might already agree that police and prisons do not make communities safer, you may still have important questions, such as, "What is abolition?" "Is abolition practical?" and "What does abolition look like in the real world?"

Mariame Kaba argues that prison industrial complex (PIC) abolition is an everyday practice constitutive of three essential components: "a political vision, a structural analysis of oppression, and a practical organizing strategy" centered on building a restructured society "where we have everything we need: food, shelter, education, health, art, beauty, clean water, and more. Things that are foundational to our personal and community safety." But what does this really mean? It means that putting abolitionist visions, analyses, and organizing into practice requires us to dream big and broadly, learn (and unlearn) how our histories have been asymmetrically shaped by the violence of carceral power, and build together in humility under an expanding vision of humanity that extends to *all* people.

"Abolition," contributor Dylan Rodríguez has written, is "the work of constantly remaking sociality, politics, economy, place, and (human) being against the duress that some call dehumanization, others name colonialism, and still others identify as slavery and incarceration."[1] And it is precisely in this context that *Abolition for the People* was born.

We began this project in the wake of the spring 2020 anti-Black, state-sanctioned lynchings of Breonna Taylor and George Floyd at a time when increasingly broad swaths of the US public were yearning for ways to uproot the devastation of policing and incarceration.

By early June—and particularly in the aftermath of George Floyd's *public* execution—we grew increasingly concerned that arguments centering a "few bad apples" as the basis of police violence predictably began to (re)monopolize mainstream discourse.

This centuries-old "few bad apples" framing—one that collapses a systems-based analysis into individual behaviorist approaches to intervention—helped to grease the wheels of public support for the reformist policy recommendations to follow: banning chokeholds and establishing a "use of force continuum" and de-escalation protocols, among others.

Not only does *Abolition for the People* serve as a rejoinder to such reformist discourses and interventions—interventions Dylan Rodríguez describes as "casualty management"—but it also provides a blueprint and vision for creating better and non-punitive ways of being together in the world.

In October 2020, we published the first iteration of *Abolition for the People* as a digital collection in partnership with Medium. This book expands significantly on our original efforts and includes three new essays, a reader's guide, a new introduction, many expanded contributions with new content, and new infographics drawn from six in-depth data stories.

As you will soon see, *Abolition for the People* is divided into four sections: I) Police & Policing, II) Prisons & Carcerality, III) Fuck Reform, and IV) Abolition Now. Parts I and II will guide you through the anti-Black foundations and histories of policing and prisons in the United States. Parts III and IV will argue against the fetishism of police and prison reform and will lay out a vision and blueprint for abolitionist organizing, respectively.

* * *

This book brings together thirty-two essays representing a broad array of voices and experiences, including political prisoners, grassroots and formerly incarcerated community organizers, scholars, and family members of those killed by the anti-Black terrorism of policing and prisons. Their experiences and analyses provide us with frameworks to better understand the violences of prisons and policing. Ultimately, we believe that *Abolition for the People* will present you with a moral choice: Will you remain actively complicit in the perpetuation of these systems or will you take action to dismantle them for the benefit of a just future?

The complexity of abolitionist concepts and the enormity of the task at hand can be daunting. To accompany you on your journey toward a greater understanding of abolitionist content, each essay in this collection is followed by a reader's guide that will help you to assess your comprehension of the material, sharpen your critical analysis, and contextualize your own lived experiences within the arguments of the text.

You won't find all the answers here, but we believe you will find useful and provocative questions—questions that can open up radical possibilities for a future where all communities can thrive.

Our hope is that you will consider using this book as an organizing tool and curricular resource for furthering the development of your and your community's political education.

Like us, we hope you find inspiration in the words of political prisoner and contributor, Mumia Abu-Jamal. "Prison abolitionists are today's freedom dreamers who seek to expand the experience of liberty for all," he writes. "[Abolitionists] posit that if we build society anew to meet the human needs of education, health care, housing, meaningful and well-remunerated employment, and community togetherness and cohesion, many of the challenges historically oppressed and ex-ploited communities face today will dissipate."

Mumia Abu-Jamal is right, of course. This is the world we're actively building together—a world where abolition is a verb. A world where abolition is understood, as Mariame Kaba has said, "not just as a horizon we'll arrive at some day" but rather as a world that's "constantly being made."[2] *Abolition for the People* represents our modest contribution to forging such a world in the yet unclaimed possibilities of the present.

We look forward to building a new world with you. ◭

Colin Kaepernick
Connie Wun
Christopher Petrella

March 2021

Believe in
New Possibilities

By Angela Y. Davis

M ovements against racist police violence and against entrenched racial injustices in this country's jails and prisons can claim a history that is almost as old as the institutions themselves. Precisely because opposition and protests calling for reform have played such a central role in shaping structures of policing and punishment, the notion of reform has superseded other paths toward change. Ironically, many efforts to change these repressive structures—to reform them—have instead provided the glue that has guaranteed their continued presence and acceptance.

Both policing and punishment are firmly rooted in racism—attempts to control Indigenous, Black, and Latino populations following colonization and slavery, as well as Asian populations after the Chinese Exclusion Act and the World War II incarceration of Japanese Americans. Attempting to undo the harm of policing and prisons without attending to these immense embodiments of systemic racism is doomed to failure. The twentieth-century militarization of the police has been further intensified by Islamophobia. More generally, the evolution and expansion of the police and the prisons are constant reminders that capitalism has always fundamentally relied on racism to sustain itself.

The insight that racism is essentially systemic and structural rather than individual and attitudinal—one repeatedly asserted by health-care advocates and anti-police and anti-prison activists over many decades—finally entered mainstream discourse in 2020 under the pressure of COVID-19 and its disproportionate impact on Black and Brown communities. Its most popular expression in the slogan "Defund the Police" was disseminated during the mass mobilizations protesting the police lynching of George Floyd in May 2020.

For those who recognize the deeply conservative repercussions of equating "reform" with change, the call to defund the police manifested an abolitionist impulse to eschew the usual calls for punishing individual police officers and instituting some form of civilian overview of the department. Instead of habitual and perfunctory calls for "reform," organizers began to think more deeply about pathways toward more radical change—in other words, change that would begin to respond to some of the root causes of why poor communities, and especially communities of color, are particularly vulnerable to the criminal legal system.

But for others it had a jarring effect, conjuring up images of chaotic, crime-ridden (Black and Brown) communities, with no force in place to guarantee order. Some people, who live in so-called high-crime neighborhoods[1] where they are preyed upon not only by the police, but also by armed individuals and groups from their own communities, and for whom the demand to defund the police was their first introduction to abolitionist ideas, were understandably bewildered. How would they survive at the mercy of malevolent groups who hardly care about the trajectory of stray bullets that have taken the lives of children and other bystanders? Their fears are real and not to be dismissed. But this is absolutely the moment to engage in the kind of educational activism that might help to encourage all of us, especially those of us who live in the most vulnerable neighborhoods, to purposefully rethink the meaning of safety and security.

Educators, organizers, artists, athletes, intellectuals—everyday people—can play a major role in introducing ways of imagining the future that are not tethered to the notion that only the police can be effective guarantors of safety or that prisons alone can assure the security of people who populate the "free" world. Anti-racist feminists have long argued that relying on conventional policing and carceral strategies exacerbates gender violence rather than eliminating it.[2] But carceral feminism, a notion that calls for the buildup of police and prisons, still dominates the mainstream. Though some education activists have challenged carceral feminism by demanding the removal of police from schools and an end to the school-to-prison pipeline, we have not yet achieved a consensus in understanding that a police presence in public schools corrupts the educational process. Police are so deeply entrenched in public schools in Black and Brown communities that their oppressive modes of discipline infect learning itself.

Security is not possible as long as the physical, mental, and spiritual health of our communities is ignored. Armed human beings, officially trained in efficient methods of administering death and violence, should not be dispatched in response to a Black woman experiencing an episode related to a psychiatric disability. She may not only not receive help, but her behavior may well be used as a pretext to kill her. Safety and security require education, housing, jobs, art, music, and recreation. If the funds currently directed toward these institutions— police departments, Immigration and Customs Enforcement (ICE), jails, prisons, and immigrant-detention facilities—were rerouted toward the public good, the need and justification for steadily expanding institutions of state violence would certainly decline. Abolitionist approaches ask us to enlarge our field of vision so that rather than focusing myopically on the problematic institution and asking what needs to be changed about that institution, we raise radical questions about the organization of the larger society.

For those who recognize that racism feeds the proliferation of police violence and the decades-old surge of prison populations but who still insist that these institutions are simply in need of deliberate reform, it might be helpful to reflect on the fact that similar logic was used about slavery. Just as there are those who want change today but fear that these institutions are so necessary to human society that social organization would collapse without them, there were those who believed that the cruelty of the "peculiar institution" was not inherent to slavery and could indeed be eradicated by reform.

Just as we hear calls today for more humane policing, people then called for a more humane slavery. Abolition—of slavery, the death penalty, prisons, police—has always been a controversial political demand, not least because it calls attention to the fact that simply reforming specific institutions without changing their foundational elements may reproduce and perhaps even exacerbate the problems reform seeks to solve.

The language of abolition evokes historical continuity. While most anti-slavery abolitionists simply wanted to get rid of slavery, there were those who did recognize early on that slavery could not be comprehensively eradicated simply by disestablishing the institution itself, leaving intact the economic, political, and cultural conditions within which slavery flourished. They understood that abolition would require a thorough reorganization of US society—economically, politically, and socially—in order to guarantee the incorporation of formerly enslaved Black people into a new democratic order. That process never occurred, and we are facing issues of systemic and structural racism today that should have been addressed more than one hundred years ago.

In the meantime, racial capitalism has become far more complicated.[3] For example, the task of solving problems rooted in colonialism and slavery requires us to recognize how the carceral system and anti-Black racism are linked to repressive border policing and detention directed at Latino communities and other immigrant communities. When we say "Defund the Police," we should also call for the abolition of ICE. And we should always keep in mind that our predicament is shared by people in many parts of the world, from Brazil and Palestine to France and South Africa.

Abolitionist strategies are especially critical because they teach us that our visions of the future can radically depart from what exists in the present. Just as trans activists have been partially successful in encouraging us to abandon the conventional gender binary—and to comprehend its structural role in defining policing and imprisonment—this current conjuncture demands that we believe in new possibilities. Such new possibilities would include rewarding jobs, critical education, decent housing, accessible health care, recreation, and art for all. It also demands that we conduct ourselves on our campuses, in our sports arenas, and in our political struggles, cultural work, and intimate lives as individuals and communities worthy of racial, gender, and economic equality—and worthy of radical, socialist futures. ◪

READER'S GUIDE

- Referring to prisons and policing, Angela Y. Davis writes, "Ironically, many efforts to change these repressive structures—to reform them—have instead provided the glue that has guaranteed their continued presence and acceptance." Please list three to four examples that come to mind.

- The author argues that in order for abolition to be successful it must not only be pursued in the United States but also globally. What are some examples the author draws upon to support this argument?

- The author writes, "Both policing and punishment are firmly rooted in racism—attempts to control Indigenous, Black, and Latino populations following colonization and slavery as well as Asian populations after the Chinese Exclusion Act and the World War II incarceration of Japanese Americans. Attempting to undo the harm of policing and prisons without attending to these immense embodiments of systemic racism is doomed to failure." Why do you think attempts to reform prisons and policing rarely, if ever, "attend to the embodiments of systemic racism"?

- The author writes, "Just as we hear calls today for more humane policing, people then called for a more humane slavery. Abolition—of slavery, the death penalty, prisons, police—has always been a controversial political demand, not least because it calls attention to the fact that simply reforming specific institutions without changing their foundational elements may reproduce and perhaps even exacerbate the problems reform seeks to solve." How would you describe the relationship between the US institution of enslavement and the development of police/policing in the US?

A Future Worth Building

By Colin Kaepernick

I n the wake of the state-sanctioned lynchings of Breonna Taylor, George Floyd, and countless others, the United States has been forced to grapple with not only the devastation of police terrorism, but also the institutions that constitute, enhance, and expand the carceral state. In response, movements that demand the defunding of the police have spread across the country with no signs of stopping. Those who have been terrorized by law enforcement, who have had enough of their very existence being criminalized, and who have dedicated their lives to the cause of liberation by any means necessary are demanding the abolition of the carceral state—the institutions, structures, and practices of anti-Black state-sanctioned violence that violate the fundamental humanity of Black and Indigenous people, and people of color.

It's been five years since I first protested during "The Star-Spangled Banner." At the time, my protest was tethered to my understanding that something was not right. I saw the bodies of Black people left dead in the streets. I saw them left dead in their cars. I saw them left dead in their backyards. I saw Black death all around me at the hands of the police. I saw little to no accountability for the police officers who had murdered them. It is not a matter of bad apples spoiling the bunch but interlocking systems that are rotten to their core and are authorized to kill Black people and other communities under the pretense of "justice."

It is only logical that systemic problems demand systemic solutions.

Predictably, the political mainstream has responded to political uprisings by shifting the demands to "defund the police" to reformist interventions centered on "acceptable" modes of enacting death and violence upon oppressed peoples. As such, conventional paths and strategies for achieving "justice" for anti-Black police terror and violence are all too often couched in campaigns and desires for convictions, punishment, and incarceration. These modes of reformist and reactionary "justice" fail to remedy the uninterrupted deaths caused by policing and prisons and frequently leave us disheartened, disjointed, and disillusioned.

Despite the steady cascade of anti-Black violence across this country, I am hopeful we can build a future that imagines justice differently. A future without the terror of policing and prisons. A future that prioritizes harm reduction, redemption, and public well-being in order to create a more just and humane world.

Abolition for the People: The Movement for a Future Without Policing & Prisons builds on a rich tradition of Black organizing and freedom-fighting. This project seeks to introduce abolitionist values, practices, histories, and ambitions to an audience that is looking for a path to a better and more just society.

Organized around four central themes—1) police and policing, 2) prisons and carcerality, 3) fuck reform, and 4) abolition now—this collection includes over thirty essays from political prisoners, grassroots organizers, movement leaders, scholars, and family members of those affected by anti-Black state violence and terrorism.

To understand the necessity and urgency of abolition, we must first understand the genesis and histories of the institutions and practices we must abolish.

*

POLICE & POLICING

The central intent of policing has and continues to be to surveil, terrorize, capture, and kill marginalized populations, specifically Black folks. In her edited collection, *Imprisoned Intellectuals*,[1] Joy James put the United States under the magnifying glass. "The world can see what goes on in the tombs of America as Black people are being slowly strangled and suffocated to death," she writes. When the world witnessed the police choke Eric Garner to death as he gasped, "I can't breathe"—that is an act of terror. When a cop car pulled up to Tamir Rice, a twelve-year-old boy, and the cop shot him in less than two seconds—that is an act of terror. When police broke down ninety-two-year-old Kathryn Johnston's front door, unloaded thirty-nine rounds, and left five bullets buried in her body—that is an act of terror. We recognize this as anti-Black violence and control while law enforcement and the injustice system see it as essential to the very nature of the job.

The political project of anti-Blackness has always been central to the enforcement of laws and legal codes in the United States. Sally E. Hadden's *Slave Patrols: Law and Violence in Virginia and the Carolinas* lays out an irrefutable case that slavery and policing are linked both in logic and philosophy. South Carolina's 1701 "Act for the Better Ordering of Slaves"[2] declared that any enslaved African "resisting" a white person could be beaten (like Rodney King in 1991), maimed (like Jacob Blake in 2020), assaulted (like Marlene Pinnock in 2014), or killed if they "resisted" (like Korryn Gaines in 2016) or took flight (like Rayshard Brooks in 2020).

The more that I have learned about the history and evolution of policing in the United States, the more I understand its roots in white supremacy and anti-Blackness. Black Panther Party co-founder Huey P. Newton once said, "The police are in our community not to promote our welfare or for our security or our safety, but they are there to contain us, to brutalize us, and murder us."[3] The omnipresent threat of premature death at the hands, knees, chokeholds, Tasers, and guns of law enforcement has only further engrained its anti-Black foundation into the institutions of policing. In order to eradicate anti-Blackness, we must also abolish the police. *The abolition of one without the other is impossible.*

*

PRISONS & CARCERALITY

As part of the reentry work I have done with Kevin Livingston from 100 Suits for 100 Men[4] at Rikers Island, I have spent time with young Black men in the facility no older than twenty. The young men explained the prison's dehumanizing conditions that range from denial of literature to physical assault. They have been criminalized and caged, in most cases, for attempting to resist being redlined into economic despair.[5]

Forever emblazoned in my memory are the words of one of the young Black men: "You love us when no one else does." The young brother was seeking love. He was seeking care. He was seeking a space that valued his life. What he received was hate and what abolitionist scholar Ruth Wilson Gilmore would call "organized abandonment."[6]

As Angela Y. Davis has written, "prisons do not disappear problems, they disappear human beings."[7] Prisons do not contain a "criminal population" running rampant but rather a population that society has repeatedly failed.

Uprisings in response to the hellish conditions Black folk have been forced to live in, both in and out of prison, have been criminalized as well. In her book *Are Prisons Obsolete?*, Davis effectively analyzes the purpose of prisons.[8] "These prisons represent the application of sophisticated, modern technology dedicated entirely to the task of social control," she writes, "and they isolate, regulate, and surveil more effectively than anything that has preceded them." An institution based on social control instead of social well-being is an institution that needs to be abolished.

*

FUCK REFORM

I recently revisited the 2016 postgame interview when I was first asked about not standing during "The Star-Spangled Banner." One of the reporters inquired about the reasoning behind my dissent. "There's a lot of things that need to change," I replied. "One specifically is police brutality. There's people being murdered unjustly and not being held accountable. Cops are getting paid leave for killing people. That's not right. That's not right by anyone's standards."[9]

Unconsciously, my critique of police terrorism was fastened to a reformist framework. My want for accountability focused on the cops receiving convictions and punishment, not acquittals and paid vacations. But I had missed the larger picture. The focus on individual punishment will never alter the outcome of a system rooted in Black death. I wanted change. I wanted it to stop. I wanted to reform what I saw. Yet, the reforms often proposed—use-of-force policies, body cameras, more training, and "police accountability"—were the same recycled interventions consistently proposed in the past. And in both the past and the present, these reforms have done nothing to stop the actions that force us to #SayTheirNames.

Similarly, suggested prison reforms—new jail construction to address crowding and dehumanizing living conditions and technological monitoring that essentially creates open-air prisons—have not and cannot eliminate the harm of the carceral state. The thread that ties all of these reforms together is the increased investment of capital into the carceral apparatus. In a recent interview on the geographies of racial capitalism, Ruth Wilson Gilmore said that "capitalism requires inequality, and racism enshrines it."[10] It made me think about the economies of exploitation, deprivation, and captivity that propel forward incarceration and the construction of prisons. These economies disproportionately target Black, Brown, and poor white people. It made me think about how the carceral state is central to the machinery of racial capitalism.

I began to ask myself the question "What is being reformed or re-formulated?"

Ultimately, I realized that seeking reform would make me an active participant in reforming, reshaping, and rebranding institutional white supremacy, oppression, and death. This constant re-interrogation of my own analysis has been part of my political evolution.

"One should recall that the movement for reforming the prisons, for controlling their functioning, is not a recent phenomenon," Michel Foucault wrote in *Discipline & Punish*. "It does not even seem to have originated in a recognition of failure. Prison 'reform' is virtually contemporary with the prison itself: it constitutes, as it were, its programme."[11] Reform, at its core, preserves, enhances, and further entrenches policing and prisons into the United States' social order. Abolition is the only way to secure a future beyond anti-Black institutions of social control, violence, and premature death.

*

ABOLITION NOW!

Abolition is a means to create a future where justice and liberation are fundamental to realizing the full humanity of communities. Practices of abolitionists are focused on harm reduction, public health, and the well-being of people. Demands to defund the police and prisons are one of the ways to first realize the goals of investing in people and divesting from punishment and, in time, progress to the complete abolition of the carceral state, including police and policing.

To be clear, the abolition of these institutions is not the absence of accountability but rather the establishment of transformative and restorative processes that do not depend upon anti-Black institutions rooted in punitive practices. By abolishing policing and prisons, not only can we eliminate white supremacist establishments, but we can create space for budgets to be reinvested directly into communities to address mental health needs, homelessness and houselessness, access to education, and job creation as well as community-based methods of accountability. This is a future that centers the needs of the people, a future that will make us safer, healthier, and truly free.

Throughout this collection, my hope is that you, the reader, squarely confront the white supremacist underpinnings of policing and prisons and the state-sanctioned oppression, destruction, and execution of Black people, Indigenous people, and people of color. You will understand the ways that reform has further legitimized the social presence of policing and prisons. You will learn about the ways that abolishing policing and prisons can create a society able to invest in the well-being of the people. My sincere hope is that you will be forced to make a moral choice by the time you finish this book: Will you continue to be actively complicit in the perpetuation of these systems, or will you take action to dismantle them for the benefit of a just future? This moment in history will not be forgotten, nor will the actions you, I, and others take.

Another world is possible, a world grounded in love, justice, and accountability, a world grounded in safety and good health, a world grounded in meeting the needs of the people.

Abolition now. Abolition for the people. ◾

Resource:

Transform Harm
  transformharm.org

READER'S GUIDE

- In his essay, Colin Kaepernick references the "institutions that constitute, enhance, and expand the carceral state." Though there is no single way to define the "carceral state," it is fair to say the term is broad and encompasses not only prisons and the police but also other institutions, agencies, practices, policies, and ideologies that see punishment and regulation as central to the maintenance of a white supremacist and hetero-patriarchal social order. According to the essay, what is the purpose of the carceral state?

- How does the author define "reformist and reactionary 'justice?'" What are the author's criticisms of criminal justice reform?

- What does the author mean by abolition? What elements of abolition does the author highlight?

- Beyond prisons and police, what other institutions and practices in your community or neighborhood are part of the carceral state?

PART

I

Police &
Policing

The Feds Are Watching

A HISTORY OF RESISTING
ANTI-BLACK SURVEILLANCE

By Simone Browne

I n October 1976, *Ebony* magazine published a story about the popularity among Black users of citizen band (CB) radio, a voice-communication technology that allowed for two-way exchanges over distance. CB radio served as a means of community organizing and entertainment, with the establishment of social clubs, the invention of vocabularies, and the use of channels almost exclusively by Black enthusiasts. The article named Redd Foxx (handle: "Redbird") and Muhammad Ali (handle: "Big Bopper") among some of the more famous users of this technology, yet also noted that "Blacks have been into CBs for years; it's nothing new."

Before the rise in CB radio's popularity on the consumer market, protesters, grassroots activists, and civil-rights organizations, such as the Student Nonviolent Coordinating Committee (SNCC) and The Congress of Racial Equality (CORE), would make use of this communication technology, along with Wide Area Telephone Service (WATS), to monitor threats, acts of intimidation, harassment, fire bombings, detentions and arrests by police, the Ku Klux Klan, [White] Citizens' Councils, and other entities deputized by white supremacy.

A caller utilizing the flat-rate WATS lines to make direct contact with the offices of civil-rights organizations would do so in an effort to circumvent local switchboard operators who could, and often would, block calls or eavesdrop on conversations and then pass along information to local police, white vigilantes, and others to enact violence. WATS calls were still listened in on by the FBI and local police, and public airwave CB transmissions were often subjected to "systematic jamming" of frequencies,[1] heightening the "risk to life and limb"[2] of voter registration workers and those staffing or assisting Mississippi's Freedom Summer enfranchisement efforts. But the data logged through these calls would be used to then dispatch assistance and protection, monitor white supremacist activities, and would also form WATS reports.[3] These compiled summaries of incidents recorded could then be shared with other organizations, movement lawyers, the Justice Department, the FBI, and news media.

Putting communication-related tools to work in the confronting of anti-Black surveillance and racial terrorism has countless historical precedents. The Negro Motorist Green Book, and others like it, charted automobile routes so that Black travelers could navigate roadways and secure accommodation within the system of segregation, sundown towns, and service stations that refused their patronage. Much earlier, disrupting the technologies of slavery became an effective way to undermine slavery itself. For example, repurposing and forging slave passes and certificates of freedom helped facilitate escapes and Black people on the move. In 1851, a broadside cautioned "colored people of Boston" to "keep a sharp lookout" as watchmen and police were authorized to act as "kidnappers" because the Fugitive Slave Act of 1850 had federalized slave catching.[4] This printed matter offered an important word of advice: "Avoid conversing with the watchmen and police officers of Boston ... [especially] if you value your liberty, and the welfare of the fugitives among you." (Sadly, more than 150 years later, a similar caution still applies.)

In another example, Harriet Ann Jacobs meticulously shared the specifics of her cunning ability to outwit her captor, Dr. Flint (a pseudonym), and eventually escape his predatory sexual harassment and enslavement in her 1861 narrative, *Incidents in the Life of a Slave Girl*.[5] Her self-emancipation began in North Carolina in 1835 when she ran off and took harbor in the homes of others, concealed herself in a swamp, and then eventually hid in a garret above her grandmother's house for almost seven years. This hiding space, where the darkness was nearly total and the air was stifling, "was only nine feet long, and seven wide" and at its highest only three feet.

She later bored a hole in one of the walls, about an inch in diameter, through which she could catch some air, peep outside, watch her children, and listen to conversations not meant for her to hear, like that of "slave-hunters planning how to catch some poor fugitive." While still confined in the garret, Jacobs would frequently out-maneuver Flint and his hired slave catchers by writing letters addressed to him and to her grandmother and then sending those letters with a trusted friend who would mail them back to North Carolina but postmarked from places like New York, Boston, and Canada. Jacobs ultimately fled her cramped cell and made her way to freedom in Philadelphia, and then on to New York and Boston.

Taken together, these rebellious acts of insurgency and stealth uses of technology—CB radios, WATS lines, counterfeited documents, artful uses of postal services—anticipate the necessary tools of subversion in the face of ongoing police violence and contemporary state surveillance. They demonstrate Black communities' inventive ways of working within the existing infrastructure to disrupt the systems that were meant to contain, objectify, and profit from them. A key part of these rebellious acts are the networks and friendships forged within a system bent on undercutting Black social life.

But what does it mean, in this moment, for corporations to capitalize on people's legitimate fear of racialized violence and the reality of surveillance by the settler colonial nation-state or otherwise?[6] Put differently, when products and innovations—like dashcams or the "Hey, Siri, I'm getting pulled over" iPhone shortcut[7]—are marketed and popularized as countersurveillance tools, they reinforce the idea that data collection technologies can help people safely navigate contact with policing. While these products might mitigate harms, or at least record them, we should read many of these moves as part of an expansion of the surveillance state.

Amazon, for example, has partnered with policing agencies to share camera footage from its Ring surveillance platform, while users of its accompanying Neighbors app can do the same by enabling in-app notification alerts when police make requests for users' video. Amazon only recently introduced an opt-in, end-to-end encryption feature for Ring video footage. Only if users choose to opt-in to this video encryption feature would their Ring footage be excluded from video sharing requests from the police.[8] Amazon's recent announcement[9] that the company will soon be selling drones that fly around the interior of users' homes as part of its Ring surveillance hardware make such video-sharing arrangements between police and consumers potentially even more troubling.

Alternatively, we could look to tools that could be imperfect, for now, but that signal a practice of abolition in their design and methods of use (see: Not911, an app created by formerly incarcerated software engineers that offers users alternatives to calling emergency services without dispatching police). Most importantly, the community care practices, toolkits,[10] and mutual-aid acts[11] done by, for example, Survived & Punished, the Bay Area Transformative Justice Collective, AAPI Women Lead, the Stop Spying LAPD Coalition, and other organizations work to produce the conditions for social transformation by stealthily disrupting anti-Black surveillance. In so being, they offer us a model toward abolition.

Undermining racialized forms of surveillance is an ongoing practice, but it's one that continually exposes the limits and weaknesses of that very surveillance. Often, corporate and state actors attempt to undermine that resistance through reforms that, rather than reducing the harm that is policing, expand its very scope, such as police body-worn cameras, "predictive" policing, and calls for community policing. What can't be fully captured and co-opted, however, are the practices of refusal and invention that hold Black liberation as the goal. ◢

Resources:

Survived & Punished:
    survivedandpunished.org
Bay Area Transformative Justice Collective:
    batjc.wordpress.com
AAPI Women Lead:
    imreadymovement.org
Stop LAPD Spying Coalition:
    stoplapdspying.org

READER'S GUIDE

- How do technologies marketed as countersurveillance tools often help to expand what Simone Browne describes as the "surveillance state"?

- The author identifies historical examples of countersurveillance technologies and strategies. Please list three to four examples.

- The author cites several contemporary community-produced abolitionist technologies and strategies that can be used to circumvent and challenge the carceral state? What are they? How do they work?

- How can countersurveillance technologies cited by the author aid in Black liberation?

The Myth of the Good Cop

POP CULTURE HELPED TURN
POLICE OFFICERS INTO ROCK STARS—AND
BLACK FOLKS INTO CRIMINALS

By Mark Anthony Neal

I f you're of a certain age—the last of the boomers or the first cohort of Generation X—and grew up Black and urban, you may have a tendency to romanticize the cops who used to walk the beat. The boys in blue who knew everyone in the neighborhood. Truth be told, the officers I most remember from my years growing up in the South Bronx were white do-gooders who appeared on TV in the 1970s. Back then, I was oblivious to the criminalization of Black bodies, the anti-Black violence that was propagated by the law enforcement community writ large, or the ideological framing about who and what the police were. I was unaware of the copaganda that pop culture had served up to an unsuspecting public for generations.

Copaganda—the reproduction and circulation in mainstream media of propaganda that is favorable to law enforcement—has long been a tool to disrupt legitimate claims of anti-Black violence. Simply put, copaganda actively counters attempts to hold police malfeasance accountable by reinforcing the ideas that the police are generally fair and hardworking, and that "Black criminals" deserve the brutal treatment they receive. Such cultural framing has been critical to buttressing the need for a more expansive criminal justice system that fuels mass incarceration.

When I was a kid, my father worked six days a week, twelve hours a day. He spent his downtime listening to gospel quartets and watching police and private detective dramas that played in the NBC Mystery Movie programming rotation: shows like *McMillan & Wife*, *McCloud*, and *Columbo*. I suppose that my father, a Black, undereducated, working-class man from the South, was drawn to the kind of folksy, down-home characters featured in these shows, in part because he found them to be comforting as examples of respectability that would be available to his young son.

The shows were often comical and pivoted on innocuous notions of morality, where "good" always won out over "bad" (the criminals were rarely "evil" on 1970s television in the ways that so-called Middle Eastern "terrorists" were portrayed in the 1980s). McCloud, for example, was a fish-out-of-water detective from the Southwest who brought his style of policing to the "big city" (he'd often chase "criminals" on horseback). Columbo, which aired intermittently for more than three decades, hinged on the "genius" of a dusty, rumpled gumshoe who constantly looked as if he'd just fallen out of bed to solve a case.

While those shows endeared law enforcement to the public, other programming from the era was more intentional in its messaging. Another staple on my dad's television was *The F.B.I.*, a show that saw actor Efrem Zimbalist Jr.—a Goldwater Republican—acting out scripts vetted by the actual FBI, which in real life was laying waste to a generation of Black freedom fighters and their organizations. FBI director J. Edgar Hoover architected COINTELPRO, which used various forms of disruption, including infiltration and violence, to undermine civil

rights, Black liberation anti-war, Native, and white radical organizations. Hoover famously identified the Black Panther Party as the biggest threat to American society; *The F.B.I.* was monumental in swaying
the public at a time when "law and order" was a rallying cry.

I also enjoyed watching the short-lived series *S.W.A.T.* (the inspiration for the 2003 Samuel L. Jackson film of the same name) and syn-
dicated episodes of *Adam-12,* both of which were set in Los Angeles.
No more than ten or eleven years old at the time, I fancied myself as
S.W.A.T.'s Dominic Luca (Mark Shera) and rookie officer Jim Reed
(Kent McCord) from *Adam-12.* Little did I know that the SWAT (Special Weapons and Tactics) unit had been designed in the mid-1960s by
Los Angeles Police Department inspector Daryl Gates in the aftermath
of the Watts Riots of 1965.

Intended as the police force's militarized arm that could address
volatile situations that needed quick and potentially violent resolution—such as snipers and the taking of hostages—SWAT teams became a means to address urban protest. Not surprisingly, one of the
first uses of SWAT was an attack on the Black Panther Party's LA
headquarters in December 1969, in which more than three hundred officers took on thirteen Black Panther members (more than half of whom
were women and children). The attack occurred only days after a similar police raid in Chicago that killed Fred Hampton and Mark Clark,
in what poet Haki Madhubuti called a "one-sided shootout." Both incidents highlight the close relationship between local law enforcement
and the FBI during the period.

The show *Adam-12* featured the Rampart Division of the LAPD,
which, two decades after the show's debut, would become the basis of
a police corruption case involving the Community Resources Against
Street Hoodlums (CRASH) unit. Also conceived of by Gates, CRASH
intimately connected to the police brutality narratives heard in gangsta
rap of the late 1980s and 1990s in songs like Toddy Tee's "Batterram"
and N.W.A's "Fuck the Police." In the case of CRASH, the narrative of
urban radicals had shifted to concerns about the "war on drugs" during
an era when crack cocaine was being introduced to Black and Brown

urban communities. Aside from the examples in rap music, most Americans were unaware of these efforts until the release of the 1988 film *Colors,* in which Robert Duvall and Sean Penn portrayed CRASH officers.

The irony was that the affable Dominic Luca and Jim Reed of the shows *S.W.A.T.* and *Adam-12,* respectively, were the public faces of the LAPD in an era in which its figureheads like Gates—who became the very symbol of racist policing in the post–civil rights era—were creating apparatuses that would have dramatic and traumatic impacts on Black communities for decades. These contradictory realities speak to how palpable copaganda was as a resource to influence public opinion and thus public policy regarding law enforcement.

With the exception of the ensemble casts of the sitcom *Barney Miller* and the melodrama *Hill Street Blues,* Black officers were largely missing as primary characters in the narratives of the '70s and '80s, a dearth that reflected the lack of diversity in station houses in the period. Charles Barnett's 1994 film *The Glass Shield,* for example, fictionalized a real-life attempt to integrate a Los Angeles area sheriff's office. Black novelists filled in the gaps, though. Chester Himes's *Harlem Detectives* series featured Grave Digger Jones and Coffin Ed Johnson, two detectives who became more prominent when they were depicted by Godfrey Cambridge and Raymond St. Jacques, respectively, in 1970's Ossie Davis–directed film *Cotton Comes to Harlem* and *Come Back, Charleston Blue* two years later.

In Raymond Nelson's 1972 essay on Himes's detective novels, he describes Grave Digger and Coffin Ed as "bad niggers"—symbols of "defiance, strength, and masculinity to a community that has been forced to learn, or at least to sham, weakness and compliance."[1] And indeed, on-screen, Cambridge's and St. Jacques's performances of the duo were given the gravitas of "race men"—these figures, often men, within Black life and culture who were committed to the "race"; they didn't simply acquiesce to the white power structure that employed them but also offered a healthy skepticism of ghetto hustlers while using their badges and relative privilege to look out for the "least of" in Black Harlem. The extent to which Grave Digger and Coffin Ed were depicted as being embedded in the very fabric of Black Harlem was a refreshing counter to the drive-by treatments of Black life found in most film and television in the era, particularly with regard to law enforcement.

The 1991 film *A Rage in Harlem,* a third of Himes's detective novels to be adapted for the big screen, found Grave Digger and Coffin Ed on the periphery of the film's focus, as if it were a metaphor for the cultural shifts that had seemingly occurred in the previous two decades. In many ways, Grave Digger and Coffin Ed were precursors to the Black-White cop buddy films of the 1980s—think Danny Glover and Mel Gibson in *Lethal Weapon,* or *48 Hours,* in which Eddie Murphy played a petty criminal working with a detective (Nick Nolte). Whereas the idea of cop buddy films with two Black actors was not tenable to Hollywood at the time—and would not be until the *Bad Boys* franchise—the Black-White cop buddy films were more marketable given the success of films like *The Defiant Ones* (Sidney Poitier and Tony Curtis) and the Richard Pryor and Gene Wilder films of the 1970s and 1980s.

Notable about these films, including the *Bad Boy* franchise with Will Smith and Martin Lawrence, is the way that Black officers were largely evacuated from Black life and community. Though Glover played a family man in *Lethal Weapon,* there was nothing inherently Black about his life. (In fact, Gibson played the role of the rogue cop.) This could also be seen in the television series *NYPD Blue,* where James McDaniels portrayed Lt. Arthur Fancy for the series' first eight seasons, yet there was little attention to his life outside of the precinct. The *Law and Order* franchise reveals little about the backstory of numerous Black officers played by the likes of Jesse L. Martin, Anthony Anderson, and Ice-T, who has portrayed Sgt. Odafin "Fin" Tutuola for nearly twenty years.

The aforementioned fictional officers exist in contrast to *Boyz n the Hood*'s Officer Coffey, a Black cop (played by Jessie Lawrence Ferguson) whose disdain for Black youth is palpable. Denzel Washington's Oscar-winning performance as Alonzo Harris in *Training Day* is yet another example of a character who is allowed to reign terror on a Black community due to the faulty logic of Black-on-Black crime and the benign neglect directed toward poor and working-class communities of color that renders those communities as complicit in their own pathologies. In such instances, it seems Black people and other marginalized communities do not deserve to be protected and served.

That such characters were featured in films by Black directors (John Singleton and Antoine Fuqua, respectively) doesn't change the fact that in much of popular culture Black officers are no longer race men at all—but, rather, stand-ins for the very anti-Black violence directed at Black communities. As a whole, these characters are complements to the purposes of copaganda, serving as examples of Black exceptionalism on the one hand while suggesting that policing is race-neutral but criminality is not. In fact, such characters help valorize and legitimize both the extra-policing and extrajudicial forms of violence directed at Black bodies.

Yet the more things change, the more they stay the same. Those beat cops on *Adam-12* that I once idolized as a kid now sit comfortably around the Sunday dinner table as three generations of officers on the police drama *Blue Bloods*. Thoughtful, introspective, and devoted to God, family, and the law—who wouldn't want them to protect and serve? ◭

READER'S GUIDE

- How does Mark Anthony Neal define "copaganda"? Do you agree or disagree with this definition? Why?

- In your opinion, what is the relationship between "copaganda" and police reform? What are the genre's potential impacts on abolition movements?

- The author writes that "Black officers are . . . stand-ins for the very anti-Black violence directed at Black communities. As a whole, these characters are complements to the purposes of copaganda, serving as examples of Black exceptionalism on the one hand while suggesting that policing is race-neutral but criminality is not." Describe the link between Black exceptionalism and the ideology of "race-neutral" policing.

- Please provide three to four examples of "copaganda" you've encountered in your own life.

My Son Was Executed by an Ideal

LOSING MY SON TO POLICE VIOLENCE

A Conversation with Gwendolyn Woods
as Told to Kiese Laymon

I t's morning. I've just gotten off the phone with Gwen Woods, the mother of Mario Woods, a young Black man executed on video by San Francisco police officers on December 2, 2015. I know that Mario's life and death helped fuel the "I Know My Rights" campaign but I'm not exactly sure how. I am terrified. I am confused. Before our conversation, I read everything I could about both Gwen Woods and her child. I watched, on silent, as Mario walked away from officers before being filled with twenty-one bullets. I heard but didn't fully understand when Colin Kaepernick told me, "Mario is why I did what I did. His mother, Mama Woods, is why I do what I do. You should talk to her. She is not a symbol, brother. You'll see."

I was still wondering why Gwen Woods refused to hang up first at the end of our conversation when she texted me two photos. In the first picture,

Mario is wearing what we in Jackson, Mississippi, call a "sweater hat,"
and a white T-shirt beneath a dark gray San Francisco 49ers sweatshirt. In
the second picture, Mario is a baby looking directly into the camera. He's
cloaked in a humongous red San Francisco 49ers jacket, the cobalt blue of
his shirt popping out of the top. At the bottom right of the picture are the
words "Mar-Man." "Just had to share Mar as a baby in his 49ers garb and
at his first game at Candlestick Park," Ms. Woods wrote in a text between
the two. "It was the first night Colin started as quarterback. He didn't
know Mar. But Mar felt he knew him as the quarterback. The irony, right?
Thank you for our conversation, K. Even more than my child leaving me, I
just never wanted to leave my child out there."

I think I understand why Gwen Woods insisted I hang up first.

* * *

Do you mind if I call you "K"? I hate to mess up people's names.

When the lawyer said he couldn't win Mario's case, even with a video, I hurt in a way I never wish on anyone except the police who executed my son. That hurt didn't stop with some settlement. After what they did to my child's body, I had my Judas moment. I felt like I sold my child for forty pieces of silver. Most of that money went to lawyers. I felt like I betrayed and abandoned my son.

I use the word "execute" because that's what they do. They execute. They annihilate. Look at the video. If they didn't annihilate my son, what did they do? If that doesn't look like an execution, tell me what it looks like? They come up with jargon for "soft targets." They told me my son was a "victim of policy."

Of course, I thought about being quiet. But when the lawyers failed to speak for us in a court of law, I said to myself, "Fine, I'll take it from here."

Then Colin came.

My first meeting with Colin was four years in the making. Mario was executed blocks from the old Candlestick Park. So, three years later, when someone asked Colin what made him take that knee. He said Mario Woods.

That's my son.

Honestly, K, it brought life back to me. It brought Mario back from the ashes. I birthed my baby. I loved my baby. They shot so many holes in my baby's body. And Colin says my baby is what gave him the strength to stand up for us and kneel. Even though my son's body is gone, I still talk to him. "Mario, someone as great as Colin Kaepernick got your back," I tell him. "He says you gave him life."

We have to start making examples of people of power and control. Nothing will change until we start dismantling that Officers' Bill of Rights. There has to be a zero-tolerance policy. No pension if you kill people who could not kill you. Right now, you can execute our children, or us, and even on the rare occasion you lose your job, you still keep your pension.

We have to dismantle that Officers' Bill of Rights.

My son was executed by an ideal. That ideal says that he, and people like him, are not redeemable. Police kill people that they believe don't deserve to live. You read what happened to his body. They pepper-sprayed my child. I know he couldn't think. Soaking wet, my child was 5-foot-4, 144 pounds.

Every parent wants their child to be seen. How can you value what you don't see? I don't think these juries see our children. Let it be juries of our peers. When I'm on jury duty, my job will only pay for two weeks because I'm not a city employee. What's the race and neighborhood demographics of most city employees? Most of them aren't our peers. Let it be people from our community, our peers. Compensate us fairly on those juries.

These police who kill our children never admit to regrets. I do. I wonder sometimes if I should have short-sold my mother's house faster and kept Mar out of prison. My father was in the Navy and bought the home when he returned from the military. Maybe that's a risk I should have taken. Maybe we would have had more resources if I did that. When we came back to California, my mother had terminal cancer. Mario was impacted by all that. I had a second job working security on the weekend.

Damned if you do. Damned if you don't.

As a Black mother, it's understandable that we go into grieving mode. You feel like you left your child out there to be executed by police and the schools and the politicians and the poverty and the addiction. But we also have to go into fighting mode. We have to fight for ourselves and our children and our communities. None of our children are one-dimensional. None of us is one-dimensional.

Mario was a kid who was always trying to help other people eat whether he had enough or not. I want to say it was me, but he was like that when he was born. They would never see this. When they executed Mario, they saw him as a nobody. They didn't love him. They didn't protect him. They executed him. It's times I didn't know who to be mad at. My mother? My estranged husband? Ultimately, some days, I'm just most mad at myself. It's schizophrenic at times.

But I am not apologizing.

I'm tired of teachable moments. I've been through that on my job my whole life. In order to talk about "Black-on-Black crime," we have to talk about the government as much as we talk about Black people. Folks want to talk about "Black-on-Black crime." Let's talk about it. And let's talk about how we are overrepresented in prisons. Let's talk about how their children never go to prison for what they do to us. Let's talk about how they're just like Trump, always deflecting. If our children mess up, and sometimes even if they don't, they go to prison. If their children mess up in ways our children can't even imagine, they become presidents of companies, politicians, and president of the United States.

So much trauma is impacted on us. We know about Oliver North and Iran-Contra. We know, throughout history, how the guns got into our community. We know how the crack came in. The government helped inflict this on us. It's like they blame us and blame our children for what they started. When I look at a young person being a knucklehead, I want to know the story behind him. We have to want to know our children's stories.

Education is crucial. But if you took my education and made me feel less than, you don't want me to love myself. You don't. You want me to love who you say you are. But I can't trust anything you say because you say I'm a nobody. You say my child is nobody. You take what made me from me and tell me all that made me ain't worth a damn in schools.

I hope that makes sense.

I'm over being apologetic about the state's failures. They want us to apologize for how we raised our children. I'm supposed to apologize to the people who killed my child? I'm going to apologize to the people who watched my child die? I am not apologizing. If my child has to go to prison, someone else's son should have to go to prison for killing my child. And they should be in general population like my child. That's how I feel sometimes. I know prisons are bad for everyone. I know that, K, but sometimes I feel like if I have to be up all night depressed, I hope those officers and their families are in the same situation I'm in.

We aren't asking for anything that wasn't taken from us. When I think of my mom's cancer, I think of environmental racism. She didn't ask for that. How do you repair what you took from her and her family? That is what reparation means. When you take something from people, whether it's health, money, security, their children, whatever, you have to repair that. But here's the truth, K. I don't know how you fully repair the hearts of mothers who watch their children be executed by people paid to protect and to serve, and then nothing happens to the executioners.

How do you repair that, K? These folks, they don't even try! That's the thing.

I've been reading a lot about alternatives to prison. I read where, in some cultures, historically, if you killed someone, you would be made to take that dead body and you'd have to carry that body around for days until you got that stench into your pores. The concept is something to think about.

I remember being a person with no hate. After seeing how they treated my child's body, I'm not going to say I don't hate. What would you feel if you saw your child with no gun executed by five officers, and none of the executioners were held responsible?

I just miss my child, K.

I remember so many things I know Mario doesn't remember. I wish I could remind him of who he was. When we were living in Houston, I met Mario one day when he got out of school. I met him at the corner. Him and my neighbor, little Johnny, were coming up the street, and he had a big black thing in his hands.

The closer he gets, I'm like, "Mario, is that a dead crow?"

Mario is telling me to save it. I said, "if you don't put that thing down…" Mario said, "When I grow up, you can't come to my house because I'm gonna have snakes." My son was so funny. He cared so much for living things that were hurt.

When he was in prison and struggling, I'd say, "The time is doing you today, Mar." I have a picture of us all at the zoo. I pull on that memory a lot. Mar was so rambunctious. I got him one of those Teddy Ruxpins when he was little. When it was time for him to do his homework, I put it way up on his bookshelf. One day, Mar climbed up there and got that Teddy Ruxpin. Whole bookshelf fell over on my child.

I got him and his brother a new winter coat to share. Mar gave it to his friend because his friend was colder than him and his brother. He was colder because he didn't have a coat at all.

None of who my child was mattered to those police, that jury, these politicians.

We have to make them uncomfortable. We have to make them uncomfortable. The police are too comfortable. Trump is way too comfortable. These politicians are too comfortable. Nancy Pelosi can sit up there with kente cloth but not say a word about Idris, Kenneth, my child, Jessica Williams, all the blood on San Francisco's hands. Now she's on TV talking about police reform, but not talking about her role in what she thinks needs to be reformed.

How?

You saw my child shot twenty-one times after posing no threat to all those police, and you don't understand why Colin took a knee. I have this great pain of losing my child. I have this great man that I consider my child now, too.

"Woman, behold thy son," scripture says. I think of Colin in that context. "Mother, behold thy son."

I love that young man, K. Not just for everything he meant to Mario. I love him because of his heart, his integrity. Colin's integrity outweighs everything popular. When you see that integrity, you must stand up. You must fight. Colin Kaepernick's story is the story of what happens to integrity and love of Black folks in the United States. This country hates integrity. I'm gonna be honest. They don't hate Colin. They think they do. They hate integrity. He told them they are responsible for a history of brutality. Telling the truth should not be a risk. But it is for us.

Colin risked it all for our children.

I miss my child every minute of every day. I am thankful that his life, no matter how short, inspired change. If he was alive, he'd say we have to do everything to keep Colin Kaepernick safe, Mama, not because he was his favorite quarterback, but because he loves us enough to fight. We can't abandon our children or the folks who fight for our children. I wish Mario was here to see what he helped continue.

Thank you for talking to me, K. Thank you so much.

You hang up first. ▲

READER'S GUIDE

- In a conversation with Kiese Laymon, Ms. Woods flips the racist ideology of "Black-on-Black crime" on its head and challenges it with several examples of anti-Black state violence. What examples does Ms. Woods cite to show that mainstream understandings of "Black-on-Black crime" have no basis in fact?

- Ms. Woods refers to an "Officers' Bill of Rights." To date, over fifteen states have enacted legislation to codify their own Officers' Bill of Rights. How do these bills of rights hamper efforts toward abolition, accountability, and harm reduction?

- What are the differences in the ways that the police and mainstream media portray Mario Woods compared to the ways his mother understands him? Why, in your opinion, is it important to center and prioritize the narratives of community members impacted by police violence?

- "My Son Was Executed by an Ideal" is the first "as told to" piece in this collection. How did reading this conversation make you feel?

The Truth About "Officer Friendly"

Scripted TV crime shows depict cops as **heroes** who do bad things for good reasons—and the criminal justice system as **race neutral**.[1]

While people of color are commonly depicted on these crime shows, the writers who shape how those characters are depicted—their behaviors, motivations, feelings—are **disproportionately white to an overwhelming degree**. Here is a representative sampling of such series:[2]

Series	Average no. of PoC characters per epidode	% total PoC writers	
Blue Bloods	3.71	0	
NCIS	4.67	0	
Goliath	4	0	
Law & Order: SVU	3.33	0	
The Blacklist	5.06	7	
Blindspot	3.29	8	
9-1-1	6.88	9	
Chicago P.D.	7.18	10	
Criminal Minds	5.41	10	
Elementary	4.81	10	
Bull	5	11	
Brooklyn Nine-Nine	4.53	12	
Bosch	5.25	14	
Hawaii Five-O	6.61	17	
NCIS: Los Angeles	4.44	18	
Narcos	11.43	20	
Lethal Weapon	4.65	20	
NCIS: New Orleans	5.17	21	
Sneaky Pete	2	25	
Orange Is the New Black	3.10	30	
S.W.A.T.	7.18	42	

In reality, **Black people are subjected to higher rates** of police surveillance, violence, and arrest:[3]

Stopped in Traffic:	Stopped in a public place or in a parked vehicle:	Experienced the threat or use of physical threat by police:	Arrested:
9.8% of Black drivers	**1.5%** of Black drivers	**5.2%** of Black adults	**0.5%** of Black drivers
8.6% of White drivers	**0.9%** of Latinx drivers	**5.1%** of Latinx adults	**0.3%** of Latinx drivers
7.6% Latinx drivers	**0.9%** of White drivers	**2.4%** of White adults	**0.3%** of White drivers

The rate at which Black people are killed by police is **more than twice** as high as the rate for white people.[4]

BLACK		LATINX		WHITE		OTHER	
Population	42M	Population	39M	Population	197M	Population	49M
Killed	1,504	Killed	1,055	Killed	2,884	Killed	239
36 per million people		**27** per million people		**15** per million people		**5** per million people	

Data stories researched and conceptualized by Tamara K. Nopper

SWAT's Paramilitary Fever Dream

WHEN POLICE PLAY SOLDIER, EVERYBODY LOSES

By Stuart Schrader

A round 1968, a "gutty little ragtag outfit" linked up on the streets of Los Angeles. This group "traded expertise" with friendly Marines and began studying guerrilla warfare. Its members soon obtained weapons just like the ones US infantry soldiers carried in Vietnam. And the group's leader came up with a snappy name to signal his desire to rule the city's streets: "Special Weapons Attack Team."

But, for a band of sworn law-enforcement officers, that name was too provocative. And the white leader of the new unit, who recounted this history in his memoir [1]—complete with hackneyed action-movie descriptions—would go on to be the chief of the Los Angeles Police Department (LAPD) for twenty-four years. Begrudgingly, Daryl Gates changed his elite group's moniker to Special Weapons and Tactics, or SWAT.

Nevertheless, "attack" was the team's primary mission, and the Black Panther Party was its highest-value target, necessitating the party's own primary mission at the time: self-defense. LAPD SWAT attacked the headquarters of the party's Southern California chapter on December 8, 1969.[2] After incapacitating the Panthers with tear gas, police officers fired five thousand rounds, wounding six Panthers. Using tear gas to make the barricaded targets easier to shoot with conventional firearms was a tactic taken straight from the US war in Vietnam, and later outlawed by executive order from use by the US military but not police.

This violent episode,[3] according to writers like Radley Balko,[4] inaugurated police militarization—the adoption of military weapons, vehicles, armor, and tactics in everyday policing activity on American streets. Police now look like soldiers, and their mission increasingly seems to resemble the types of "counterinsurgency" that the United States has pursued in Iraq and Afghanistan: heavily armed raids, often based on electronically gathered intelligence.

Critics of militarization typically argue that using this gear alienates police from regular people, increases the likelihood of violent encounters, and has no place in a democracy that cherishes a strict division of domestic policing and foreign military action. Yet looking more closely at the LAPD's response to political protest indicates that thinking about the police as a domestic body and the military as an international one is too reductive. Police in the United States have long looked beyond borders and to the military for help resolving problems of their own making. Police militarize when they are in crisis, relying on innovations that are a product of the US empire—the ongoing effort to force the rest of the globe to accede to the designs of Washington and Wall Street.

* * *

In the 1960s, before Daryl Gates created SWAT, some of the LAPD's top officers were already operating far beyond city limits, as I've illustrated in my book *Badges Without Borders: How Global Counterinsurgency*

Transformed American Policing.[5] At the request of the attorney general in 1962, Los Angeles sent a pair of Spanish-speaking cops to the Dominican Republic to impart lessons on "riot control" to the police force there, fearing that Communist subversives were planning to foment civil unrest. The LAPD maintained a reputation for expertise in controlling unruly crowds. These officers brought LAPD training manuals to the Caribbean, while also introducing tear gas and recommending the use of batons.

In the short term, these LAPD efforts seemed to pay off. At a large demonstration in Santo Domingo less than two weeks after the officers began training local cops, the police did not turn too violent, and the crowd dispersed without much trouble. But in April 1965, there was a coup. A revolutionary upsurge overwhelmed the police, leading to a brief civil war. President Lyndon Johnson feared that Communist forces were gaining the upper hand. He ordered the US military to invade. When open hostilities ceased, the Dominican Republic's police were reconstituted as a far more vicious force. Soon, the US-trained police would be responsible for political persecution of leftists, including torture, forced disappearance, and cold-hearted murder in the streets.

Compare this sequence of events to what happened in Los Angeles in the 1960s, culminating in SWAT. There are eerie parallels when looking at the Watts rebellion of 1965 and its aftermath: In both instances, police were overwhelmed, the military got involved, and then police returned even more vicious.

* * *

After an incident of police brutality involving Black motorist Marquette Frye, and his brother and mother on August 11, 1965, exaggerated but plausible rumors began to spread about police attacking a pregnant Black woman. Watts residents began protesting—and in response, cops ran wild, acting even more unhinged than usual. Looting, shooting, fires, and mass arrests ensued. The situation quickly became the most destructive "civil disorder" the twentieth century had yet seen. The National Guard patrolled in jeeps and cargo trucks, wearing helmets and carrying bayonet-tipped rifles. And then, once an uneasy calm returned to the streets, the LAPD became even more venomous against Black and Chicano activists.

Determined never to be caught off-guard again, the LAPD created two new units in ensuing years: SWAT was joined by the Public Disorder Intelligence Division, a secretive outfit that spied on activists and even on some elected officials. By the early 1980s, one of the officers the LAPD had sent to the Dominican Republic, in fact, became the leader of that division. Meanwhile, Gates touted SWAT's successes at adopting military tactics, offering blueprints for other police forces around the country to militarize when they run into trouble.

This pattern is global. American police commanders declare that their officers are so well trained and experienced that they should teach cops elsewhere how to do their jobs. When those cops inevitably falter in a crisis—whether civil unrest or apparent "crime" surges—officials come to believe more aggressive approaches are necessary.

Then, the military gets involved. The police commanders, in turn, take new lessons from the more militarized approaches. These become the new baseline, and anyone who opposes them becomes an enemy.

Police militarization is the way police forces compensate for their own failures and mistakes. Police admire the military because it models what they want to be: an extremely well-resourced, technologically sophisticated, tactically effective, and widely respected instrument of state violence. So when police seem insufficiently trained, undisciplined, or even corrupt, commanders will look to the military for models on how to improve. Those improvements rarely occur, but in the process, the police adopt military weapons. (The Pentagon has transferred $7.4 billion[6] in surplus weapons and supplies to police since 1997, while additional materials[7] come from private donations, other federal sources like the Department of Homeland Security, or state and local budgets.) Accompanying this gear is a martial mentality that makes leaving the precinct house seem like a mission into hostile enemy territory.

At almost any point[8] in the past 120 years, we can find examples[9] of this cycle, as police seek help and guidance from the military. And each round of police militarization at home has built upon a foundation already forged abroad. The question before us right now is whether the cycle will continue after the 2020 rebellions in Minneapolis, Nashville, New York, Los Angeles, and many other cities.

In recent protests against police violence and racist abuse, police have frequently worsened the situation. In city after city, protesters faced violent assault by heavily armed police, from officers in Brooklyn using their vehicles as battering rams on crowds to cops in Philadelphia firing tear gas at fleeing demonstrators pinned against a barrier. In only a few cases has the National Guard intervened, and military leaders balked when the Trump administration considered using soldiers to crush demonstrations in 2020.[10] But the baseline, as everyone has seen, is already a highly militarized force. And it failed miserably at lessening the intensity of protest. In fact, police accomplished the opposite: spurring the most sustained and widespread period of political unrest in the United States in decades, if not ever.

After the proverbial smoke clears, when the expert studies are finalized, the re-training is complete, and a newly equipped force is unleashed, we must ask, what will the next iteration look like? Will the police militarize even further, taking inspiration from overseas operations?

Police crises like the current one inevitably cause police to look for outside help.[11] The demand to defund police is a prophylactic measure against this possibility.[12]

When protesters chant "Defund the police," cops respond, "But who will come to rescue you when you're in crisis?" We could turn the question back on the police: What if you didn't have the military to rescue you in your moments of crisis? And this new question opens onto a new horizon of abolition, and of hope: a world without police or soldiers. ◼

READER'S GUIDE

- Stuart Schrader traces the history of SWAT teams to Los Angeles in the 1960s and writes that the Black Panther Party was SWAT's first target. He writes, "LAPD SWAT attacked the headquarters of the party's Southern California chapter on December 8, 1969. After incapacitating the Panthers with tear gas, police officers fired five thousand rounds, wounding six Panthers. Using tear gas to make the barricaded targets easier to shoot with conventional firearms was a tactic taken straight from the US war in Vietnam." How does this history help to cement the link among the militarization of police, anti-Blackness, and anti-communism?

- How, according to the author's research, do police respond to political protests? What are your thoughts on these responses?

- The author writes that "Police in the United States have long looked beyond borders and to the military for help resolving problems of their own making" and cites several examples. Can you think of any additional examples from your own life?

- The author ends their essay with a new hope: "a world without police or soldiers." In your opinion (and based on this essay), what could that look and feel like?

Disability Justice Is an Essential Part of Abolishing Police & Ending Incarceration

By Talila A. Lewis

W hile it is well known that policing in the united states was originally developed and later honed to control Black and Indigenous people's lives (these are not mutually exclusive groups)—our movement, labor, speech, ownership, family, and more—most are unaware that disabled people (and those labeled disabled) have always been primary among the carceral machine's intended targets. In fact, there is evidence that disabled people have the most frequent and catastrophic encounters[1] with carceral systems, and that ableism[2] has long been central to the nation's economic, political, legal, and social anatomy. Indeed, no social justice issue, including abolition,[3] can be properly addressed without intentionally centering disability and ableism,[4] and no social justice movement can be successful without disability justice at its heart.

*

UNDERSTANDING DISABILITY, ABLEISM, POLICING, AND INCARCERATION

Most have come to understand disability through a lens of whiteness, wealth, and other power and privileges that actively exclude the experiences of Black/Indigenous and low- and no-income people.[5] Importantly, people who experience deprivation, violence, oppression, and/or precarity also experience disability at disproportionately higher rates. These environmental factors and socioeconomic experiences are a cause, complicator, and even consequence of all manner of disability.[6] Notably, disabled people disproportionately experience deprivation, violence, oppression, and precarity.

More importantly, one *does not* have to be disabled to experience ableism. Rather, ableism[7] is a systemic oppression that allows social systems and individuals to assign value to people based on their appearance and their ability to re/produce, excel, and behave, among other things. Ableism evaluates people on their divergence (whether actual or perceived)[8] from constructed ideas of normality, intelligence, excellence, and productivity.

In the united states, these constructions are necessarily rooted,[9] as is the country itself, in anti-Blackness, anti-Indigeneity, misogyny, eugenics, colonialism, imperialism, and capitalism. For example, enslavers, scientists and doctors, economists, religious leaders, and others claimed that Black people were less intelligent, capable, and sentient, and were therefore naturally suited for slave labor. To this day, Black/Indigenous people and low- and no-income people, regardless of their disability status, are depicted as biologically inferior, less capable of making societal contributions, and more likely to be dependent on others. These ableist ideas are used to justify violence, discrimination, and oppression, including medical rationing,[10] labor exploitation, incarceration and institutionalization, family regulation, deprivation of resources, and more.

Still, most people in social justice movements are unable to recognize ableism[11] and are unaware of just how ordinary yet lethal it is. But policing, incarceration and institutionalization, labor exploitation and impoverishment, forced familial separation and deprivation of resources, climate and environmental injustice, and other state and corporate violence disproportionately affect disabled and other marginalized people while creating and exacerbating disabilities.

Disability justice[12] is a requisite for abolition[13] because carceral systems medicalize, pathologize, criminalize, and commodify[14] survival, divergence, and resistance.

The past and present connections between disability and all forms of carceral violence are overt and overwhelming. Disabled people comprise just 26 percent[15] of the united states population—but represent up to half of the people[16] killed by police, over 50 percent[17] of the incarcerated adult prison population, up to 85 percent[18] of the incarcerated youth population, and nearly one hundred percent of those incarcerated in medicalized carceral spaces[19] like nursing facilities, group facilities, and civil commitment, "treatment" facilities, and "hospitals." Whether under the pretense of "care" or "corrections," disabled people are highly represented in *all* carceral populations. History explains this phenomenon.

The united states government and corporations have always used constructed ideas about disability and criminality alongside and intertwined with constructed ideas about class and race to classify, criminalize, cage, and disappear its "undesirables." In this way, those in positions of power maintain the white supremacist status quo and create an exploitable labor pool while sowing discord within and across marginalized communities.

For instance, mainstream doctors and scientists diagnosed Black enslaved people who engaged in work stoppages, "property" destruction, or "theft"[20] with *dysaesthesia aethiopica*,[21] or "rascality." Similarly, mere thoughts of escaping enslavement was dubbed *drapetomania*.[22] In both cases, these purported mental illnesses could only be had by Black people and could only be "cured" by yet more unpaid hard labor and insufferable violence. These legitimate acts of resistance to enslavement (one of the first forms of incarceration) were not only labeled as mental illnesses, but they were simultaneously deemed criminal/delinquent. Or take the 1880 census's[23] "3D schedule," which described the so-called "dependent, defective, and delinquent classes"[24] using terms rooted in eugenics, now considered disability slurs, to label people as: "idiots; insane inhabitants; deaf and dumb; blind; homeless children; inhabitants in prisons; paupers and indigent inhabitants in institutions, poor houses or asylums, or boarded at public expense in private houses." Forced institutionalization/incarceration[25] and sterilization[26] of people in all of these "classes" was not uncommon, and continues to this day.[27] Carceral classifications premised on sex assigned at birth operate as a form of eugenics where people labeled deviant, disabled, and/or dependent are confined in conditions that rob them of their ability to conceive during their most fertile years.

If this is not evidence enough, disenfranchisement of people with felony records and people with disabilities can often be found within the same section of many laws.[28] Many felon/disabled disenfranchisement laws were enacted in the years immediately following the 1840 us Census. This census falsely claimed that Black people had higher incidences of "idiocy" and "insanity" than white people, and that free Black people had even higher incidences of these disabilities than enslaved Black people.

Supporters of enslavement were committed to proving that Black people could not handle freedom. White doctors and scientists were interested in honing eugenics theories and practices to prevent Black/Indigenous people and others labeled "dependent, delinquent, and defective" from reproducing and freely moving in and around "civilized" society. All the while, white legislators used the same ableist/racist/classist arguments to justify civic, social, economic deprivation to the same groups of people. Legislators crafted false narratives of laziness, ignorance, and uncivility to collectively disqualify people labeled "idiots" or "insane" or felons from voting. What many now call collateral consequences[29] of incarceration—being barred from voting or holding public office, even after release—are often still called "civil disabilities."[30] Modern coronavirus criminalization,[31] resisting arrest,[32] and disorderly conduct[33] laws, and police officers and unions together with the medical-carceral industrial complex using pseudoscience diagnoses like *excited delirium*[34]—a modern pseudoscience diagnosis that is used as legal justification for unjustifiable law enforcement murders of mostly multiply marginalized people—all help illuminate the unbroken chain between past and present carceral logics and practices.

These warped and circular rationales are used to justify horrific exploitation, experimentation, and extermination. They also quell public outcry over what otherwise would be deemed indefensible theft of dignity, life, and liberty.

The goal of criminal and medical incarceration has always been civic,[35] social, economic, and physical marginalization and death of people who society deems unfit. The categories of what constitutes "unworthy" are intentionally broad and intersected as to be endlessly applicable. The nimble, timeless, and comprehensive nature of structural and systemic oppression demonstrates that power holders deeply appreciate how identities intersect and illustrate why intentionally intersectional responses to state violence are necessary.

When abolitionists do not have a strong disability justice analysis, systems of incarceration simply recategorize and redistribute people into other violent carceral institutions for other manufactured reasons, often based on purported health concerns, criminality, and vulnerability. Knowing this, we are left no choice but to view carcerality much more broadly, through a disability-justice lens. If we fail to fill this gap in our collective consciousness, ableism will continue to be used as an excuse for inflicting violence upon marginalized people under the guise of care, treatment, and rehabilitation.

*

THE DIFFERENCE BETWEEN DISABILITY RIGHTS
AND DISABILITY JUSTICE

Whereas disability rights[36] seeks to change social conditions for some disabled people via law and policy,[37] disability justice moves beyond[38] law and policy. Disability justice seeks to radically transform social conditions and norms in order to affirm and support all people's inherent right to live and thrive. All social justice movements, then, must put the needs of disabled people—especially those at the margins of the margins—front and center. This work begins with unearthing and understanding the inextricable links between ableism and other systems of oppression.

Abolitionist movements must contend with how disability and ableism interact with[39] carceral-medical systems. These movements must be committed to abolishing *all* spaces to which marginalized people are disappeared. Disability rights communities must begin to practice disability justice[40] and disability solidarity.[41] Both of these frameworks demand a radical reorientation of our collective understanding of systems of oppression, especially as related to disability, inter/dependence, and carcerality. Advocates for any other form of social justice, especially racial, environmental, and economic justice, must work to understand how ableism interacts with other oppressions and violence to create, perpetuate, and exacerbate inequities.

Such a comprehensive approach would challenge carcerality at its core.[42] No longer could arbitrary concepts of class, criminality, or disability serve as a wedge between disability and abolitionists' struggles, for they are one and the same.

Similar to transformative justice[43] and abolition frameworks, disability justice fundamentally alters our approach to everything we think and do. It provides meaningful and necessary context[44] for marginalized people's responses to their lived experiences. It helps us politicize our disabilities, love ourselves and others more fully,[45] creatively dismantle oppression, and uplift people who are perpetually marginalized within our own communities and movements. It honors Black/Indigenous disabled wisdom,[46] builds strong care networks,[47] and develops community/cultural health and healing workers. It helps foreground the necessity of harm reduction, healing, and transformative justice, and supplants punitive responses that find refuge in carceral logics and spaces. And it develops the requisite relationships,[48] knowledge, and tools to help us practice accountable advocacy across identities, communities, and movements.

Abolition depends on racial, economic, and healing justice—all of which depend on disability justice. We have an opportunity to bring to the fore experiences and connections that have largely been invisibilized in the abolition movement. Now is the time to challenge dominant narratives about disability, ableism, policing, and incarceration—to invite people to revisit everything they think they know about interlocking systems of oppression, and to commit themselves to disability justice. Successful abolition strategies will weave communities together by highlighting the ties between oppressions that lead to seemingly intractable structural and systemic inequity. ◼

Resources:

The Abolition and Disability Justice Coalition:
   abolitionanddisabilityjustice.com
Disability Justice Culture Club:
   mutualaiddisasterrelief.org/co-conspirators/disability-justice-culture-club
HEARD:
   behearddc.org
Elandria Taught Us:
   docs.google.com/document/d/1xRutOaEUG_KB3Nslkvq
   -RODS5eJhdXljCOr9oHGH1Mo/edit

READER'S GUIDE

- What is "disability justice" and how does it differ from "disability rights"?

- Talila A. Lewis writes, "The united states government and corporations have always used constructed ideas about disability and criminality alongside constructed ideas about class and race to classify, criminalize, cage, and disappear its 'undesirables.'" What does the author mean by this? Provide examples to support your explanation.

- The author argues that "disability justice" is a requisite for abolition. Why? What are some historical and contemporary examples the author uses to support their case?

- What is "disability solidarity" and how can you participate in this work?

Snaps!

COLLECTIVE (QUEER) ABOLITION
ORGANIZING CREATED THIS MOMENT

By Erica R. Meiners

round fifteen years ago, a handful of queer students at a Southwest Side high school in Chicago invited me for a school visit. These young folks likely reached out because I was critical of (school) policing, flamingly out, and most importantly—easy to find.

According to these students (and a few teachers I talked to at that time), there were no out lesbian, gay, bisexual, transgendered, or queer (LGBTQ) adults at their school. Yet despite a culture of relentless homophobic and transphobic harassment—and other systemic forms of oppression such as white supremacy and ableism,[1] which are inseparable from gender- and sexuality-based violence—these young folks formed a PRIDE club.

What did they plan and dream about in their lunch hour and after school gatherings? A queer prom. An end to being beaten up under the stairways and then punished by school police and administrators as the instigator. More possibilities for queer intimacies and joy beyond the rigidly punishing binaries. Freedom from being treated as if they were *predatory, disposable, deviant* in their own neighborhood. A halt to the routine indignities—goaded and mocked for their hair, clothing, their *walk*—and the sanctions that always followed any attempt at self-defense. (I use *queer* as both a proxy or shorthand for LGBTQ— lesbian, gay, bisexual, transgender, and queer/questioning—but also to encompass a political stance that pushes back on *equality* and *normal* as goals or values, and to recognize that queer liberation always requires the end to other forms of domination such as misogyny and capitalism, which also diminish queer lives.)

These students knew that another world was possible—already unfolding—but wasn't within reach in their schools and communities. Collectively, they stretched to try to find, feel, and build something different.

Of course, I wasn't any solution—but I did support this cluster to forge their own bridges and connections to others, particularly to groups pushing back on the violence queers experienced in schools. And I got out of their way.

As the movement to remove police from schools—and to defund police more widely—heated up over the summer of 2020, my memory flashed back to this handful of young folks who, with commitment and style, inhabited something still often marked as unimaginable and toxic—*queer*—and both attempted to pushed back on school police, administrators, and security guards while insisting on gender and sexual self-determination. Often extinguished as a precursor to this political moment, tiny clusters of queer students named the false promise of safety embedded in policing, and as importantly with fierce joy and without any permission, imagined and demanded something different.

As scholar and poet Gloria Anzaldúa reminds us, "Nothing happens in the 'real' world unless it first happens in the images in our heads."[2] Abolition requires the desire and the capacity to imagine—

collectively—that something different is possible. The project of both dreaming and acting as if another world is possible is queer labor, indeed.

Yet campaigns for police-free schools—or more widely our abolitionist present—are rarely recognized as queer struggles.

"There are no single-issue struggles because we don't live single-issue lives," as Audre Lorde wrote in 1984, yet queerness and queer lives are often erased in most mainstream recitations of the violence of the criminal legal system. While research about sexuality and gender identity across the criminal legal system is uneven, available data flags the grotesquely high numbers of queer youth of color across every facet of detention.[3] LGBTQ students, particularly students of color, overflow all categories of school discipline—detention, suspension, and expulsion. Approximately 20 percent of people surveyed[4] in a youth detention center identified as something other than heterosexual and cisgender, 39.9 percent of girls in detention in California identify as LBQ/GNCT (lesbian, bisexual, queer/gender-nonconforming and transgender), and 85 percent of these youth are of color. The tentacles of the carceral state also includes child and family services or what Dorothy Roberts names the "family regulation system."[5] For instance, "19 percent of youth in LA's [Los Angeles's] foster care system identify as LGBTQ."[6] Again, an intersectional lens—or an analysis that race, gender, sexuality, ability are co-constitutive—is imperative: 95 percent of the youth in foster care are also nonwhite.

While these numbers are staggering, these "facts"—usually distilled, vetted, and archived by the very institutions that sanction and reward harm—mislead as often as they illuminate. The deployment of these statistics suggests that there is an acceptable or a not "disproportionate" rate of LGBTQ incarceration. Absent from these statistics are how homophobia and transphobia force underreporting—*I can't tell anyone who I am*—and all the queers not formally in the child welfare system who couch surf and build mutual aid networks and "stay with friends" because home, foster care, and group homes are unsafe.

The specificity and intensity of the violence of anti-Black racism and transphobia is often elided within datasets summarizing the experiences of "LGBTQ" or "queer" youth. Also erased in this snap-shot is that law enforcement—police, Immigration and Customs En-forcement officers, corrections staff, school security guards—are often key perpetrators of gender and sexual violence.[7] Most centrally, these statistics don't offer the *why* and the creative forms of resistance and survival[8] telegraphed by people's real lives: In 2012, after years of be-ing spit on and dodging rocks, empty bottles, and an endless parade of derogatory names, Dynasty Young was expelled from school after firing a stun gun in the air as a form of self-defense.[9] School leadership had repeatedly refused to intervene, arguing that Dynasty's "flamboyance" justified any harm. While national pressure forced school leadership to rescind this punishment, few get this opportunity for a wide platform. And let's not forget that the public circulation of Dynasty's pain only delivered an impoverished state response: *we will no longer expel you.*

To survive and flourish, some queer folks intimately recognize that the tools the state provides in the name of safety or protection—police and social work, to name a few—create harm. By necessity, queers, in-cluding young people, have often been at the forefront of abolitionist, or proto-abolitionist, organizing. In the 1960s, the San Francisco–based "homosexual and transsexual" youth organization, Vanguard, orga-nized against the routine police practice of harassing and arresting poor people (including unhoused youth) from neighborhoods such as the Tenderloin—a practice colloquially known as "street sweeping."[10] In the early 1970s, the Ann Arbor–based group Youth Liberation Organization organized against "adult chauvinism" and imperialism and for commu-nal families and the "unhindered" right of sexual self-determination (among other radical goals), publishing and distributing a newsletter for middle and high school students.

Over the last decade, a queer youth of color organization in New Orleans, BreakOUT!, spotlighted the routineness of the policing, pro-filing, and punishing of queer youth of color through campaigns such as "We Deserve Better," and illustrated that law enforcement personnel are often the primary instigators of harm for young queer folks: Break-OUT!'s research found that fifteen out of fifteen trans youth reported being propositioned by a New Orleans police officer for sex.[11] In 2013, New York City's queer youth network FIERCE! worked collaboratively to challenge a routine police practice: condom possession functioned as evidence to detain or arrest queer youth of color on the charge of "intent to solicit or engage in prostitution."[12]

Decades of this local organizing, propelled by collectives of young queer folks of color and shaped by national networks such as Critical Resistance and INCITE!, chipped away at the false "common sense" that prison and policing (and compulsory heterosexuality and gender conformity) make our communities safer. (Notably the campaigns and organizing did not, and still do not, demand more gay social workers or lesbian cops, or trans-specific beds in youth prisons.) As this genealogy of critical abolitionist organizing reminds us: making freedom is everyday queer labor.

And yet we must avoid romanticizing any network, campaign, or project, particularly those led by young people. "Youth" is a flexible and often dangerous category gifted to some, denied to others, and a burden to many: People with disabilities are perpetually infantilized, Black/Brown folks—*as early as Kindergarten*[13]—are "aged up,"[14] or assumed to be older, and punished as adults, while twenty-year-old affluent white people are "aged down" and marked as "emerging adults"[15] with a get-out-of-jail-free-card. Far from static, these categories mask the wildly uneven and harmful ways that life-giving attributes—innocence and culpability—are unevenly distributed across race, gender, and ability.

Many forms of organizing use these age-related categories uncritically and/or tokenize young people's participation and also center campaigns directly on ideological cul de sacs rooted in these flexible artifacts. For example, the innocence of (some) children, their innate ability to "rehabilitate," fuels criminal legal *reform* campaigns to close *youth* prisons. Yet these same logics—youth as exceptional, innocent, changeable—also buttress the rationale for insidious forms of carcerality: Public registries, mandated reporter laws, and criminal background checks expand in the name of (white) child protection but fail abysmally to protect any child. Fetishizing youth also neatly elides adult accountability; *that is work for the young, let them lead the way.* The empty elevation of young folks can also produce the perpetually awkward question—what of the grown-up youth activist?

The goal is not to exceptionalize or romanticize any organizing, but rather to name and proliferate all the radical, feminist, queer, autonomous, Black and/or Indigenous, and other overlapping movements that deeply inform our abolitionist present *without* triggering these trip wires of the carceral state. These radical genealogies continue to shape our landscape: Today, in Chicago, collectives of queer young folks, disproportionately Black and Latinx and feminist—Assata's Daughters, Black Youth Project (BYP) 100, Brave Space Alliance, Chicago Freedom School—are at the forefront of pushing abolitionist thinking and practice. From the #nocopacademy campaign that challenged the city's decision to build a ninety-five-million-dollar police academy on the west side of Chicago, to the organizing that is demanding the removal of police from public schools, queers continue to be a militant, joyous, and visionary force.

And like the queer high school students who reached out years ago— we are not waiting for anyone's permission to imagine and build flourishing communities where no one is disposable. Queer labor, indeed. ◢

Resources:

Youth Liberation Organization:
    youthliberation.com
Critical Resistance:
    criticalresistance.org
INCITE!:
    incite-national.org

READER'S GUIDE

- How does Erica R. Meiners define and use the term "queer"?

- The author writes that "campaigns for police-free schools—or more widely our abolitionist present—are rarely recognized as queer struggles." Why is this often the case? And how does the author argue that the two political projects—abolition and queer struggle—are inextricably intertwined?

- The author argues that the "tools the state provides" create harm. How?

- The author writes that "queers, including young people, have often been at the forefront of abolitionist, or proto-abolitionist, organizing" and cites organizations like Vanguard, BreakOUT!, and FIERCE!. Please take some time to explore these organizations and learn about their histories. How does their work help to usher in a world that is safer and freer?

Schools as Carceral Spaces

Police entered schools in the 1950s as **School Resource Officers** (SROs) to build "friendly" youth-police relations. With the "War on Drugs" and zero-tolerance policies, their presence grew.

In 1975, **only 1%** of schools were **patrolled by police officers**.[1]

By 2018, **58%** of schools had either a SRO or sworn officer.[2]

Today, **14 million** students are in schools with police but no counselor, nurse, psychologist, or social worker.[3]

"Black students from pre-kindergarten through twelfth grade are overrepresented in every form of discipline— from teacher-issued referrals to corporal punishment to suspensions, expulsions, and police arrests."

DR. KIHANA MIRAYA ROSS

■ Black or African American ☐ White ▨ Latinx ▨ Asian ■ Other [4]

TOTAL ENROLLMENT
15% 49% 26% 5%

PHYSICALLY OR MECHANICALLY RESTRAINED
27% 48% 17%

ARRESTED/REFERRED TO LAW ENFORCEMENT
31% 36% 24% 5%

EXPULSION
33% 37% 22%

In the 1990s, Black and Latinx youth were portrayed as **superpredators** in the media and the White House:

"The kinds of kids that are called superpredators. No conscience. No empathy. . . . We have to bring them to heel."

HILLARY CLINTON

Black youth, perceived as superpredators, were twice as likely to be sentenced to **life without parole** or LWOP. [5]

In April 2021, the Supreme Court ruled that sentencing juveniles to life is not cruel and unusual punishment.

"The harm from these sentences will not fall equally. The racial disparities in juvenile LWOP sentencing are stark: 70 percent of all youths sentenced to LWOP are children of color."

JUSTICE SONIA SOTOMAYOR [6]

Black youth—and adults— are subjected to higher rates of arrest.

- ■ Black or African American
- ☐ White
- ▨ Other

ADULT ARRESTS [7]

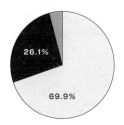

26.1%

69.9%

YOUTH ARRESTS

33.9%

62.5%

TOTAL OF POPULATION [8]

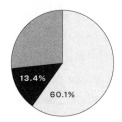

13.4%

60.1%

Data stories researched and conceptualized by Tamara K. Nopper

How Abolition
Makes Schools Safer

FUNNELING OUR CHILDREN
FROM CLASSROOMS TO CAGES ENDS NOW

By kihana miraya ross

I was sixteen years old, stopped at a red light, the first time I saw sirens flashing in my rearview mirror.

Stomach tight, breath stifled, and heart pounding, I looked over at my friend in the passenger seat. The same terror trying to close my throat stared back at me through his eyes. I could hear a muffled voice over a loudspeaker telling me to pull over. Instead, I hit the gas, bolting through the red light and racing down the street. My friend yelled at me, "What are you doing? Pull over!" I didn't know what I was doing. It didn't make logical sense. All I knew was that we were in imminent danger and I had to get away. But my friend was right. Escape was impossible. My barely running old-school Tercel's horsepower was no match for a police cruiser, and capture after a chase was even more dangerous. I pulled over. I rolled my window down as the cop quickly approached demanding an answer. "I got scared," I said. "I'm sorry."

While I have since learned how to navigate the constricting terror I feel when I see flashing lights behind me (this hasn't changed despite nearly three decades and a professorship at a prestigious university), I want to be clear that this panic isn't limited to when we recognize the shape of a police car in our rearview mirror. It isn't limited to the myriad other activities people racialized as Black are brutalized for, such as walking or swinging or singing or laughing or playing or watching television or sleeping or breathing. It is also something many of our babies feel as they walk into their schools, as they sit in classrooms, as they navigate hallways between classes. It is what happens when you feel your body tighten as you realize cops are not in schools to protect you. They are there to protect schools from you.

Beyond the ways this understanding manifests in our bodies, the relationship between Black children and the school's larger disciplinary structure is clear: Both principals and teachers in US public schools are over eighty percent white,[1] and nearly seventy percent of police in schools[2] are white. Regardless of the discipliner's gender (the majority of teachers and principals are women, and the majority of police in schools are men), Black students from pre-kindergarten through twelfth grade are overrepresented in every form of discipline—from teacher-issued referrals to corporal punishment to suspensions, expulsions, and police arrests.

Even Black toddlers in pre-school, as young as three years old, are disproportionately[3] sent out of the classroom, suspended, and expelled. What they can look forward to as they enter elementary school are cops who think they are old enough to be arrested: Kaia Rolle,[4] a six-year-old girl in Florida, was handcuffed, placed in the back of a police cruiser, and taken to a juvenile detention facility simply for throwing a tantrum in class. By the time her grandmother became aware of what happened, young Kaia had already had her mugshot taken and fingerprints recorded.

Six years old. Hopscotch, jump rope, and mud pies years old. Let that sink in.

Kaia is only one of the thousands of Black students harassed, assaulted, and arrested in schools every year—the very beginning of a school-to-prison pipeline that, through a system of discipline and marginalization, feeds children directly into the carceral system. Perhaps even more terrifying, however, is the fact that these experiences are too often normalized as part of Black students' reality in schools. Having learned early on about the unrelenting violence police unleash on those racialized Black, these children enter school with survival sensibilities based on a recognition of how police see them and what this means for how they must necessarily see police.

In fact, Black students are most likely to report not feeling any safer[5] with an officer on their campus and least likely to agree with positive statements about the police in their schools. As a part of my own ethnographic work with Black high-school girls, I interviewed students extensively about their experiences in schools—including with school police. One of my students remarked, "We're a target. And they see us as a threat, so you know we see them as a threat." If the police are threatened by Blackness more broadly, this signals the impossibility of a protective relationship[6] between the police as a structure and Black people as human beings.

Students also shared numerous stories of their own negative interactions with police. Students discussed being followed, male family members being called the N-word, having guns put to their heads during raids of their homes, and being fondled inappropriately during unprovoked searches at school. Their own experiences, and the experiences of Black people *en masse*, led students to believe that police were against them and that police would either be unnecessarily brutal, or unhelpful and certainly nonprotective, in the event their assistance may have been needed.

Another one of my students commented, "I feel like police officers show different feelings toward Black people then they would to a normal, like, white person." A normal white person. While this student's words speak for themselves, I want to emphasize the way in which she understands police to be able to see the humanity in white people (look, a normal person) while they look at Black people "differently." This student understands that for police, Black people are not quite normal; they are something else entirely.

It is precisely this inability to recognize Black humanity that permeates students' broader anti-Black experiences in schools. Indeed, anti-Blackness in education is not simply about the ways Black students are disproportionately punished by teachers, administrators, and actual gun-toting police officers. It is also about the ways Black students are policed more broadly—the attacks against our hair in locs, braids, and even the Afros that grow naturally from our heads. The ways Black girls are hypersexualized and dress-coded disproportionately. The ways Black boys' bodies are adultified and rendered criminalblackman.[7] The ways LGBTQ and gender-nonbinary Black students are erased, marginalized, and othered. The ways our bodies—our skin, our hair, our clothes, our voice, our body language, our cadence, our minds—have always represented a dangerous intrusion within educational institutions structured by anti-Black solidarity. It is about the policing of the boundaries of our existence—the way our very presence, let alone our struggle, our brilliance, our creativity, and our ingenuity, are misrepresented and/or effectively stamped out of the curriculum and denied space in schools more broadly.

So while the decades-long fight led by students, parents, activists, and organizations[8] alike to abolish police in schools is perhaps more readily understandable, we must also be calling for the abolition of policing in schools more broadly. The abolition of policies, practices, and structures[9] that facilitate and support the narrative that Black students are a problem. The abolition of a system that uses our tax dollars to wield both Tasers and textbooks against us. The abolition of the pipeline that funnels our babies from classrooms to cages.

Renowned Black feminist activist and scholar Angela Y. Davis[10] recently remarked[11] that "abolition is really about rethinking the kind of future we want." What we want is for schools and classrooms to be spaces of love. Not just a love for the Harlem Renaissance or the civil rights movement but love for loud colors and loud voices. Love for sagging pants, hoodies, and corner store candies. Love for gold grills and belly laughs on hot summer porches. We want schools to be sites of struggle, to engage with Black folks' historical and contemporary yearning to be at peace. To seek refuge from an anti-Black world, where Black children can dream weightless, unracialized, and human. Where language flows freely, where existence is nurtured, and resistance is breath. Where the Black educational imagination dances wildly into the night—quenching the thirst of yearning and giving birth to becoming. ◪

READER'S GUIDE

- kihana miraya ross argues that for Black youth, cops in schools are "there to protect schools from you." What does ross mean by this statement?

- The author demonstrates that school disciplinary structures are racialized as fundamentally anti-Black. What evidence does the author draw on to support this argument?

- The author writes, "Indeed, anti-Blackness in education is not simply about the ways Black students are disproportionately punished by teachers, administrators, and actual gun-toting police officers. It is also about the ways Black students are policed more broadly—the attacks against our hair in locs, braids, and even the Afros that grow naturally from our heads." Do your own experiences confirm ross's depiction? Why or why not?

- What steps can you personally take to support, in the words of the author, "the abolition of policies, practices, and structures that facilitate and support the narrative that Black students are a problem"? Further, what does a relevant and liberatory education look like for Black students? Can you cite any examples from your own life?

We Must Center Black Women

BREONNA TAYLOR AND BEARING WITNESS TO
BLACK WOMEN'S EXPENDABILITY

By Kimberlé Crenshaw

Why #SayHerName is crucial to the struggle for Black freedom

On September 23, 2020, Kentucky Attorney General Daniel Cameron delivered the much-anticipated decision[1] on whether Breonna Taylor's killers would be prosecuted. Guided by Cameron's judgment of the legality of the officers' actions, a grand jury decided that none of the officers involved in killing Breonna Taylor would stand trial for her death.

Cameron's gut-wrenching announcement[2] came on the sixty-fifth anniversary of another jury decision that absolved white men for a murder that transformed the nation: On September 23, 1955, twelve white jurors took less than two hours to acquit two white men of torturing and killing fourteen-year-old Chicago native Emmett Till[3] in Money, Mississippi.

Mamie Till's decision to hold an open-casket funeral for her son—in order to, in her words, "Let the people see what they did to my boy"—awakened an entire generation of young African Americans to take up the centuries -long struggle for Black freedom. Her simple act demanded that the world bear witness to the profound savagery of white racism and to reckon with the complicitous legal system that effectively facilitated its ongoing horrors.

Indeed, the galvanizing dimension of Emmett Till's murder was not the shock that a lynching had happened in 1955, but that such a gruesome, unspeakable killing was licensed by a legal system that would hold no one accountable. Similarly, the state's judgment that no legal or moral harm had been done to Breonna Taylor offers an abject lesson in the contemporary ways that law has facilitated a particularly lethal relationship between Black bodies and the police. The fact that the officers who killed her would be subject to no consequences for taking her life uncloaks both the failed structures of our legal system and the long-overdue confrontation with how the contours of acceptable police practice are shot through with anti-Black racism.

This unveiling could well be a ground-shifting moment in the epic struggle against anti-Black violence. Like the murder of Emmett Till three generations ago, the police killing of Breonna Taylor and the legal judgment that lent it legitimacy may inspire a new generation to repudiate policing, illegitimate state power, and its legalized facilitation against Black bodies.

If Breonna's story serves as the cornerstone for a generation of activism, like Emmett's did, it will foreground something new in the Black freedom struggle, something that the #SayHerName Campaign has been fighting for since 2014: It will make all Black women central to any analysis of and challenge to anti-Blackness.

Some will seize on differences between the two killings to discount the relevance of Emmett Till's death to Breonna Taylor's. Emmett was tortured and killed by vigilantes enforcing Southern codes of white supremacy, and his killers were acquitted after a full trial by an all-white jury. The trial's faux-murder-mystery frame belied the fact that jurors had every reason to know that the two accused had conspired with others to kidnap and kill the fourteen-year-old.

Their hasty acquittal amounted to a brazen act of jury nullification.[4] Breonna, by contrast, was killed by sworn officers who were executing a warrant. Her death was ultimately framed by a grand jury—sealed proceedings headed up by Kentucky's African American Attorney General—as a permissible homicide, committed during the course of law enforcement.

In both Breonna's and Emmett's deaths, the state blamed the victims for alleged behaviors that triggered the murderous responses by white men empowered to exercise their prerogative to kill. Pretense abounded in both the assertion that there really was reasonable doubt that J. W. Milam and Roy Bryant killed Emmett Till and that Myles Cosgrove, Brett Hankison, and Jonathan Mattingly really had no choice but to shoot into Breonna Taylor's home—stopping to reload—after they encountered one shot from an occupant who had the right to fire it.

The overkill on display in these murders renders the racially punitive aspects of both exceptionally legible: Neither death would be remotely imaginable had the racial roles been reversed. The contemporary failure to hold police accountable for their wanton disregard for Black lives is as much of an expression of embedded racial power as was the legal facilitation of white supremacist vigilante violence. And it has forced every Black woman to confront a horrifying fact: "Breonna could easily be me."

Like so many of us, Breonna had curled up in the arms of a loved one after a long day of work to watch a movie as she drifted off to sleep. In the wee hours of the morning, she was abruptly awakened by an attack on her home from persons unknown. It escalated after a single gunshot fired from her boyfriend in self-defense prompted at least thirty-two rounds from the plainclothes firing squad attempting to annihilate them both. After being struck by a fusillade of bullets, she took her last breath as her boyfriend begged her to stay with him, never knowing that the very men who took her life were the same men sworn to protect her.

Those of us who have chanted "We are Breonna Taylor!" are saying that we can imagine our lifeless bodies left in the hallways of our homes. We can imagine ourselves exposed for hours[5] while uniformed vultures pick through the remnants of our lives, seizing upon choices we made and those that were made for us in order to quiet the qualms that might otherwise arise had we been another woman in a different body, in a different part of town, living a different life, with a different man endeavoring to protect us.

We can watch in our minds' eye the belated but widespread saying of our names to insist that our shuttered futures should be made to count for something. We can feel the hope that with the gaze of the world finally upon us, that the fact that we had done nothing wrong would make it wrong that we'd been reduced to nothing. And we can taste the tears that mark our bitter awareness that despite the countless demands to arrest the cops that killed us, our deaths would ultimately be dismissed as just one of those things that happens: A no-harm, no-foul misfortune that counts among the acceptable costs of maintaining the anti-Black foundations of police and policing.

Reduced to collateral damage, our deaths can seem so natural that some Black men dismiss them with the same breezy equation that Charles Barkley and Shaquille O'Neal did: A man had shot at intruders in self-defense, and for his mistaken belief that the right to self-defense applies to us, our deaths are justified. Black women like Breonna Taylor have been shunted—by race, class, and gender—into a place far from the gated neighborhoods men like Barkley and O'Neal have been permitted to occupy. It's hard to believe that the same violence and the same justification would be accepted had it been their wives or girlfriends whom they'd sought to protect.

This double loss of life—first at the hands of police, and then in the justification of death—might otherwise have continued unaddressed were it not for the fact that this time the whole world has borne witness. The open and notorious exposure of the brutal truth that lays beneath the surface of law-and-order justification is fully legible with unprecedented clarity. Breonna, like Emmett, lost her life according to the false imperative that this is just the way things have to be. It's a lie built around a contingent set of practices that reflect and sustain a historic pattern of police power that is racist and patriarchal.

Breonna Taylor's murder stands as a potential historical parallel to Emmett Till's only if the gendered racism that Black women have always faced is understood to be as vital to our justice demands as was the gendered racism that killed Emmett Till. Emmett's body forced us to confront the volcanic reservoir of white supremacy that was fed a boy's life—a ritualist sacrifice born out of the white male ownership of white women. His murder was a blood sport that was inhumane even if the claims that preceded it had been true. That it was predicated on a lie adds but an asterisk to the horror it unleashed.

That the murder was situated as a conflict between men—supposedly between a Black boy and white men over the sexual ownership of a white woman's body—did not diminish that Emmett's death was a symbol of the overarching subordination of the entire Black community. Its gendered specificity only enhanced the virulence of anti-Black racism, writing Emmett into a long history of legal and extra-legal lynchings that was understood as the quintessential embodiment of white supremacy. His murder helped frame a zoomed-out view of how lost lives in the 1950s were linked to lost lives in the 1930s, 1920s, 1870s, and 1610s. It was a murder that connected a chain of tyranny expressed from within law and at its margins.

Emmett Till's death continues to ground a particular vision of anti-Black racism rooted in patriarchal white supremacy. But the telling remainder of that story is in the discarding of Black women as subjects of anti-Black racism. For us to mobilize around Breonna Taylor in the same way our foremothers and forefathers mobilized around Emmett, we must bear witness to the ways that Black women's precarity is a continuous enactment of surveillance and punishment[6] grounded in slavery's logics.

To bear witness to this buried history, we must equip ourselves with tools to excavate and recover. This is the work of the African American

Policy Forum and our #SayHerName Campaign: to re-center Black women's vulnerability as the subject of anti-racist mobilization.

Turning back the clock on #SayHerName links Breonna's vulnerability in her own home to the fact that Black women were unsafe in the slave quarters, in the fields, and in the homes of white people that they worked for. It regrounds anti-racism in the reality that Black women have never had the right to self-defense—at least not one that the state was bound to respect.

Thinking of #SayHerName within this broader historical context opens up the possibility of reclaiming what's been forgotten and recalibrating our imaginations in a way that broadens the scope of what we are fighting for today. It expands the scope of the state's role in facilitating, licensing, and authorizing multiple forms of violence against us.

Imagine how integral the fight against misogyny might have become had Fannie Lou Hamer's struggles against forced sterilization been as centered in the discourses against racism as her struggle to vote was. One can only dream about how sexual harassment and assault would be centered as a form of anti-Black racism if Rosa Parks's entry into the American imagination began when she was a rape crisis advocate for Recy Taylor. And one can only envision the world we would be living in now if race and gender had not been violently torn apart when Anita Hill came forward and told her story.

Building on #SayHerName and imagining safe futures for all Black women would be a firm step toward a new social order without the terror of the anti-Blackness that suffuses policing in the United States. It would mean not simply becoming witnesses of history, but being activists contesting the consequences of that history in the here and now. It would mean ensuring that the Emmett Tills, Eric Garners, Tamir Rices, George Floyds, Tony McDades, and Mike Browns are linked to the Breonna Taylors, Michelle Cusseauxs, Tanisha Andersons, Kayla Moores, and India Kagers—all Black lives lost to police violence. It would mean that all Black women are fully centered in every effort to dismantle the barriers to Black freedom.

It is now up to those of us invested in confronting and challenging this vicious history to decide whether Breonna's killing will mobilize an entire generation to foreground and challenge the many gendered dimensions of anti-Black racism. For our #SayHerName Campaign, this means working directly with the mothers and sisters of Black women, girls, and femmes killed by police, and amplifying their testimony to inform our activism.

These mothers, like Mamie Till sixty-six years ago, are fighting to show the world what the law did to their children and to seed a movement to do something about it. Join them, and us, in fighting for a history that could be. One in which all Black lives mattered. ◾

Resources:

African American Policy Forum:
    aapf.org
#SayHerName Campaign:
    aapf.org/sayhername

READER'S GUIDE

- Kimberlé Crenshaw writes, "If Breonna's story serves as the cornerstone for a generation of activism, like Emmett's did, it will foreground something new in the Black freedom struggle, something that the #SayHerName Campaign has been fighting for since 2014: It will make all Black women central to any analysis of and challenge to anti-Blackness." What is the #SayHerName campaign the author describes, and why is centering all Black women central to the goal of challenging anti-Blackness?

- The author argues, "In both Breonna's and Emmett's deaths, the state blamed the victims for alleged behaviors that triggered the murderous responses by white men empowered to exercise their prerogative to kill." What other similarities do you see between these two murders and trials? What differences?

- The author writes, "The contemporary failure to hold police accountable for their wanton disregard for Black lives is as much of an expression of embedded racial power as was the legal facilitation of white supremacist vigilante violence." What is the relationship between racial power, white supremacist vigilante violence, and police impunity?

- What examples does the author cite for centering and being more accountable to Black women and femmes? How can you support and amplify the #SayHerName work?

PART

II

Prisons & Carcerality

Stolen Freedom

THE ONGOING INCARCERATION OF CALIFORNIA'S INDIGENOUS PEOPLES

By Morning Star Gali

A bolition is more than an idea. Abolition is decolonization. Abolition on stolen land, as is the case for Indigenous communities, is a radical dismantling of the carceral state. Carceral Colonialism[1] is defined as the policies, practices, and institutions, rooted in colonialism, in which the criminal justice system has continued to incarcerate Indigenous peoples for expressions of cultural and ceremonial practices.

For twenty-five years, Indigenous rights activists fought for an official UN declaration on the[2] rights of Indigenous peoples—for a document that doesn't just affirm our individual human rights, but asserts our inherent and inalienable collective rights as Indigenous peoples.

In 2007, that document was finally adopted by the UN's General Assembly. Article 10[3] of the UN Declaration on the Rights of Indigenous Peoples[4] states that "Indigenous peoples shall not be forcibly removed from their lands or territories. No relocation shall take place without the free, prior and informed consent of the Indigenous peoples concerned and after agreement on just and fair compensation and, where possible, with the option of return."

Yet, in the United States, Indigenous communities continue to be impacted by historical and ongoing forms of settler colonialism—the violent uprooting, removal, and displacement of Indigenous peoples through criminalization and dispossession from our lands, communities, culture, and traditional lifeways. It was not until August 11, 1978, with the passage of the American Indian Religious Freedom Act, that Native peoples were allowed to openly practice ceremonies, utilize sacred objects and materials, and gain access to sacred places. Up until this time, Indigenous peoples throughout the United States were not afforded the rights of religious exercise and cultural protections as listed in the US constitution. And that settler colonialism, while familiar to so many Indigenous people throughout the country, has played an outsize role in the history of California. Since the Spanish and Mexican colonial periods of missionization and the Gold Rush–era,[5] Anglo military occupation of the state, the criminalization and incarceration of Native peoples through racial and gendered violence has been deployed as a tool of colonial control and genocide.

* * *

Indigenous peoples have always migrated across our sacred lands and continue to do so. It is only the Indigenous people of the Americas, though, who have been forcibly removed, caged, and interned on reservations and throughout California's rancheria systems,[6] a system that deemed California Native peoples as homeless on our Tribal lands and designated allotments in the form of checkerboarded and privatized[7] "trust lands" that constitute a fraction of our ancestral territories.

Oppression came long before the rancherias, however. California's first prisons existed through the mission system: twenty-one of them, built between 1769 and 1823, and stretching from San Diego to Sonoma along what was known as California's "El Camino Real," held Indigenous people as laborers[8] while Franciscan missionaries attempted to convert them to Christianity. The mission system[9] created an entirely new social construction of "Mission Indians," which led to forced assimilation, cultural erasure, and the homogenization and destruction of Tribal identity.

Our California Indigenous ancestors were the first to experience incarceration and chattel slavery[10] within the state of California and endured eight decades of incarceration between the mission and Gold Rush eras (1769–1849). Mostly forced into residence in and near satellite forts and missions, California Tribal communities such as the Ohlone, Coast Miwok, Chumash, Kumeyaay, Pomo, and Patwin relatives had to stay under the threat of violence. The workers included the local Indigenous population pressed and enslaved as draft labor for farms and ranches under the management of the church or Spanish Military personnel and settlers.

This triad of military, church, and colonial settlements weren't simply institutions of imperial power and settlement: They had the specific purpose of policing, forced religious conversion and reeducation, and enslavement and population control so as to exploit local resources through Indigenous people's forced labor.

In 1850, California became a state under the so-called Compromise of 1850. At the time, some of the state's first civilian police departments were established within the greater San Francisco Bay Area and San Jose. A new pattern of violence and repression emerged and a campaign of near-total genocide commenced against the state's native population.[11] Whereas the US Army/Navy Shore Patrols, US Army Cavalry, and the California Rangers had succeeded Spanish Conquistadors and Mexican Militia in rounding up Indigenous peoples for forced labor and enslavement,[12] a new doctrine of "red skin" genocide and scalp bounties produced roving gangs of vigilantes and terrorists.

A succession of wars, skirmishes, and massacres decimated California's Indigenous bands to such an extent that roughly within fifty years entire Tribal groups and extended Indigenous family lines had ceased to exist. This violence was met with forms of resistance including seeking shelter in farms and ranches, as well as survival tactics like Indigenous intertribal marriage and adopting the identity of ethnic Mexicanos in order to escape the genocidal pogroms targeting the native Indigenous population. For nearly a century, to be an Indigenous California Native was to live a life in hiding, anonymity, and denial of one's own identity. Life in a prison—a prison of secrecy.

To bring attention to yourself usually resulted in some form of punishment. This still affects our population numbers as determined by the US Census and accounts for the undercount of Tribal peoples.[13] As 80 percent of Tribal peoples now live within Urban environments, every time that a Tribal member is not included equates to a loss of already scarce infrastructure such as health care and housing.

* * *

The continued genocidal laws and policies that exist today, are a continuation of the mass genocide and erasure of the "founding" of California as a state over 170 years ago.

"That a war of extermination will continue to be waged between the two races until the Indian race becomes extinct must be expected," said California's first governor, Peter Burnett, in an 1851 state of the state address.[14]

The Indian Wars have never ceased. In addition to biological weapons used against Indigenous populations in the form of smallpox-infested blankets and strychnine-laced food, California Tribal peoples have faced an onslaught of genocidal practices enacted to ensure the fracturing of our Tribal lands and communities.

We are the only people in the United States for which the federal government requires proof of blood quantum to prove ancestry,[15] a government-imposed system to intentionally limit Tribal enrollment and control the definition of who is and who is not considered to be a Native American person. This process—paper genocide,[16] as it is commonly known—is violent and dehumanizing and should be considered nothing less than a method of extermination. Whereas the definition of an Indigenous person anywhere else in the world is based on self-identification, the definition in the US context creates a complex application system to determine who can and cannot prove on paper their indigeneity.

Blood quantum requirements were employed to negate the US government's treaty obligations[17] by ensuring that there wouldn't be enough verified people to meet the treaties' conditions. As the burden of proof lies on the individual to provide documentation, such requirements lead to extinction of our Tribes. Settler-colonial systems such as Tribal governance over enrollment of Tribal membership were designed to decrease our membership base, as individuals would not be able to meet such complex requirements, such as meeting varied requirements for housing, education, and health care.

California Tribes exist today under rubrics of Federally Recognized, Non-Federally Recognized (NFR), State Recognized, Terminated, Unacknowledged, Disenfranchised, Disenrolled, and Indigenous peoples. In addition to California's unratified eighteen treaties[18] that created a complex and precarious political position for California Tribes and Tribal peoples, these fractured designations contribute to the lateral violence within our communities between the "haves and the have-nots," result in violent disruptions within our communities, and contribute to the overrepresentation of incarcerated Indigenous populations.[19]

To exist under the confinement of federal recognition status is in actuality a genocidal practice perpetuated by settler colonialism that targets Indigenous women, girls, and two-spirit (2Spirit)[20] trans and nonbinary relatives. This also contributes to the ongoing crisis of Missing and Murdered Indigenous Women, Girls, and Two-Spirit People[21] (#MMIWG2S), which began with the trafficking of Indigenous bodies by US soldiers. The result is a double marginalization within a justice system that criminalizes Native people but provides little to no resources when we ourselves are victims of violence. As the onus is placed on the survivor, classifications such as Non-Federally Recognized, State-Recognized, Terminated, Disenfranchised, and Disenrolled Tribal peoples provide challenges and barriers to accessing available services.[22] Many Tribal Nations are only allowed to allocate Tribal funding based on the service area that's in proximity to ancestral Tribal lands, rancheria, and reservation areas. By experiencing forms of violence that are racialized, gendered, and classed, the settler-colonial narrative upholds the burden of proof to provide documentation—for example, federal recognition status.

While missions, forts, reservations, and rancheria systems[23] together constituted the first institutions of incarceration within California, carceral practices continued through boarding schools and foster homes, group homes, and juvenile detention. This genocidal legacy of violent removal and cultural erasure continues today in forms of incarceration, family separation, and border militarization to divide and confine Indigenous families and communities. Today, such forms of criminalization and dispossession include the grotesque treatment of our Indigenous relatives at the southern border.

The ongoing criminalization of Indigenous peoples—whether through forced removal from our lands, family and community separation, or destabilizing our traditional and cultural knowledge—is intertwined with the way carceral institutions continue to forcibly remove Indigenous peoples. Oil pipelines, the lumber companies clear-cutting our sacred forests, and the prison industrial complex (PIC) all exist as extractive industries, dispossessing Indigenous peoples of both land and what settler colonialism refers to as resources.

The lineage of uninterrupted settler colonial violence remains present in the state's relationship to Indigenous peoples of California. California currently incarcerates over 241,000 people,[24] with Native peoples imprisoned at nearly four times the rate of White people, and almost double the rate of Latinxs, yet we comprise 2 percent of California's population. (The California Deptartment of Corrections and

Rehabilitation categorizes American Indian peoples under racial categories of "other.")[25]

* * *

In California, there may be no more established symbol of the carceral state—and resistance—than Alcatraz. For Ohlone peoples, its original inhabitants, it was considered unfit for human habitation, whereas for the US government, it was the paragon of incarceration.

In 1864, California Native leaders were captured and sent to Alcatraz[26] for resisting the dispossession and displacement of our lands and lifeways. Numerous California Tribes, including Yuki, Wailacki, Concow, Little Lake Pomo, Nomlacki, Pit River, Maidu, and Nisenan were forced to march to the Round Valley Reservation[27] on foot under fatal conditions. By 1868, Alcatraz had its first formal jailhouse facility for the long-term detention of military prisoners—Confederate prisoners of war. During the 1870s, Hopi, Apache, and Diné (Navajo) prisoners of war were incarcerated in Alcatraz for refusing to send their children to boarding school. "The Rock," as it became known, continued to be an ongoing location for the incarceration of insurgent anti-colonialists and Indigenous people well into the twentieth century.

Yet, long a place of misery, Alcatraz was given new meaning in 1969 during an extended nineteen-month-long occupation by Indigenous people organized by the then ad hoc organization "Indians of All Tribes" (IOAT).[28]

Alcatraz is not simply an island. It is a symbol of resistance and solidarity.

Every year, on the second Monday of October, I gather in solidarity with Indigenous peoples[29] from across the world in celebration and to honor the Alcatraz Occupation that took place fifty years ago. We gather with a community of twelve hundred to five thousand people and offer sunrise prayer offerings in remembrance of our ancestors who were imprisoned on the island, in honor of our family members who held the rock, and in resistance to all that we have endured and continue to carry for our children and all of our future generations.

During the sunrise prayers on the island, I often think of my own father and how he used to carry me on the island during those cold mornings over thirty-five years ago. I think about his time of incarceration, and the many incarcerated relatives that are separated from their families, children, and Tribal communities. I think of how fractured it is that punitive carceral practices have always been unfamiliar to Indigenous practices, and how our ceremonies of restoration and bringing the world back into balance are extrinsic to a settler-colonial framework.

My late father, Isidro Gali Jr., was incarcerated for over seven years at San Quentin State Penitentiary. Upon his release, he returned to California Department of Corrections and Rehabilitation (CDCR) as an American Indian spiritual advisor,[30] working on death row to offer ceremonial healing for other imprisoned Indigenous peoples. Redemption and healing of our peoples and communities is possible. Justice for Indigenous peoples outside of the confines of settler colonialism is a close reality. From my father's incarceration to his advocating for abolishing the death penalty, my family has carried on the struggle of freedom and justice, for all peoples.

We have sought to resist this alien and repressive carceral system for over five centuries. Traditionally, when Indigenous peoples have caused harm to one another, our cultural system dictates that payment is made in the form of money, fines, restitution, service, and banishment to the individuals and family members we have harmed, whether intentionally or not. This peacemaking and restorative justice model continues today in Tribal courts such as the Yurok Tribal Justice Center, founded by Yurok Chief Justice Abby Abinanti.[31]

Our healing is justice. Our healing is resistance. Our healing is meeting our prayers with action.

The castigative foundation of the United States is cracking, exposing a carceral system that we need to abolish. Our Afro-Indigenous relatives are on the front lines of experiencing state-sanctioned violence—and as Indigenous peoples, it is our responsibility to advocate and support the survival of our relations. One of my volunteer roles is co-leading the Healing Justice Committee for Anti Police-Terror Project Sacramento,[32] which provides support to families impacted by police terrorism and models community alternatives to policing, and its MH First Project. When I advocate for our Indigenous youth, both in my family of four children and within our community, I state that all of our Indigenous youth are considered system-impacted due to the institutional incarceration and generational impacts that have created fractures with our family unit.

Elimination of the settler colonial carceral state is necessary for a free and safe future. To this end, how do we address punishment and harm in a nonpunitive way? How do we utilize an Indigenous Justice[33] and decolonized abolitionist framework[34] to transition to holistic and survivor-centered practices? How can we heal ourselves individually and collectively in a way that does not further harm and contribute to the fracturing of our families and communities? I do not have all of the answers. I do know, however, that we could start by following Indigenous peoples' practices of restorative and transformative justice.[35]

By undoing the violent patriarchal practices of caging humans, and practicing rematriation—the restoration and healing of the land[36]— we and our communities can build an abolitionist future free from the fetters of settler colonialism. ◼

READER'S GUIDE

- What is decolonization and how does it relate to 1) the UN's 2007 Declaration on the Rights of Indigenous People and 2) the abolition of the carceral state?

- Morning Star Gali defines "settler colonialism" as "the violent uprooting, removal, and displacement of Indigenous peoples through criminalization and dispossession from our lands, communities, culture, and traditional lifeways." How do you believe settler colonialism works in practice? Please cite a few examples relevant to your own life.

- What, according to the author, constitutes the "first institutions of incarceration within California"? How do those institutions play out today?

- According to the author, what is healing? How does the author's analysis of healing relate to abolition? And how does the author's definition of healing relate to your own life?

Queer & Trans Liberation Requires Abolition

By Dean Spade

I n recent years, more and more police departments have rolled out rainbow-painted cop cars[1] for Pride, "Safe Place"[2] campaigns with rainbow cop-shield stickers, and other messaging that portrays cops as pro-LGBT. Is this progress? Are the police a positive force for queer and trans well-being?

Queer and trans activists have a long history of protesting against police violence. In fact, annual Pride celebrations mark the anniversary of the Stonewall Rebellion:[3] In June 1969, at a bar called the Stonewall Inn in New York City, queer and trans people fought back against the ongoing violence[4] they faced at the hands of the police. For a long time, queer and trans people, especially Black and Indigenous people and other people of color, have been some of the boldest leaders in movements for police and prison abolition (think of Angela Davis,[5] Kuwasi Balagoon,[6] Laura Whitehorn,[7] Miss Major,[8] Andrea Ritchie,[9] adrienne maree brown,[10] Mia Mingus,[11] Alisa Bierria,[12] Angélica Cházaro,[13] Tourmaline,[14] and Beth Richie[15]).

In the half-century since Stonewall, much has changed for queer and trans people. Social norms, media representations, and some laws have reduced the stigma associated with our communities. However, poverty,[16] housing insecurity,[17] discrimination,[18] and violence[19] are all still a reality for queer and trans people, especially trans people of color, queer and trans immigrants, and queer and trans people with disabilities. Unfortunately, police harassment[20] and violence,[21] as well as brutal violence in prisons,[22] jails, and detention centers,[23] remain a central source of violence in the lives of queer and trans people.

For these reasons, many queer and trans activists have rightfully pushed back on law enforcement's new pro-LGBT branding. Grand marshals and awardees at Pride celebrations have withdrawn[24] in opposition to police participation at Pride. Protesters[25] have blocked police contingents and created alternative events rejecting the idea[26] that police are LGBT-friendly and should be part of Pride celebrations. The fight over whether police belong in the annual celebrations that mark the anniversary of fighting back against the NYPD at Stonewall are but a sliver of the broader work queer and trans people are doing to abolish police, prisons, and borders.

Why is abolition so important to queer and trans resistance, and why have queer and trans people and communities been leaders and visionaries in the fight for abolition? First, because queer and trans people have been and remain targets of the police. Forty-eight percent of LGBTQ people responding to the National Crime Victimization Survey[27] report experiencing police misconduct. Other studies have shown that trans people are nearly four times more likely than cisgender people to experience police violence and seven times more likely[28] to experience physical violence when interacting with the police.

This violence is even more severe and targeted for Black and Latinx trans people. According to the National Center for Transgender Equality,[29] 38 percent of Black trans people report having been harassed by police, and 15 percent report having been assaulted by police. Trans people are particularly vulnerable to police violence and criminalization because, facing discrimination and exclusion in many schools and jobs and from our families, we often work in underground economies to get by. Sixteen percent of all trans people are involved in underground economies or criminalized work like sex work to survive, and those numbers are even higher for Latinx trans people (34 percent of whom work in underground economies) and Black trans people (53 percent of whom do criminalized work). Even trans people who are not engaged in sex work or other criminalized work are frequently profiled, harassed, and arrested by police who perceive trans women of color as criminals routinely. In places like New York and New Orleans, activists have been fighting to get rid of the laws that have facilitated this profiling and criminalization, but regardless of what the law says, the day-to-day anti-trans, racist practices of police remain common.

Queer and trans people are also more vulnerable to immigration enforcement because of their criminalization. Reduced pathways to citizenship through family due to widespread family rejection means that queer and trans migrants are more likely to be undocumented. High rates of police profiling and targeting mean increased vulnerability to detention and deportation. In juvenile and adult jails and prisons, and in immigration prisons, queer and trans prisoners are targeted[30] for violence and have an increased likelihood of solitary confinement. Our communities live with the stories of Tony McDade,[31] Layleen Polanco,[32] Patreese Johnson,[33] Renata Hill,[34] CeCe McDonald,[35] Ky Peterson,[36] Johana Medina Leon,[37] Roxana Hernández,[38] and many others—queer and trans people who have died in ICE custody, were killed by police, or were criminalized for defending themselves.

We don't trust the police. We fear them.

Second, queer and trans people fight for abolition because we refuse to have our movement for liberation co-opted by law enforcement as a public relations strategy. Hundreds of cities have adopted the police-initiated Safe Place campaign[39] since it was invented in 2014 by Officer Jim Ritter at the East Precinct of the Seattle Police Department (SPD). Ritter created the pro-SPD propaganda campaign four years after Seattle erupted in protests over the police killing of Native woodcarver John T. Williams[40] and three years after the Department of Justice launched an investigation[41] of the SPD that found "systemic use of force violations" and bias. Activists call this "pinkwashing" —when institutions that are facing criticism try to make themselves look progressive through a "LGBT-friendly" PR strategy. The Safe Place campaign encourages businesses to put a rainbow police-shield sticker in their windows to let anyone fleeing anti-LGBT attacks know that if they come inside, the business will call the cops for them. Like rainbow-painted cop cars,[42] the Safe Place logo takes a symbol of the queer and trans liberation movement—the rainbow flag—and puts it on a police badge to declare that the police are our protectors.

But the police are leading perpetrators of violence[43] against queer and trans people, not our protectors. Instead of putting a rainbow police badge in the window, we want businesses to agree not to call the police as a way to make our communities safer. We don't want our lives and the violence we experience used to legitimize the police or expand their ever-growing budgets in our names.

The third reason queer and trans resistance is tied up with abolishing prisons, police, and borders is that our movement emerged from and is completely intertwined with movements for racial and economic justice and against colonialism worldwide. The uprising at Stonewall happened in the context of widespread resistance to policing[44] in the United States, and to war and colonialism globally. Queer and trans liberation is inextricable from other leftist liberation movements— feminism, migrant justice, Black liberation, disability justice, environmental justice, and more. All marginalized and targeted groups face not only poverty and housing insecurity, but also police violence and targeted criminalization and deportation. All these movements imagine another world where all people have what they need, no one is exploited to enrich others, and we don't live with a violent standing army of police endangering our lives and using resources[45] that could be better put toward housing,[46] health care,[47] and childcare.[48]

For decades, we have watched as police budgets and the numbers of people locked up have grown.[49] A 2017 study[50] showed that Oakland spent 41 percent of the city's general fund on policing that year— and that Minneapolis spent almost 36 percent, Houston 35 percent, and Chicago nearly 39 percent. Many of us live in cities where more than half the budget goes to policing people, processing them through courts, locking them up, forcing them into electronic monitoring[51] or mandatory services,[52] or other forms of racist control.[53]

Often police and prison expansions have happened in the name of fixing[54] or reforming purportedly "broken" systems. They have hired cops of color, women cops, even LGBT cops. They have added training. They have created countless policies prohibiting police violence. They have created special cages[55] for vulnerable groups. Each reform adds more cops, more cells, or more dollars to a system that is devouring our communities.

We are abolitionists[56] because we know it is not a broken system that needs to be fixed—it is a system operating exactly as it was designed to operate[57] and hurting the people it has always hurt, and it needs to be dismantled. We want to see police, ICE, courts, and cages defunded[58] so that everyone has a safe place to stay, food on the table, and health care. That is entirely achievable, and it is the only pathway to real safety[59] for queer and trans people and everyone. ◼

READER'S GUIDE

- Dean Spade writes that disproportionately "queer and trans people have been and remain targets of the police." What evidence does the author use to make this argument?

- What was the Stonewall Rebellion and why is it an important flashpoint in the long history of queer and trans activists protesting against police violence?

- The author discusses "pinkwashing" and argues: "Often police and prison expansions have happened in the name of fixing or reforming purportedly 'broken' systems. They have hired cops of color, women cops, even LGBT cops. They have added training. They have created countless policies prohibiting police violence. They have created special cages for vulnerable groups. Each reform adds more cops, more cells, or more dollars to a system that is devouring our communities." Please cite a few real-life examples of these types of reforms in action. Further, what is the relationship between these reforms and police violence?

- Where does the author suggest funding for police should be reallocated? What are your thoughts on this proposal?

Challenging E-Carceration

ABOLITION MEANS NO DIGITAL PRISONS

By James Kilgore

O n my second day home from prison, a cheery middle-aged white woman from the Illinois Department of Corrections showed up and locked an electronic monitor (EM) around my left leg. "Your parole agent will tell you the rules," she informed me. "Until then, you are on lockdown."

The agent phoned the next morning and told me I would be allowed out of the house Monday through Friday from 6 a.m. to 10 a.m. "You should be able to complete all your business in those hours," he assured me. Those sunset walks and restaurant dinners with my family that I had dreamed of for six years suddenly turned into setting the alarm for 5:30 a.m. to use my full four hours of movement before the e-lock on the cage of our house clicked shut.

I spent a year on the monitor. Eventually they loosened my restrictions, but I still couldn't leave the house without advance permission. In fact, I had to submit a list of all my movements two weeks at a time, leaving no room for spontaneity or emergencies. When I told people how frustrating life on the monitor was, they all had the same reply: "It's better than prison." They were missing the point. I wasn't free, I had moved to e-carceration.

Fast forward ten years and a mass movement has arisen to get people out from behind the walls. Many of us are talking about prison abolition. Formerly incarcerated people have come together to form organizations like All of Us or None and the National Council for Incarcerated and Formerly Incarcerated Women and Girls. In response, authorities across the country are offering to release people on monitors as a "solution" to mass incarceration. In Chicago,[1] and the state of Massachusetts,[2] the use of monitors is skyrocketing. Though data is scarce, the number of people on monitors has risen from 55,000 in 2005[3] to an estimated 250,000+ in 2019. BI, the largest electronic monitoring company in the US, a subsidiary of the world's largest private prison operator, the GEO Group, has secured its third five-year contract with US Immigration and Customs Enforcement (ICE) to place thousands awaiting adjudication of an immigration case on a GPS tracker. The deals have brought[4] over six hundred million dollars to the company.

Despite the growth of monitors, the "better than prison" trope is losing ground. In a 2017 interview with me, Johnny Page, who was given electronic monitoring after twenty-three years in prison, offered a typical analysis, "You get to pay your own bills, you don't have to wait in line for the telephone, you don't have to wait in line for the shower, but you're still in jail. It's just another form of incarceration."[5]

Survivors of the shackle are fighting back. In Alameda, California, Robert Jackson and three plaintiffs launched a lawsuit[6] against LCA, an EM company that forced them to pay $250 a week to be on the device. Jackson had landed on the monitor as part of a mercy release when his wife suddenly died of meningitis while he was serving 120 days in the county jail. The EM fees, plus feeding his three kids, quickly sunk him into debt. He lost his car and his apartment, and had to send his children out to stay with relatives. Currently, the suit is dragging through the courts.

Apart from individual litigation cases, there is organized resistance. Community Justice Exchange, a national network of more than 100 local bail funds, has pushed back against electronic monitors and is fighting for the freedom of people awaiting trial. In 2019 MediaJustice's[7] Challenging E-Carceration project joined with other nonprofits and people who had experienced EM to craft a law[8] to ban the use of monitors on people released from prison in Illinois. The bill passed the House but COVID-19 intervened before it could reach the Senate. The resistance to what we are now calling ankle shackles continues to grow.

Those fighting for criminal justice reform as well as abolitionists have discovered that these devices don't create alternatives or offer any dimension of freedom. They are extending and redefining our understanding of prison and incarceration. Monica Cosby,[9] who spent twenty years in prison before landing on a monitor, described the situation, "any residence where you are living while on a monitor becomes like a satellite prison." For many Black people the ankle band also triggers historical memories. Jean-Pierre Shackelford, who was on an ankle monitor for nearly three years in Ohio, reflected[10] "when you think about it, it's nothing but twenty-first-century slavery and control, electronic style."

*

E-CARCERATION AND ABOLITION

But e-carceration is not just about ankle shackles. While shackles are the most common form of e-carceration, phone apps are on the rise. A number of companies have jumped into this market. Predictably, BI is at the cutting edge with SmartLINK, which not only does GPS location tracking but can monitor respiration rate and heart rate while incorporating voice and facial recognition for log in. Since developing apps requires far less capital investment than producing shackles, startups like Acivilate, Outreach SmartPhone, and Guardian by Telmate are scrambling to secure contracts with local jails and state departments of corrections. Promise, a company funded by Jay-Z and Roc Nation, offers a similar app, one which founder and CEO Phaedra Ellis-Lamkins suggested[11] would provide "'liberty and justice for all' to millions." Her language of caring and patriotism provides cover for what abolitionists label carceral humanism, the marketing of tracking and controlling as a service rather than punishment.

*

E-CARCERATION, SURVEILLANCE, AND BIG DATA

Once ankle shackles developed GPS capacity, they became part of the surveillance state. Location tracking doesn't just supply information to parole agents or courts. It ends up in the cloud, central control for racial capitalism. Dominated by Big Data giants, including Amazon, Microsoft, and Google, these megastorage sites create databases that house everything from GPS tracking details to criminal history to credit scores and school disciplinary reports. Processed via racialized algorithms, the data on the cloud target the criminalized sector of the population—a population that is disproportionately Black, Latinx, Indigenous, LGBTQ+, and poor that land in prisons, jails, and on ankle shackles. They are the vulnerable surplus of a rapidly diminishing employed working class.

Big Tech also markets this data, facilitating the systematic exclusion of the criminalized from housing, education, jobs, programs, and services. We find the cutting edge of this e-carceration in the Intensive Supervision Appearance Program (ISAP) run by ICE. Here the tracking data from individual migrants on ankle shackles blends with the data of millions in the ICE database, tracking their social networks, linking their organizing efforts, and monitoring their usage of state-funded services.

Abolitionists must call out the technologies of e-carceration—ankle shackles, facial recognition, risk assessment—along with the racist algorithmic formulas that target and punish the criminalized. We must call for technologies of liberation that open new opportunities, not technologies that confine us to our houses and neighborhoods with geo-fences. Rather than accommodate new forms of punitive data gathering, we must build on the existing efforts of activists and grassroots organizations to apply technology to the systemic problems of inequality and environmental destruction that are endemic to racial capitalism. These technologies of liberation will not come from Jeff Bezos or Bill Gates but must arise from the struggles and organizations that emerge as we carry the struggle for abolition forward. ◼

Resources:

Community Justice Exchange:
communityjusticeexchange.org
Challenging E-Carceration:
challengingecarceration.org
Media Justice:
mediajustice.org/issue/high-tech-policing

READER'S GUIDE

- What is "e-carceration"? Describe some key features and characteristics of the "e-carceration" movement.

- What is racial capitalism? How does James Kilgore describe the relationship among "e-carceration," surveillance, and racial capitalism?

- The author gives examples of resistance to "e-carceration." Please list them.

- The author urges that we must "call for technologies of liberation that open new opportunities, not technologies that confine us to our houses and neighborhoods with geo-fences." In your view, what might some of these technologies in support of abolition look like?

The Carceral State

2.3M | 5M | 1 in 40

people are incarcerated in the US.[1]

people are on probation or under parole supervision at risk of imprisonment.[2]

US residents is currently under some form of correctional control.[3]

Mass incarceration is part of the **carceral state** but not its limit. The carceral state "includes police, criminal courts, probation and parole, criminal records databases and risk-assessment tools, brick-and-mortar incarceration, and 'e-carceration' with electronic shackles."[4]

The **incarceration rate** in the United States (which includes prisoners in local jails, state prisons, federal prisons, and privately operated facilities) has increased dramatically over the last four decades.[5]

1980	**220** per 100,000
2020	**698** per 100,000 [6]

And among those incarcerated, Black and Latinx people are grossly overrepresented relative to their national population share.

RATE OF INCARCERATION IN PRISONS

Black people	**1,096** per 100,000
Latinx people	**525** per 100,000
White people	**214** per 100,000

RATE OF INCARCERATION IN JAILS [7]

Black people	**592** per 100,000
Latinx people	**182** per 100,000
White people	**187** per 100,000

The massive misdemeanor system contributes to **overcriminalization** and **mass incarceration**. Black people are particularly vulnerable to misdemeanor arrests. [8]

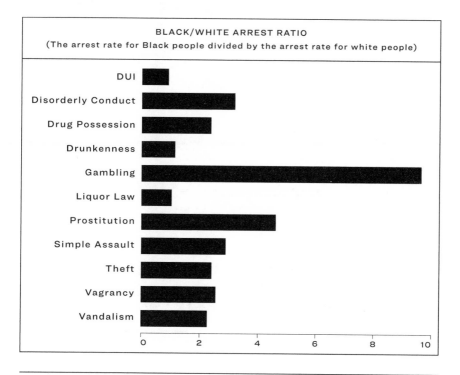

BLACK/WHITE ARREST RATIO
(The arrest rate for Black people divided by the arrest rate for white people)

Immigration enforcement is part of the carceral state—
and it is **expanding**. [9]

APPREHENSIONS BY PROGRAM

Program	2017	2018	2019
Total	461,540	572,566	1,013,539
CBP Border Patrol	310,531	404,142	859,501
ICE Homeland Security Investigations	7,539	9,843	10,939
ICE Enforcement and Removal Operations	143,470	158,581	143,099

Data stories researched and conceptualized by Tamara K. Nopper

The Fight to Melt ICE

WHY WE'RE FIGHTING
FOR A WORLD WITHOUT ICE

By Cristina Jiménez Moreta
and Cynthia Garcia

Immigrant youth and our families courageously left everything behind in our countries of origin to move to the United States. Some of us fled poverty, military coups, violence, and wars, while others simply wanted to go after a better life. While adapting to a new place, we've experienced some of the worst this country has to offer: workplace exploitation, wage theft, racial profiling, fear of deportation, and police violence. But as part of the immigrant youth movement at United We Dream (UWD), we've also experienced the power of people coming together, taking action, and winning change.

The seeds of our movement began with the idea that we have to protect and defend our families from deportation and fight for our right to access higher education. In the early 2000s, tens of thousands of undocumented students were graduating[1] from high school each year. All of us lived with the fear of deportation and the looming possibility that our families could be torn apart, while simultaneously facing barriers to college education, exploitation at work, and a future filled with uncertainty.

This fear of deportation was heightened after September 11, 2001, as we witnessed how immigration enforcement and national security were being conflated in new and troubling ways. In the name of fighting terrorism, President George W. Bush created the Department of Homeland Security (DHS) in 2002, within which immigration and immigrants were considered matters of national security. This not only led to increased racial profiling and xenophobia, but as a result, local and federal law enforcement were targeting Muslims, Black immigrants, and non-Muslim immigrants of color at higher rates, often leading to detention and/or deportation.

Nationwide, thousands would be implicated by the post-9/11 enforcement regime, which produced an expanding infrastructure that supported local and federal law enforcement efforts to criminalize, target, detain, and deport immigrants. Within this infrastructure, we saw increases in racial profiling, greater policing of Black and Brown communities, enhanced militarization of the US-Mexico border, and the implementation of racist federal policies, such as the National Security Entry-Exit Registration System,[2] which targeted immigrants from twenty-five countries.

Among the thousands who were affected by the post-9/11 regime were Kamal Essaheb and Walter Barrientos in New York and Marie Gonzalez in Missouri—three young undocumented immigrants who were threatened with deportation.

Their deportation cases spurred some of our first advocacy efforts that would eventually carry us forward in forming UWD in 2008. Together, along with activists and organizers from across the country, we mobilized people to write letters and telephone elected officials to demand that the government allow Kamal, Walter, and Marie to stay in the United States, winning extensive media attention. Although

Marie's parents were deported, our organizing efforts stopped the deportations of Marie, Walter, and Kamal. This was a bittersweet moment in our fight to protect immigrants, as it further exposed the human impact of the enforcement regime in not only deporting immigrants but also tearing apart families.

This moment also taught us that people closest to the pain are closest to the solutions our communities need. At the time, undocumented immigrants publicly fighting against deportations were unheard of. Yet, in defiance of conventional wisdom, undocumented youth and their families launched campaigns to share their stories, pressure those with decision-making power, and win deportation relief. It was clear that our movement had the power to create real change.

This was even more evident in 2012, when the Deferred Action for Childhood Arrivals (DACA) program was created as a direct result of our organizing efforts. Under the Obama administration, enforcement programs and collaboration between ICE and local police were aggressively expanded, leading to an increase in the number of immigrants being detained and deported even for minor violations, such as traffic infractions. Under the political calculation that ramping up enforcement would bring members of Congress from both parties to the negotiating table, the Obama administration deported a record number of immigrants from the United States. During Obama's eight years in office, more than 3 million individuals and families were deported and separated from their loved ones. His administration failed to pass legislative immigration reforms, while the enforcement regime steadily grew in resources and power.

As organizers and directly affected people, we recognized this as a moment of leverage: By sharing our stories, we could pressure President Obama to take action. Our movement successfully created the conditions that led President Obama to implement DACA, which protected close to 800,000 young immigrants from deportation. The program continues to be the most significant policy breakthrough and victory on immigration in almost three decades. By sharing our stories and leading direct action and civil disobedience to get ICE agents out of our communities, we recognized the power we had in winning protection from deportation through policy changes.

This and other victories have strengthened our movement and brought hope to our communities—but as we have seen, mass detention and deportation have not stopped. ICE and US Customs and Border Protection (CBP), the two agencies primarily responsible for immigration enforcement, have continued to carry out a racist and white supremacist agenda, targeting immigrants—particularly Black and Brown immigrants—for detention and deportation with little oversight or accountability. Clearly our fight is not over.

Year after year, failure at the immigration-policy negotiation table has been followed by near-silent acceptance of growing annual budgets and authority for ICE and CBP.[3] Together, the two agencies employ more than 80,000 people, with a massive budget of $25.3 billion in 2020[4] ($8.4 billion for ICE and $16.9 billion for CBP), which is more than all other federal law enforcement agencies combined. Yet, while resources for the deportation force have grown, schools and hospitals in our communities often remain underfunded and suffer from a lack of federal support.

The deportation force of ICE and CBP, built by administrations on both sides of the aisle, was completely unleashed under the Trump administration. During Trump's time in office, ICE and CBP carried out a list of attacks against immigrant communities, including putting children in cages; targeting immigrants in their workplaces, schools, places of worship, hospitals, and homes; and breaking down doors and abducting parents from their children. But the Trump administration didn't stop there.

Throughout his four years in office, Trump consistently tried to dismantle DACA, reduce refugee programs, and detain and deport an increasing number of immigrants. Under his administration we saw fifty-seven immigrants, including children, die in detention camps,[5] the deportation[6] of a woman who served as a key witness into reports of sexual assault and harassment inside ICE facilities, reports of forced hysterectomies being performed on immigrant women,[7] and eight immigrants who have died as a result of COVID-19[8] while in ICE custody.

Facing these and a number of other attacks, UWD has fought tirelessly to protect and demand justice for immigrant communities. Over the past decade, UWD alone[9] fought on behalf of more than one thousand people threatened by deportation. Facing hundreds of calls per week on our community "Migra Watch" free hotline, UWD community organizers responded to immigrant families reporting interactions with ICE and CBP agents and needing help when their friends and loved ones faced detention and deportation.

In one instance, Tania, a cancer survivor in Georgia, was taken to a detention camp after a traffic stop. ICE agents kept Tania locked away for four months, away from her children and the cancer treatment she needed to live. UWD has fought on behalf of individuals like Hector, who was taken away after being stopped for expired tags on his license plate, and high school students like Dennis, who was dragged away by ICE agents after reporting being bullied at school.

Our history and the present moment have shown us that the risk of harm, detention, and deportation will always exist wherever police and federal law enforcement do. Our vision is for all people in this country, regardless of immigration status, to be able to live freely, with full dignity, and thrive. To get there, we must unite in the larger struggle against white supremacy and racism, which are rooted in interlocking systems of policing, mass incarceration, and immigration enforcement that, by design, target and further dehumanize immigrants, especially people of color.

At the same time, we must also acknowledge the historic erasure of Black and Indigenous people from immigration conversations and center these communities in our fight for immigrant justice. The United States' legacy of genocide and colonialism cannot be ignored, as the impact of this continues to be felt today. We have seen Indigenous immigrants die as a direct result of the US immigration system's failure to provide interpretation and translation services to immigrants who speak Indigenous languages. In 2018, two children from Indigenous Maya communities in Guatemala died[10] in CBP custody after not receiving proper medical attention, as medical services were not translated in Q'eqchi' and Chuj, the two Indigenous languages that the children and their families spoke.

This is why, over the past decade, UWD leaders have made the demand of abolition and justice for all central to our vision, work, and movement strategy. Grounded in our lived experience, we know that ICE and local police work together to racially profile immigrants. For many in our communities, a traffic stop or any other contact with local police is the first entry point into the deportation pipeline.

Thus, when we call for the abolition of ICE, we are also calling for the abolition of enforcement on all levels and the systems that support it, from detention facilities to prisons. The abolition of ICE is inherently tied to the abolition of all other forms of enforcement and incarceration. Hence, UWD stands unequivocally with the Movement for Black Lives and its demands to defund the police, because we know that the police, ICE, and CBP work together to disproportionately target Black[11] and Brown immigrants.[12] We also know that the same people who profit from the mass incarceration of US-born Black and Brown people also profit from immigrant detention and deportation.

We are engaged in a lifelong journey toward racial, gender, and economic justice. With each victory, our sense of what is possible should grow and our understanding of the vulnerabilities of our adversaries should deepen. A world where our communities do not have to live with the fear of deportation and detention is possible. A world in which we and others in the movement have abolished ICE—and where the safety, health, education, and well-being of our communities is a priority. We have witnessed and participated in a movement of undocumented people who have transformed the politics and policy of immigration with a bold vision of freedom and dignity for all people, regardless of immigration status. That movement has proven that when we follow the leadership and vision of those closest to the pain and injustice, a new world is possible. ◼

READER'S GUIDE

- Cristina Jiménez Moreta and Cynthia Garcia write that with bipartisan support Immigration and Customs Enforcement (ICE) and US Customs and Border Protection (CBP), the two agencies primarily responsible for immigration enforcement, have continued to carry out a racist and white supremacist agenda, targeting immigrants— particularly Black and Brown immigrants—for detention and deportation with little oversight or accountability." How has their organization, United We Dream, sought to challenge the xenophobia and white supremacist agenda of ICE and CBP?

- In 2002, then-President George W. Bush created the Department of Homeland Security (DHS). The establishment of this department has had negative cascading consequences for immigrant communities—particularly immigrant communities of color. Please describe.

- Based upon this essay's arguments, what are the connections between the prison system, anti-immigration policies, xenophobia, and racism in the United States?

- In your view, how have the Obama, Trump, and Biden administrations' immigration policies and impacts overlapped?

The Hidden Pandemic

PRISONS ARE A PUBLIC HEALTH CRISIS—AND
THE CURE IS RIGHT IN FRONT OF US

By Kenyon Farrow

s we deal with the scourge of COVID-19, which at this writing
has killed more than 600,000 people in the United States and
rising,[1] policy and public health experts are clamoring for strategies to stop the spread of the virus after dealing with the absence of
credible and competent leadership at the federal level under the Trump
administration. Now, the country awaits the Biden administration to be
able to fully implement a better federal strategy to end the pandemic,
which now includes the rollout of three vaccines (with possibly two
more in the pipeline) that we know can stop severe illness and death
from COVID-19, and likely slow the spread of the virus to eventually
open venues that had to be fully or partially closed. However, the rollout of vaccines has been very uneven, with many Republican governors

flagrantly thwarting public health guidance on offering vaccines to people most vulnerable to mortality and morbidity, preferring to ensure wealthy and/or white constituents have first dibs.

There is inspiring work happening in the US and globally around how to reduce transmission of COVID-19 (or any future airborne pathogens) in settings like prisons, jails, and detention centers. Yet much of what is being discussed by city, county, state, and federal officials has been mostly meager reforms that would only slightly reduce the number of people in carceral settings, or releasing people who have comorbidities such as old age, asthma, and heart disease that may make them more vulnerable to illness and death should they contract COVID-19. Some of the reforms, like the use of biometrics and regular temperature taking (despite the fact that many people can carry and transmit COVID-19 even while asymptomatic), introduce more forms of surveillance[2] into prison and jail settings.

Very few of these plans acknowledge that these spaces create opportunities for the spread of infectious diseases. If we know that to be the case, public health activists who are truly interested in social and racial justice should in fact be calling for the abolition of the prison industrial complex as part of a strategy to reduce the possibility of current and future epidemics.

On March 31, 2020, the US Bureau of Prisons announced the next phase of a plan[3] to help curb COVID-19 exposure in federal prisons. Those measures included a fourteen-day confinement in cells. The memo states that "to the extent practicable," incarcerated people would be allowed to participate in some education and mental-health services, and provide labor in areas that required workers to keep the facilities running. The memo also noted that "asymptomatic inmates are placed in quarantine for a minimum of fourteen days or until cleared by medical staff" and "symptomatic inmates are placed in isolation until they test negative for COVID-19 or are cleared by medical staff as meeting CDC criteria for release from isolation."

The original memo made no mention about providing masks or any other personal protective equipment to incarcerated people, nor medical treatment to those who tested positive for COVID-19, until several days after the CDC's recommendation.

Activist groups and some elected officials called for stronger measures to protect those in prison. Rep. Jerrold Nadler, D-NY, advocated for the release of incarcerated people who are pregnant, older, or suffering from other conditions that would make them more vulnerable to COVID-19 complications and death. At the time, former Attorney General William Barr issued such an order, but only focused on federal facilities in Louisiana, Connecticut, and Ohio—all of which had already shown extremely high rates of COVID-19. (State facilities and local jails have all had their own protocols for testing, treatment, and early release.)

But these measures have not been enough. In August 2020, the *New York Times* reported[4] that the top 10 COVID-19 transmission clusters in the country were in prisons, jails, and detention centers. According to a December 2020 report issued by the National Commission on COVID-19 and Criminal Justice, COVID-19 infection rates were four times higher than the general population (noting that in some states it's up to seven times higher), and people in carceral settings are twice as likely to die from COVID-19 than people on the outside. As alarming as those numbers are, they are incomplete: Several states have not reported key data including the breakdown of infection rates among incarcerated people and prison staff, or demographic data (for instance, the race of those diagnosed or who died from the disease).

"There's no way to social distance," Adamu Chan, an incarcerated person inside California's infamous San Quentin prison, told the *New York Times*[5] in a story published on June 30, 2020. "We all eat together. We have a communal bathroom. There's no way to address a public health issue in an overcrowded facility."

Vaccine rollout was a mess during Trump's last few months in office. As the first two vaccine candidates were approved by the Food & Drug Administration (FDA), it's been widely reported that the Trump Administration just dropped off vaccines to states without resources, guidelines, or any assistance on how to implement the much-needed massive campaign to vaccinate people. But that lack of guidance and planning has made it much worse for people in carceral settings. According to a story in *The Guardian* from February 9, 2021, only 39,000 people out of the more than 2 million in US prisons had been vaccinated by January of the same year, despite the higher rates of COVID-19 in carceral settings compared to the general population. And the vast majority of states have not added people in prison and jails to their high-priority populations for vaccination.

The disproportionate impact of COVID-19 in carceral settings, the incomplete reporting of data, and the minimal public health and health care standards (including vaccine access) being uniformly implemented is no surprise to anyone who has been inside a facility, has a loved one who is or was imprisoned, or works as staff. Prisons, jails, and detention centers themselves are well known to be incubators of infectious disease outbreaks. This is not the fault of those confined in carceral settings, but rather is a result of how societies view people whom they send to such places of forced confinement. To condemn one to such a facility is to judge not just their actions but their person.

Punishment is not just taking away freedom of movement. It is forcing people into conditions of squalor—places that are overcrowded, violent, and without access to adequate (let alone high-quality) health care—all intended to be part and parcel of the sentence itself. It's a sentence to violence, deprivation, illness—physical and psychological, and spiritual—and sometimes premature death. According to the Bureau of Justice Statistics,[6] 40 percent of all people in prison reported having a current chronic health condition, while over half said they have had a chronic medical condition at some point in their lives. And 21 percent of people in prison and 14 percent of people in jail reported ever having tuberculosis, hepatitis B or C, or other STDs. HIV rates in prisons are five to seven times higher than in the general population.

At the state and local levels, public health officials most often have no legal authority to implement or enforce sanitation, medical care, food, water, and air quality inside facilities, despite what might be written into state law or the codes of operation for carceral settings. It usually takes lawsuits on behalf of incarcerated people to enforce medical care, basic sanitation, or other public health measures. Groups like Caring Collectively for Women Prisoners, Interrupting Criminalization, and the NYC COVID-19 Working Group have stepped up pressure on authorities to ensure people in prisons, jails, and detention centers are released, or at least protected from COVID-19 in custody, or are not left out of vaccine access programs.

Federally, the Centers for Disease Control and Prevention only provides guidelines for public health policies and procedures for carceral settings and has no enforcement authority over the Bureau of Prisons. The Federal Bureau of Prisons has stated that they have begun vaccinating many federal prison staff, and some in those facilities. But most people held in carceral settings are imprisoned in state-run facilities, where the CDC and BOP have no authority to enforce any public health measures. Therefore, the decisions about public health and health care are mostly left to state departments of corrections—often down to the whims of the warden to implement or not. Medical staff are often part-time and may not be qualified to provide care to people.

The lack of any accountability around public health and health care access in prisons is the rule and not the exception, and it has disastrous consequences. The 2020 scandal at an immigrant detention center in Southern Georgia demonstrates this. Dawn Wooten, the licensed practical nurse who worked at the center, is the whistleblower in the case against the facility where Mahendra Amin, MD, allegedly performed nonconsensual hysterectomies[7] on scores of women. If true, not only is this a serious abuse of power, and in fact a violation of medical ethics and human rights, but Amin is not certified by any of the twenty-four member boards of the American Board of Obstetrics and Gynecology, according to news reports.[8] While forced sterilization has a long history and has been fought primarily by reproductive and disability justice activists (mostly Black and Brown feminists), people in prisons, jails, and detention centers are often the most vulnerable still to these practices.

But this is not surprising. It is not uncommon for many facilities to employ doctors who do not have the training to perform certain kinds of medical care in carceral settings. Also, some doctors may take those jobs to abuse populations that have little power or access to systems of accountability. Wooten also alleged in her complaint that the conditions in the facility did not meet standards to best prevent the spread of COVID-19, nor did it even meet the standards for basic human decency. There is an unknowable number of cases of people who die in custody every year for being denied access to lifesaving care. In recent years, several people with HIV in immigrant detention facilities were denied access to their antiretroviral medication, and subsequently died, most notably transgender activist Roxana Hernandez in 2018.

Whether it's COVID-19, hepatitis, tuberculosis, or other infectious disease outbreaks that are regularly occurring inside carceral settings, we have to begin to think about these issues as constitutive of the prison industrial complex, not as aberrant. And the best strategy to help curb the spread of infectious diseases and promote health among all people residing in the US is to begin to put the same kind of energy, resources, and intellectual thought into what role a future without prisons can play in a future without COVID-19, or other pandemics. Bacteria and viruses will always exist and cause disease—but the conditions that breed pandemics are most often human-made.

Ending pandemics is going to take not only calls to defund the police or abolish the prison industrial complex, but to also plan for a new social contract.[9] One that devises community-developed systems that provide for lives of dignity and joy, and minimize violence, greed, and deprivation. Our carceral system renders those who are locked in it as outside the parameters of citizens, of community members, and even outside notions of "the public." And the effect is that it renders people inside carceral settings as not just invisible, but expendable, and enshrines illness and premature death into the experience of carceral forms of punishment.

In order for public health to not ring as a meaningless phrase, we have to begin to tackle public health from an abolitionist framework, and not only express care or concern for the people on the outside who are not in prison now or are not rendered as reasons for the carceral state to exist in the first place—Black, Latino, Native American, poor, homeless, queer, immigrant, transgender, sex worker, drug user, or dealer.

Our planning for future life should not end with our desire for the return of boozy brunches and taco Tuesdays. We should be planning for a future for human life. Prisons, jails, and detention centers are the antithesis of that by design. ◼

READER'S GUIDE

- Given the disproportionately severe ways COVID-19 has impacted incarcerated people, Kenyon Farrow writes that "public health activists who are truly interested in social and racial justice should in fact be calling for the abolition of the prison industrial complex as part of a strategy to reduce the possibility of current and future epidemics." What are some examples the author uses to support this assertion?

- According to the author's essay, what are the public-health concerns regarding conditions in prison? Provide three to four concerns.

- The author argues, "In order for public health to not ring as a meaningless phrase, we have to begin to tackle public health from an abolitionist framework, and not only express care or concern for the people on the outside who are not in prison now or are not rendered as reasons for the carceral state to exist in the first place—Black, Latino, Native American, poor, homeless, queer, immigrant, transgender, sex worker, drug user, or dealer." Please cite three to four ways you believe an abolitionist worldview may be applied to public health policies and practices writ large?

- The author argues that prisons, jails, and detention centers are the antithesis of a future for human life. What do you think the author means by this? Do you agree or disagree? Explain.

The Long Grip of Mass Incarceration

Almost **149 million** people— **45%** of the population— have had an immediate family member incarcerated.

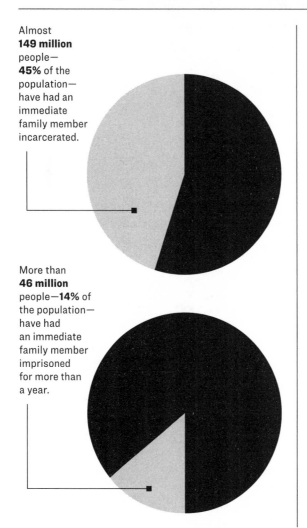

More than **46 million** people—**14%** of the population— have had an immediate family member imprisoned for more than a year.

This is a more pronounced reality for people of color...

63%

of **Black people** have had immediate family members incarcerated.

48%

of **Latinx people** have had immediate family members incarcerated.

42%

of **white people** have had immediate family members incarcerated.[1]

Less than a third of people incarcerated in state prisons receive visits. This can be for various reasons, including the lack of family or strained relationships. But geography plays a key role as many prisons are built in rural areas, making family members and friends travel hundreds of miles for visits.[2]

Among people incarcerated in state prisons...

A little over **50%** are imprisoned **101–500** miles from their home communities

Almost **8%** between **501–1000** miles

And a little over **2%** more than **1000** miles.[3]

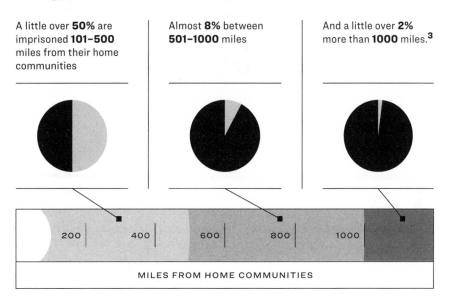

MILES FROM HOME COMMUNITIES

The most recent data show that about **150,000** people incarcerated in state correctional facilities are **55 or older**. And more than **20,000** people incarcerated in federal prisons are **56 or older**.[4]

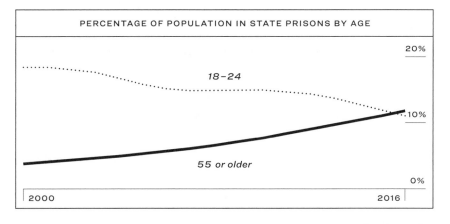

PERCENTAGE OF POPULATION IN STATE PRISONS BY AGE

20%

18–24

10%

55 or older

0%

2000   2016

Data stories researched and conceptualized by Tamara K. Nopper

My Father Deserves to Be Free

A SON'S FIGHT FOR HIS FATHER'S FREEDOM

By Russell "Maroon" Shoatz *and*
Russell Shoatz III

R ussell "Maroon" Shoatz is an activist, writer, founding member of
the Black Unity Council,[1] former member of the Black Panther Party,
and soldier in the Black Liberation Army.[2] Incarcerated since 1972
and now seventy-eight years old, Maroon is serving multiple life sentences
in Pennsylvania as a US-held political prisoner of war. After escaping
prison twice, in 1977 and 1980, he earned the name Maroon from fellow
incarcerated men, a nod to Africans who fled chattel slavery and created
autonomous communities throughout the Americas. His son, Russell
Shoatz III, is a longtime activist, educator, and live-event producer. For the
past three decades, he's worked tirelessly for his father's freedom and that of
all US-held political prisoners.

Below, Maroon and Russell discuss their life together while being kept apart, the traumas they've suffered at the hands of the carceral state, and how, in spite of all of this, they still have an unbreakable relationship as educators, as freedom fighters, and as father and son.

This conversation has been edited and condensed for clarity.

* * *

RUSSELL "MAROON" SHOATZ: From as far back as I can remember, my son has intrigued me with his analysis on a multitude of different subjects. I guess it should come as no surprise since the Shoatz family is steeped in a long tradition of education and profound thinkers.

RUSSELL SHOATZ III: Some of my earliest memories are of attending Samuel B. Huey Elementary School on 52nd and Pine in West Philadelphia. My mother worked at the school.

MAROON: My mother, Gladys Shoatz, was a trailblazer in supporting her community and her neighbors' families in Philadelphia. She made sure that the educational systems worked for her community and that the people knew exactly what they were supposed to receive from the school board. My now-deceased sister, Ida Shoatz, also became an educational icon in Philadelphia and abroad. In Peru, she helped organize school lunch programs for over a dozen villages in the Andes. When she returned home, Ida channeled her experiences back into her own community, challenging the educational system to properly serve poor and disenfranchised communities in ways few, if any, African American women had before. My other sister, Dr. Suzette Hakeem, also became a lifelong education advocate and supported countless students of all ages.

So over forty years ago, when my son, Russell, began to ask me about a myriad of topics—my criminal case and why I was incarcerated, my spiritual beliefs, my cultural beliefs, what books I was reading, my relationships with women—I immediately knew we would be engaged in a lifetime educational journey.

RUSSELL: From my formative years until I was a preteen, my mother was extremely diligent in shielding me from any harm or danger and specifically making sure that any of the political actions that my father was involved in from the turbulent sixties didn't affect my growth, development, and abilities to prosper, in general. In elementary school, though, I first began to recognize that I was a little different than most children around me. My good friend Reginald Barnes, whose father was a police officer and a pastor, would occasionally invite me over to do homework. Mr. Barnes told me that every time I came over to study with Reggie, he would bring us pizza. I was more than obliged to take him up on this offer. Shortly after, my father escaped from prison for the first time. It was a surreal experience, especially in the context of Philadelphia in the seventies, widely experienced by Black and disenfranchised communities as a police state. Frank Rizzo was the police chief, and police terror reigned. That day started off as usual, but just as first period was beginning, we were all alerted by the sound of a three-toned xylophone over the public announcement system. Usually, the xylophone would be followed by a fire drill or some other school-specific message. This time, however, it was considerably different as the principal began delivering what can only be described as a student's dream: He stated that there would be an early dismissal that day! The entire school, myself included, erupted in joy at his proclamation. But that joy would soon turn into bewilderment. As my classmates and I exited the building, we discovered our school was surrounded by Rizzo's police force, armed to the teeth. A teacher walked me across the street to my home. But it wasn't the home that I had known. My home was filled with intruders. The intruders were police officers—police officers who I immediately saw as a threat. I witnessed my mother intensely arguing with them. I watched those intruders set about destroying everything in the house, from furniture to framed family photos. They claimed that they were looking for my father. From that day on, school at Samuel B. Huey would never be the same. Nonstop, classmates would ask me how my father got on TV. Regularly, some of my childhood friends would bring up that my father was on the front page of the newspaper.

What stays with me the most, though, is classmates casually saying, "Tell your father to escape again so that we can have another early dismissal." I was only ten years old. I was ten, trying to navigate anger and sorrow over my father's absence. I was ten, trying to make sense of the little information I'd overheard from family members about my father taking up arms to defend our community against police violence. I was ten, dealing with flashbacks of law enforcement forcing their way into my home, claiming to be looking for my father. Yet, to some of my peers, all that mattered about him was the possibility of getting another day off from school.

MAROON: Like most people, Russell wanted to know the in-depth specifics of how I ended up with a sentence of life without parole and all of the gritty details surrounding my involvement with the Black Unity Council and, later, the Black Liberation Army. I explained to him, as I've been explaining to people until now, that those details, if exposed, could incriminate me and others. He recognized early on that phone calls and letters would limit him in the information for which he was mining. This led to relentless visitations and many hours of travel. I was always considered an escape risk, so I remained in solitary confinement for nearly thirty years—twenty-two of them consecutive.[3] At Dallas, Pennsylvania, they forced my family to unsafely travel through the entire prison in order to visit me in my dark, dank basement cell, as if I were Hannibal Lecter.

At one point, my son even traveled to Fort Leavenworth, Kansas, where I was illegally transported following the Camp Hill prison uprising of 1989,[4] in which incarcerated people in Pennsylvania rose up against overcrowding and inhumane conditions. After days of skullduggery, mental jousting, intense questioning, and eating all of the vending machine food, including my favorites, coffee and cake, Russell sat quietly in that Kansas prison, staring downward. Then he raised his head to ask a question that took me by total surprise: He said that based on the bulge in my pants, it seemed that he was not endowed with the same size penis as me. I chuckled and explained to him that the bulge came from repeated beatings, where my attackers would all kick me in the groin until I was completely disfigured. Still thirsting for more, he would ingeniously pry information from me and intensely debate me.

RUSSELL: Historically, these conversations with my father have been like mentally battling one of the greatest mixed martial arts fighters of all time. Gracie Jiu-Jitsu[5] has nothing on the mental warfare I've endured and the ingenious ways by which the crafty old veteran has forced me to tap out!

MAROON: I was never bothered by his mental attacks, as this was common amongst the younger men in prison who, after failed physical attacks, would resort to the intellectual bum-rush. I welcomed these opportunities and created African-centered solitary confinement study courses. As the hardened young men would be sent to the hole, my comrades and I would immediately engage them about why they were in prison and stress how important it was that they educate themselves before leaving. It was literally a mental boot camp in which I shared my personal library of books that family and supporters would send me. The young students were engaged, encouraged, and tested on what they had read until we felt they had properly retained the information. Similar to the ongoing mental battles I endured with my son, these young men became some of my greatest teachers. A recent debate I had with Russell focused on Marvel's movie *Black Panther* and the character Killmonger. I proposed that someone had done some intense research of our movements in the sixties, including the Black Panther Party and Black Liberation Army, and had synthesized our rage and anger into this uncoincidentally Oakland-reared character.

RUSSELL: I had to agree that, due to the Hollywood budget and cultural context of the Marvel movie, there seemed to have been some significant research of movements and strategies by our most recent freedom fighters. But I've challenged some of my father's analysis of the film, in particular his overarching critique of Killmonger.

MAROON: I believe he is an example of how militants can be blinded by thoughts of physical and military conquest as retribution. This blind rage is a gateway to a host of schisms, from misogyny to power-hoarding to an overall loss of focus on what Che Guevara famously stated as the reason why we fight: "a love for the people."

RUSSELL: Most people that I've engaged with, be they activists, academics, or everyday folks in my world, love Killmonger for his desire to fight the oppressor and channel his anger, even if some in the village didn't understand his tactics. Personally, I'm a fan as well, though I do have my share of questions surrounding the portrayal of some not-so-glamorous details about his past, namely his father's dirty dealings with a mercenary and the sweeping trauma that defines his childhood as a result of his father's brutal death. Hollywood continues to give credence to the stereotype of Black men not being present in crucial ways and not being able to overcome particular challenges. It's not lost on me that I'm calling this convention to task as a Black man whose own father was locked up or on the run since I was three years old. But lurking beneath all of the great fight scenes and the machismo and bravado that Killmonger embodies is his dysfunctional childhood, which feeds his blind rage. This narrative of the traumatized Black male child whose only outlet is self-destruction, which in most cases leaks out onto his very own community, is well-worn and cliche. Think about how this storytelling technique shows up consistently throughout Hollywood depictions of Black communities. I'm not knocking *Black Panther* as a whole. There's plenty to admire in its script, enactment, and production. But while I support the broadening representation of Black folks in Hollywood and our ability to shape our own narratives and tell our own stories, the critic in me can't help but point out these striking contradictions. What good is increased access to large-scale cultural production if we're reproducing outdated tropes anchored in pathologizing Blackness? I suppose, then, my critique of how Killmonger's childhood is represented in the film ultimately overlaps with some of my father's concerns about the character as an adult.

Some years ago, my father encouraged my sisters and me to take on African names. He urged us all to do it as a reclamation of cultural heritage erased by our upbringing and socialization in the US. I picked "Jela," which in Swahili means "father was troubled around the time of my birth." Killmonger's past also involved his father facing trial and tribulation rooted in a commitment to liberating Black people when he was young. Unlike the Hollywood caricatures, though, I've spent forty years learning from my father's struggles. We don't see eye-to-eye on all topics related to our people's fight for liberation. But when it comes to character, courage, commitment, and critical thinking, I must admit that those disgruntled teachers, authority figures, and police officers from my youth were spot on: I have proudly ended up being just like my father—and my father deserves to be free.

It is 2021. My father was born in 1943. He's seventy-eight years old. He is a grandfather. He is an elder suffering from stage 4 colorectal cancer. He is a threat to no one. He is a prisoner of a war waged against Black people[6] by the US government. The only threat that he serves is to anyone who believes that Black people are unworthy of defending themselves against state-sanctioned acts of terror. He is a human being who has been dehumanized, confined in a cage, alone,[7] and tortured.[8]

My father deserves to be free. All political prisoners deserve to be free. Free. Them. All. ◪

READER'S GUIDE

- Russell Shoatz III describes his father, Russell "Maroon" Shoatz, as a "prisoner of war." Provide three to four examples from their conversation to support this understanding.

- How did Maroon's activism influence the development of his young son's political consciousness?

- What was the role of education in both Shoatzes' lives? How did this influence their politics? How has your education (informal or formal) shaped your own politics?

- What was the debate that the older and younger Shoatzes had around the film *Black Panther*? And what are your own thoughts on their analyses?

We're All Living in a Future Created by Slavery

Ameer Hasan Loggins

hen I was nineteen years old, I was arrested.

Instead of a dungeon, I was held in an overcrowded holding cell. Instead of being shackled and transported across the ocean on a floating prison, I was handcuffed, sitting shoulder to shoulder with another young Black male being hauled across the county on a prison bus.

During intake, I was stripped of my clothes, forced to stand naked as officers stripped me of both my pride and my dignity. I tried to cover my genitals. It was my last grasp at holding on to my humanity. I was commanded by officers to remove my hands. They had guns. I had nothing. I complied. The officer barked, "Lift up your nut sack."

I had no choice. I was ordered to "squat down and cough." When I was finally handed a pair of state-issued boxer shorts, I was so desperate to have on anything to cover my exposed body that I did not give a damn that the underwear had been passed down, circulated among others who had been stripped naked before me.

I think about the African diaspora. I think about my family. I think about myself.

In the summer of 2017, I visited the continent of Africa. While there, I basked in the beauty of the lively Ramadan nights in Morocco. I stood in the searing sun of Egypt. I took pictures with the great pyramids as my backdrop, mimicking Malcolm X during his visit in 1964. When I made it to Ghana, I visited the final resting place of Kwame Nkrumah. While standing at his tomb, I thought about Nkrumah writing, "All people of African descent, whether they live in North or South America, the Caribbean, or in any other part of the world, are Africans and belong to the African Nation."[1] I stood there thinking about the divide between being identified as African and being of African descent. I was in the homeland of my ancestors, and yet I knew none of their names or faces.

But I did know why they were forced to leave. I had reached a point where I could not return home to the United States without experiencing the carceral castles on Ghana's Gold Coast.

My feet were firmly planted, affixed to the weather-beaten ground of the Castle of St. George in Elmina. I stood in front of a cell, designated for incarcerated Ashanti, Mandinka, Hausa, Wolof, Fula, and Susu from various kingdoms who had been deemed as deserving of death because they fought to live in freedom. I stood there in front of a thick black wooden door hauntingly marked by a human skull and a set of crossbones carved into stone.

Behind that door was a darkness I never experienced.

In the 7 x 10 prison cell, there was a total absence of light. There was also an abject emotional darkness that came with knowing folks wrapped in the same skin that I'm in were left there to starve and rot to death.

The captives imprisoned at the Castle of St. George were a part of what I call the carceral class. I am a member of this class.

The carceral class is made up of persons of African descent who are systematically stigmatized as unfit for freedom and deserving of the dehumanization that comes with being incarcerated. The idea of the carceral class is the product of an anti-Black framework that represents Black people as the locus of crime and Blackness as synonymous with criminality. As a classification, the carceral class denotes that, at any given time, your freedom can be ripped from underneath your feet. That you can be torn away from the people you love and the places you love to be.

Although he didn't name it, Malcolm X knew about the carceral class, too.

In Malcolm X's blistering 1963 speech, "Message to the Grassroots,"[2] he spoke of the systemic condemnation of Black folks in the United States. He lasered in on the uncomfortable bond of being Black in America. Malcolm made it plain and uncompromising. "We are all Black people, so-called Negroes, second-class citizens, ex-slaves," he said. "You are nothing but an ex-slave. You don't like to be told that. But what else are you? You are ex-slaves. You didn't come here on the Mayflower. You came here on a slave ship—in chains, like a horse, or a cow, or a chicken."

I wrestle with what Brother Malcolm said. Not because I disagree with the troublesome truths that he spoke, but because I feel his analysis can be extended.

His words still ring in my mind on a loop.

"You are nothing but an ex-slave."

You are nothing but a slave.

You are nothing.

You are a thing.

Malcom's speech takes me back to Achille Mbembe's *On the Postcolony*.[3] In it, Mbembe lays bare his views on what it means to be branded, burned with the mark of being a slave. He viewed slave as the "forename" one must "give to a man or woman whose body can be degraded, whose life can be mutilated, and whose work and resources can be squandered—with impunity."

I think about a time before enslavement. Before Africans were ensnared in the wretchedness of having both their labor and their lives exploited from can't-see in the morning to can't-see in the evening, they were prisoners of a particular kind.

Those who were captured and eventually enslaved were regular folks: commoners, farmers, wage workers, domestic servants, and artisans who worked with their hands. Two-thirds of those held captive were young African men. As Marcus Rediker recounts in *The Slave Ship: A Human History,* slave raiders targeted "'the roughest and most hardy,' and avoided the privileged 'smooth negroes.'"[4] The class-based vulnerability of the common folks figured centrally in their capture and confinement. Rediker continues:

"Second to war as a source of slaves were the judicial processes in and through which African societies convicted people of crimes ranging from murder to theft, adultery, witchcraft, and debt; condemned them to slavery; and sold them to African traders or directly to the slave-ship captains . . . . Many Africans and (abolitionist) Europeans felt that judicial processes in West Africa had been corrupted and that thousands had been falsely accused and convicted in order to produce as many tradeworthy bodies as possible."

A judicial system of injustice had waged war on African commoners, criminalizing them into a world of carcerality.

Malcolm's raspy tone echoes again in my mind. I hear him saying, "You didn't come here on the Mayflower. You came here on a slave ship—in chains, like a horse, or a cow, or a chicken."

And again, Brother Malcolm was correct.

We did not willingly travel to the Americas on the Mayflower. We were forced here on the White Lion[5] and the Clotilda.[6] It is not hyperbole to suggest that the slave ship was an aquatic prison. Its European captain was the warden. Its European crew were the prison guards. And in handcuffs and leg shackles were the formerly free Africans, eaten alive, buried in the belly of vessels of mass incarceration.

The largest wave of forced African diasporic movement was anchored to punishment and carcerality. Everywhere the descendants of the Middle Passage were forced to find footing, a carceral-class status and the struggle for liberation followed.

Malcolm knew the global connectedness of Black folks' oppression. He knew that in the United States, the African diaspora's carceral-class status is still branded to our being.

Forty percent of the ten million incarcerated Africans brought to the Americas and sold into chattel slavery ended up in Brazil. Today, it is estimated that 75 percent of Brazil's prison population are Brazilians of African descent. In the country's capital Brasília, Afro-Brazilians make up 82 percent of those incarcerated. Although only 11 percent of the country's total population is between eight and twenty-four years of age, this age group represents approximately one-third of those imprisoned.[7]

In the United States, Black adults are 5.9 times as likely to be incarcerated than white adults.[8] As of 2001, one out of every three Black boys born in that year could expect to go to prison in his lifetime. Black girls are far more likely to be incarcerated than Asian or white girls. As the Sentencing Project shows us, "The placement rate for all girls is 43 per 100,000 girls (those between ages 10 and 17) but the placement rate for Asian girls is 3 per 100,000; for white girls is 29 per 100,000 . . . . Black girls are more than three times as likely as their white peers to be incarcerated (94 per 100,000)."[9] While 14 percent of all youth under 18 in the United States are Black, 42 percent of boys and 35 percent of girls in juvenile detention facilities are Black.[10] Among Black trans folks, 47 percent have been incarcerated at some point in their lives.[11]

The criminalization of Black folks in the United States is both a pathologizing and totalizing practice. No group is spared. No group is left unvictimized. These are the progeny of the commoners, the prisoners of war, and the freedom fighters who made up the original carceral class. Malcolm also knew that as a Muslim, "There is nothing in our book, the Quran, that teaches us to suffer peacefully."

On Christmas Day in 1521, twenty enslaved Muslims, wielding machetes, attacked their Christian masters on the island of Hispaniola.[12] It was the first recorded enslaved African revolt in the Western Hemisphere.

Four years later, enslaved African Muslims rebelled against the Spanish on the coast of present-day South Carolina.[13] It was the first rebellion by enslaved folks in the history of North America.

In 1729, Granny Nanny,[14] a self-liberated African Muslim leader and warrior, led her army of Maroons in Jamaica into the battle with the British—and crushed them in combat. On August 14, 1791, an enslaved African Muslim named Dutty Boukman[15] led other enslaved folks in an uprising against the French. This rebellion and the death of Boukman are marked as being one of the sparks that lead to the Haitian Revolution.[16] On the twenty-seventh night of Ramadan in January 1835, a group of enslaved African Muslims in Salvador da Bahía, Brazil, organized one of the largest slave rebellions in the history of the Americas.[17] After being forced aboard on June 28, 1839, Sengbe Pieh, an enslaved African Muslim, led the aquatic revolt on the Amistad.[18]

For members of the carceral class, resistance is in our blood. Resistance is a binding component of our collective experience. Resistance is in our history. This is the history of Black folks like Safiya Bukhari, Iya Fulani Sunni-Ali, Kamau Sadiki, Jamil Al-Amin, Mutulu Shakur, and Russell "Maroon" Shoatz.[19]

This is why we resist to this day.

In the end, I return to where I started, thinking about Saidiya Hartman's words. We live in a time created by the original mass incarceration—the transatlantic slave trade. The "peculiar institution" that is rooted in carcerality.[20] Malcolm X knew this. Political prisoners in the United States today, who need to be freed, know this. I, too, know this. There has not been a point in my life where I have not been intimately impacted by the carceral state. We know this because we have all been subject to and subjugated by the carceral state. It is this experience of knowing that informs my fight to abolish the carceral state. ◼

Resource:

https://thejerichomovement.com/prisoners

READER'S GUIDE

- Ameer Hasan Loggins introduces a new term to the Black freedom lexicon: the carceral class. Loggins writes, "The carceral class is made up of persons of African descent who are systematically stigmatized as unfit for freedom and deserving of the dehumanization that comes with being incarcerated. The idea of the carceral class is the product of an anti-Black framework that represents Black people as the locus of crime and Blackness as being synonymous with criminality." Identify three to four examples the author uses to show how the carceral class has operated throughout history?

- The author writes, "A judicial system of injustice had waged war on African commoners, criminalizing them into a world of carcerality." What does the author mean by "world of carcerality"? Do you agree or disagree? Explain.

- The author conceives of the carceral class as an anti-Black global phenomenon. Why do you believe the global scope of his analysis is important? What do you think this might say about struggles for global abolition?

- How do you see the idea of the carceral class manifesting in the everyday life of your community?

PART

III

Fuck
Reform

Reforms Are the Master's Tools

THE SYSTEM IS BUILT FOR POWER, NOT JUSTICE

By Derecka Purnell

P ocket change.

That was the difference between a cold bus ride or a freezing walk during Boston's brutal winters. But my client traveled to his weekly group meeting any way that he could with the quarters in his worn brown wallet. We did not discuss what he said in the circle when he went. Or what any other man confessed or kept secret. Our conversations were mostly about whether he signed in for attendance. To finish his probation, we had to show the court that he completed the class.

The probation officer warned me that my client had violated the terms of probation and would be facing jail time. He would lose his weekly meetings, his part-time fast-food job, his corner bunk at a shelter, and more. Completely shocked, I called the nonprofit where my client went for meetings and asked about his attendance. The person who answered explained that my client, in fact, rarely missed a class. But each session had a fee and my client only paid a fraction of the total cost. He owed a balance. Attendance wasn't the issue. Money was.

A couple hundred dollars.

That's about what I spent to get my locs retwisted and styled where I lived in Cambridge, Massachusetts. A semester worth of Uber rides to nowhere. The tab at law firm recruitment lunches. Yet for my client, it was the difference between a bed in a jail and a corner bunk in a shelter.

The day of the hearing, I prepared to argue that my client had successfully completed each class, and that payment should be an arrangement between him and the nonprofit, not to be used to violate his terms of probation. He's literally homeless, I screamed inside my own throat. Isn't this situation obvious? But the court is not for truth or justice. Just power and persuasion. The probation officer and judge still needed to be convinced that my client should not go to jail because he's poor. Jail doesn't stop poverty or homelessness, it exacerbates it. According to the Prison Policy Initiative, up to 15 percent of people confined to prisons and jails experience homelessness before they enter and are five times more likely than the general public to experience homelessness upon their release.

Right before the clerk called the case, my client bustled through the hall beaming and proud that he made just enough after saving several paychecks to cover his debt. He had nothing left except pocket change.

My client was in a diversion program. He could delay or avoid jail by completing court-mandated group counseling classes. This was better than jail, and my law clinic professors wisely trained students to request diversion for our clients, so I did. Diversion is among the "best" reforms in the criminal legal system, yet it still kept people trapped. My client was not in jail, but he was not free. The power of the probation office was extended to the organization, who had planned to deny the completion of the terms due to payment. He was diverted from jail, but still under carceral control.

Additionally, even if my client had emotional health challenges, going to jail could exacerbate them. According to the World Health Organization,[1] incarceration is detrimental to mental health due to "various forms of violence, enforced solitude or, conversely, lack of privacy, lack of meaningful activity, isolation from social networks, insecurity about future prospects (work, relationships, etc.), and inadequate mental health services." Ironically, the shelter where he slept shares many of these same qualities. Rather than ridding society of the oppressive conditions that can cause our anger, the burden of improvement is on individuals under the threat of imprisonment.

Diversion and other "reformist reforms"—changes that increase the power, scope, and legitimacy of the criminal legal system—often sound like a great alternative to sitting in jail. We want to believe that these reforms are gentle or perhaps that a more diverse system will alleviate the suffering of the people who bear the brunt of the badge and the cage. As Maya Schenwar and Victoria Law detail in their book, *Prison by Any Other Name*,[2] reformist reforms encourage judges and cops and prisons to enter into our most sacred spaces, our homes, therapy sessions, jobs, schools, hospitals, even places of worship. Your shelter manager or employer now surveils your whereabouts. Your landlord dangles an eviction card over your head for new and arbitrary reasons. Your court-mandated therapy group leader determines that you violated your probation because you are too poor to pay for classes you didn't sign up to attend.

Counterintuitively, reforms do not make the criminal legal system more just, but obscure its violence more efficiently. Why spend money to jail someone when you can charge them hundreds of dollars for wearing an electronic ankle shackle forcing them to stay home? Florida's probation officers collected more than $90 million from people on probation, and $11 million worth of forced labor called community service.[3] Diversion, probation, and ankle shackling are certainly not jail, but we can build better options to reduce, stop, and prevent contact with the criminal legal system altogether.

This level of systemic oppression reminds me of Audre Lorde's popular quote that the master's tools will not dismantle the master's house. For me, the full quote is quite compelling:

"For the master's tools will never dismantle the master's house. They may allow us temporarily to beat him at his own game, but they will never enable us to bring about genuine change. And this fact is only threatening to those women who still define the master's house as their only source of support."[4]

While Lorde was originally criticizing white feminists, her assessment can apply here, too; many people believe that the current legal system is our sole source of support for justice, accountability, and even jobs. This belief is bipartisan. Rural residents in Republican districts protest prison closures to avoid job loss. In criticizing social justice calls to defund the police, Democratic mayor Lori Lightfoot explained that Chicago protesters were "eliminating one of the few tools that the city has to create middle-class incomes for Black and Brown folks." The amorphous, multiracial middle class is managerial, filled with politicians, lawyers, judges, cops, probation officers, prison guards, and nonprofit employees whose job security is predicated on maintaining an unjust system.

If the criminal legal system is our sole source of support, then reform might also be attractive to the ever-growing exploited classes that experience the most injustice, especially if they are Black, Indigenous, immigrant, or have a disability. They likely rely on the criminal legal system mostly out of desperation because their social, economic, and educational supports have been undermined or decimated. For example, a Black teenager in Michigan, once incarcerated[5] for not completing her virtual schoolwork, was originally on probation because she stole a cell phone and bit her mom's finger in a fight over not being allowed to go to a friend's house. Her mom called the police three times on her daughter because she did not know where else to find help.

Even people who police primarily put in prisons experience the carceral state as a sole source of support. Without jail, they would not have health care, therapy, beds, chances to go to school or recover from an addiction—all of which should be plentiful, optional, high-quality, and available for anyone, anywhere, anyway.

The criminal legal system is like the master's house. Reforms are the master's tools. Sometimes, Black public defenders will be able to use a tool or two to get their client free, or a Black prosecutor or judge will even appear to be in charge of the house, which was true in my client's case. But this will never bring about genuine change. Reforms do not solve the root causes of harm—individual or institutional. The master's house is on fire, and the more that we try to reform, diversify, and resource it, the more people will suffer as it collapses. Dr. Martin Luther King Jr. was right to fear, as he once told Harry Belafonte,[6] that he was integrating Black people into a burning house.

Unlike reform, abolition is about dismantling oppressive systems and expanding or creating sources of support for people like my former client, for Grace and her mother, for me and you. Abolition might feel threatening because it upends the status quo and delusive comforts of cops and cages. Fighting for a society where Black people and our oppressed siblings can thrive is not "normal" in a country built on genocide, theft, slavery, patriarchy, homophobia, xenophobia, ableism, and militarism. The fight is forged. What abolitionists dream and build is more promising than diversifying police departments or expanding probation. Abolition creates more just societies where we don't need masters' houses, masters' tools, or masters at all.

In a more just world, my client's pocket change could be the difference between a walk or train fare to his favorite restaurant. Perhaps he could have a corner apartment instead of a corner shelter bunk, and he would feel overwhelmed because he had too many green jobs or too many therapists or too many schools to choose from. He wouldn't have run in the halls to greet me about paying off his balance for his freedom. His freedom would be free. ◪

READER'S GUIDE

- Derecka Purnell juxtaposes reform and abolition. Please identify three to four key differences between reform and abolition.

- According to the author, what is the relationship between incarceration and emotional/mental health?

- The author writes, "Abolition might feel threatening because it upends the status quo and delusive comforts of cops and cages." Have you experienced people (yourself included) feeling threatened by these arguments? How have you responded to these threats? Using the author's essay, how could you challenge these concerns?

- The author shows that houselessness and incarceration are often intimately related. According to a 2018 report authored by the Prison Policy Initiative, "formerly incarcerated people are almost ten times more likely to be homeless than the general public." Conversely, research recently conducted by the Urban Institute shows that experiencing unsheltered houselessness increases one's interaction with the carceral state. How have you seen these phenomena play out in your community?

No Justice, No Freedom

CRIMINAL JUSTICE REFORM
COST ME 21 YEARS OF MY LIFE

By Derrick Hamilton

I n 1994, New York State convicted me of a murder I didn't commit. Like countless others, I was found guilty of causing harm, when in fact I was victimized by a system that often uses fabricated evidence to fill prison cells with Black men just like me.

For twenty-one years, I languished in prison, my time stolen by Bill Clinton's infamous 1994 crime bill,[1] a bill then-Senator Joe Biden helped to write. The legislation was publicized as a much-needed reform to get drugs off the street—but like so many other reform efforts framed as ways to make our criminal legal system fair and equal for all, it gave police and the prison system the means to incarcerate people without concern for justice itself.

In 2015, I was exonerated.[2] Some years previous, a woman whose testimony had helped secure my conviction recanted it, claiming that one of the investigating detectives had coerced her into testifying. The same detective, Louis Scarcella, has had sixteen cases overturned.[3] Ultimately, a Brooklyn district attorney investigating old cases[4] overturned my conviction.

While incarcerated, I studied law and was able to find paths to freedom not just for myself, but for other incarcerated people who had been wrongfully convicted. I learned that the average lawyer has too many cases and not enough time to litigate zealously; if I were ever to get out of prison, I realized, I would have to file motions on my own and assist my lawyers in proving my innocence. While I was incarcerated, no one else had a vested interest in me achieving this goal. This is by design.

One of the most daunting hurdles I encountered as a person incarcerated by the New York State Department of Corrections and Community Supervision was the Antiterrorism and Effective Death Penalty Act (AEDPA), a 1996 bill that President Clinton signed into law. This law—also publicized as an important reform—made it the case that once a person held in a state facility has exhausted their state remedies, they can no longer pursue federal recourse unless they can prove that an unreasonable application of United States Supreme Court precedent occurred. This effectively creates an extremely narrow legal window and takes away the power of judges to release someone who they know is illegally confined.

Clinton's 1994 and 1996 bills were essentially designed to do three things: 1) give police and government officials the tools to fight what they deemed an extended "war on drugs"—a set of policies most lawmakers today are perfectly comfortable not repealing—in Black and Brown communities, 2) build more prisons, particularly solitary confinement units, and 3) lock up more Black and Brown people in the process, pushing them through the difficult-to-understand criminal legal system.

For example, the 1996 bill imposed a one-year statute of limitations for filing for *habeas* relief. This provision created an undue burden on non-lawyers to understand the complexity of this new enactment.

President Clinton's reform law took away federal review of state court convictions to incarcerated people who perhaps have not had the luxury of years of formal legal training. They could not understand what an unreasonable application of United States precedent meant, let alone how to apply it.

The so-called truth-in-sentencing bill that President Clinton signed in 1994 was publicized as a way to curb drug offenses. This gave police—both in New York City and beyond—the power to conduct illegal stop-and-frisk searches, plant evidence, and falsify reports to justify an arrest. It created a quota system in which police felt the only way to move up the ranks was to make more arrests. The racist quota system was later exposed[5] by members of the NYPD in 2016.

We must abolish any system that permits prosecutors and judges to be protected by the 11th Amendment, which gives them immunity when they abuse their power. By holding prosecutors and judges accountable, police will then have to answer for their actions because the prosecutor or judge can't protect them. Accountability would entail removing them from office when there is proof that they have violated their oath of candor to the courts and fairness to the accused—an ethical oath all judges and prosecutors swear to uphold.

It should come as no surprise that other amendments also uphold anti-Black racial hierarchies. The 13th Amendment should also be abolished because it permits and legalizes incarcerated people to be treated as slaves. Many incarcerated people[6] become mentally ill from many years in punitive housing—myself included. I spent ten years in segregation housing where I was confined for twenty-three hours a day. If we are to make a fairer society, where all people are treated with dignity, then we must start with eradicating any laws and institutions that discriminate against individuals. Institutions like prisons destroy families, don't make communities safer, and intensify poverty. As long as any member of society can be treated as a slave, there will be abuse of power by the slave owner. History has taught us no less.

Together, President Clinton's 1994 and 1996 reform laws led to my spending twenty-one years in prison. In the absence of such laws, the officer that framed me for murder would not have had the powerful resources and ability to do so. He still receives a pension[7] from New York City and has not been held accountable for any of his actions—despite the fact that dozens of his past murder cases are currently under investigation.[8]

Reform may sound appealing, but we must abolish laws and institutions that have been enacted to give police and prisons more power and immunity. A society that holds everyone accountable is the only one worth living in—and is the first step toward honoring the dignity and fundamental humanity of Black and Brown people. ◼

READER'S GUIDE

- Derrick Hamilton cites two Clinton-era "crime" bills that have disproportionately criminalized Black people: 1) The Violent Crime Control and Law Enforcement Act of 1994 and 2) Antiterrorism and Effective Death Penalty Act of 1996. Based on this essay, describe the two features of each of these bills and their outcomes.

- The author writes, "While I was incarcerated, no one else had a vested interest in me achieving this goal. This is by design." What does the author mean by this? Do you agree or disagree? Explain.

- The author references the 11th Amendment. In your own words, describe why the 11th Amendment is important to the author's argument that "criminal justice reform" does not constitute progress for those most impacted by the carceral state.

- After spending twenty-one years in prison, the author was exonerated in 2015. What emotions does the author's story evoke in you?

Police Reform as Counterinsurgency

HOW REFORMIST APPROACHES TO
POLICE VIOLENCE EXPAND POLICE POWER
AND LEGITIMATE THE NEXT PHASE
OF DOMESTIC WARFARE

By Dylan Rodríguez

*

THE LOGIC OF "REFORM"

Reform is best understood as a logic rather than an outcome: an approach to institutional change that sustains existing social, economic, political, and/or legal systems, including but not limited to policing, two-party electoral politics, heteronormativity, criminal justice, and corporate destruction of the natural world.

To reform a system is to adjust isolated aspects of its operation in order to protect that system from total collapse, whether by internal or external forces. Such adjustments usually rest on the fundamental assumption that these systems must remain intact—even as they consistently produce asymmetrical misery, suffering, premature death, and violent life conditions for people and places targeted by anti-Black criminalization, white supremacist police profiling, gendered racist displacement, and colonial occupation.

While modern policing has emerged through the institutionalized violence of anti-Black apartheid and the long genocidal legacies of chattel slavery and frontier warfare, contemporary efforts at "police reform" nonetheless suggest that policing can be magically transformed into a non-anti-Black, non-racial-colonial ("racist") system. As the story goes, this white magic is to be performed by way of piecemeal changes in police administration, protocols, "officer accountability," training, and personnel recruitment.

The #8CantWait[1] campaign, widely publicized[2] on social media by the nonprofit organization We the Protestors and its Campaign Zero effort during the early days of the June 2020 global rebellion against anti-Black police violence, exemplifies the foundational fraudulence of this magical ambition. Premised on the untenable, poorly researched,[3] and dangerous notion that adoption of its eight improved "use of force" policies will result in police killing "72 percent fewer people,"[4] the #8CantWait agenda attracted immediate and widespread support[5] from celebrities and elected officials, including Oprah Winfrey, Julián Castro, and Ariana Grande. Such endorsements are inseparable from the political logic of the nonprofit industrial complex:[6] The infrastructure of liberal philanthropy commodifies simplistic narratives of reform into tidy sound/text bites that are easily repeated, retweeted, and reposted by public-facing people and organizations. This dynamic not only insults the intelligence of those engaged in serious, collectively accountable forms of struggle against state violence—it also glorifies clout-seeking laziness as a substitute for actual (abolitionist) activism.

One of many glaring problems with #8CantWait—which advocates de-escalation, "warning before shooting," banning chokeholds, and installation of a "use of force continuum"—is that many of its proposed policy reforms were incorporated by the most homicidally anti-Black police departments in the United States (including the notorious Chicago PD) well prior to the state-sanctioned killings of Breonna Taylor, George Floyd, and so many others. Against all historical evidence, #8CantWait attempts to convince those questioning and rebelling against a violent, misery-making system that policing is reformable— that it can be modified and refurbished to protect and serve the very same places, communities, and bodies it has historically surveilled, patrolled, intimidated, and eviscerated.

As Project NIA director and abolitionist organizer Mariame Kaba wrote in a June *New York Times* editorial,[7] "There is not a single era in United States history in which the police were not a force of violence against Black people." A recent amicus brief[8] in *Harvard Civil Rights–Civil Liberties Law Review* echoes Black radical feminist and abolitionist[9] analyses like those of Kaba, Rachel Herzing,[10] Alisa Bierria,[11] Sarah Haley,[12] Beth Richie,[13] and Ruth Wilson Gilmore[14] by considering how #8CantWait amounts to a liberal reaction to and attempted appropriation of an emerging global mass movement that radically confronts the foundational, gendered, anti-Black logics of modern policing. The brief suggests that "Campaign Zero's decision to move forward with a middle-of-the-road proposal, just as abolitionist organizers have begun to garner increased public support in their demands to defund and abolish the police, is questionable."

It is vital to ask why such reform campaigns consistently emerge with special intensity in historical moments of widespread (Black) revolt against normalized systems of state power and undeclared domestic war. The 2020 global rebellions against anti-Black policing, acceleration of abolitionist and proto-abolitionist organizing, and spread of Black feminist and queer radicalisms in our midst are, as the late Cedric Robinson[15] might say, a brilliant, messy, beautiful totality that seeks to overthrow conditions of terror. These conditions are both deeply historical and acutely present, encompassing the deadly forces of criminalization, housing and food insecurity, incarceration, targeted environmental toxification, sexual violence, and cultural demonization. Yet, reform movements tend to simultaneously obscure and reproduce normalized conditions of terror by deferring and/or repressing militant collective confrontation with the historical foundations of gendered anti-Black and racial-colonial state violence. Put another way, if the foundation of such violence is policing itself, rather than isolated acts of "police brutality," or criminal justice rather than the scandal of "mass incarceration," then reform is merely another way of telling the targets of such asymmetrical domestic warfare that they must continue to tolerate the intolerable.

What might it mean, in moments of widespread rebellion against normalized conditions of terror, to conceptualize reform campaigns like #8CantWait as a liberal-progressive counterinsurgency?[16] How do such reformist counterinsurgencies serve to undermine, discredit, or otherwise disrupt oppressed, freedom-seeking (Black, Indigenous, incarcerated, colonized) peoples' growing struggles for abolitionist, anti-colonial, decolonizing, and/or revolutionary transformations of existing social, political, and economic systems?

*

"REFORMISM"

Reformism[17]—the ideological and political position that fixates on reform as the primary if not exclusive engine of social change/justice—is another name for this soft form of counterinsurgency. Reformism defers, avoids, and even criminalizes peoples' efforts to catalyze fundamental change to an existing order, often through dogmatic and simplistic mandates of "nonviolence," incrementalism, and compliance.

Moreover, reformism sees the law as the only legitimate form of protest, collective cultural/political expression, and/or direct intervention on systemically violent conditions. (It is worth noting that the interpretation of violent vs. nonviolent acts requires discussion and debate, particularly in response to oxymoronic notions of "property violence" that rarely account for gendered anti-Black and racial-colonial state violence.) Reformism limits the horizon of political possibility to what is seen as achievable within the limits of existing institutional structures (electoral politics, racial capitalism, heteronormativity, formal citizenship, established forms of government and state authority, etc.).

While abolitionist, revolutionary, and radical forms of collective analysis and movement frequently create irreconcilable confrontation with oppressive institutions and systems, reformism seeks to preserve social, political, and economic orders by modifying isolated aspects of their operation. A peculiar assertion animates contemporary forms of this liberal-progressive counterinsurgency: that the long historical, systemic, institutionally reproduced asymmetries of violence produced by existing systems are the unfortunate consequences of fixable "inequities," "disparities," "(unconscious or implicit) biases," corruptions, and/or inefficiencies. In this sense, reformism presumes that equality/equity/parity are achievable—and desirable—within existing systems.

The reformist counterinsurgency pivots on a fervent belief that the spirit of progress, national improvement, and patriotic belief will prevail over a fundamentally violent order. In practice, this belief approximates a form of dogmatic liberal faith—a kind of pseudo-religion. Thus, increased "diversity" in personnel and bureaucratic infrastructure, shifts in the legal and policy apparatus, and individualized "anti-bias trainings"[18] ascend as some of the principal methods for alleviating state violence. There is yet another layer of fatal assumption that structures the reformist position: that those targeted for misery, displacement, and premature death under the existing social order must tolerate continued suffering while waiting for the reformist "fix" to take hold.

*

ABOLITION

An abolitionist analysis and collective praxis, on the other hand, offers an urgent rebuttal to the bad-faith incrementalism of the reformist position. Two parts of the spreading abolitionist response are worth emphasizing: First, that the internal logic of the existing social, political, and economic order (following Sylvia Wynter,[19] let us call this "Civilization"[20]) amounts to a long historical war on specific peoples and places. Second, that the transformation of such an order not only requires its upheaval, but also must be guided by the liberation, collective health, and self-determination of African-descended peoples, Indigenous and Aboriginal peoples, and other peoples and places targeted by the long history of Civilizational war.[21] Considering the anti-Black, genocidal, and proto-genocidal[22] logic of racial capitalism, the (US) nation-state, white supremacy, and settler-colonial[23] domination, reformism is not merely inadequate to the task of abolishing anti-Black, racial-colonial warfare; it is central to Civilization's expansion, sophistication, and deadliness.

To be fair, some rare reform campaigns seek immediate institutional adjustments that directly address the asymmetrical casualties of anti-Blackness and racial-colonial violence. Abolitionist approaches to reform,[24] for example, endorse short-term measures that defend the existence of vulnerable and oppressed people while allowing organizers, teachers, scholars, and other activists to build greater capacity to completely overturn and transform existing systemic arrangements. #8toAbolition,[25] the abolitionist response to #8CantWait, exemplifies such a program of immediate local reforms, which include defunding/redistributing police budgets, decriminalizing survival-focused economies and communities, decarceration of jails and prisons, and universal access to safe housing. Yet, the campaign nonetheless asserts that "the end goal of these reforms is not to create better, friendlier, or more community-oriented police or prisons. Instead, we hope to build toward a society without police or prisons, where communities are equipped to provide for their safety and wellbeing." Reform is, at best, a stopgap emergency tactic that abolitionists undertake with principled suspicion.

The historical moment of the 2020 rebellions momentarily obliterates the reformist script and poses an ongoing challenge to the centrist pivoting signified by the Biden-Harris administration's patriotic restoration of respectable, dignified, "normal," anti-Black, colonial, white supremacist state power. While much of the 2020 US electoral discourse was funneled into a false (and frequently blurred) opposition between piecemeal police reform/defunding and varieties of pro-police nationalism, the contemporaneous proliferation of grassroots abolitionist, proto-abolitionist, and Black freedom/self-defense organizing refuses to concede ground. Growing numbers of people, communities, and organizations are unapologetically, militantly rejecting the contemporary sociopolitical and economic order. This period is animated by widespread Black and Indigenous revolt, audacious visions of a future against/after Civilization, and a disciplined mass refusal to surrender to the intimidation of right-wing reactionaries and the open repression of the state. Proliferating grassroots activity, language, thought, and collective learning expose the brittle ideological claims of reformism, which wilt in the face of the surging art, movement, and poetry of abolition, revolution, reparation, and radical community that define periods like the summer of 2020. Readers of this and other contributions to Abolition for the People may already be engaged with such collectives, but if they are not, they can likely find ways to connect themselves with mutual aid, abolitionist, and other community accountable organizations with reasonably minimal effort.

Finally, at a time when the United States is reacting to this insurgent, self-liberating swell of humanity by openly moving toward a twenty-first-century version of white nationalist fascism, it is helpful to revisit the words of Black revolutionary writer, teacher, and organizer George Jackson, from his book *Blood in My Eye*:

"We will never have a complete definition of fascism, because it is in constant motion, showing a new face to fit any particular set of problems that arise to threaten the predominance of the traditionalist, capitalist ruling class. But if one were forced for the sake of clarity to define it in a word simple enough for all to understand, that word would be 'reform.'" [26]

Fatal and terrorizing state violence is not containable to isolated incidents. It draws from and actively expands a long Civilizational history that is based on the evisceration and negation of Black life; the occupation and destruction of Indigenous peoples and places; the criminalization of queer, trans, and disabled people; the flourishing damage of state-sanctioned sexual violence; and the stubborn omnipresence of violent misogyny—which are the everyday order of things under the conditions of normalized (domestic) war.

Reform is at best a form of casualty management, while reformism is counterinsurgency against those who dare to envision, enact, and experiment with abolitionist forms of community, collective power, and futurity. Abolition, in this sense, is the righteous nemesis of reformism, as well as the militant, principled, historically grounded response to liberal counterinsurgency.

Abolition is not an outcome.[27] Rather, it is an everyday practice, a method of teaching, creating, thinking, and an insurgent ("fugitive") community-building project that exposes the pitfalls of the reformist adventure. It demystifies reformism's cheap magic and summons an embrace of the dynamic Black radical and revolutionary tradition that informs collective labors of freedom,[28] structures notions of justice and collective self-defense, and induces a political and ethical obligation to fight unapologetically, in whatever ways are available, effective, and historically accountable. Anything less is a concession to the logics of anti-Black and racial-colonial genocide. ▲

READER'S GUIDE

- According to Dylan Rodríguez, what is reformism? How does it differ from reform? How is reform a form of counterinsurgency?

- What is the author's criticism of #8CantWait? Do you agree or disagree? Explain.

- What does the author mean by asymmetrical domestic warfare? Provide three to four examples from the author's essay and provide three to four examples from your own observations.

- "Abolition is not an outcome," the author argues. "Rather, it is an everyday practice, a method of teaching, creating, thinking, and an insurgent ("fugitive") community-building project that exposes the pitfalls of the reformist adventure." Please provide three to four concrete examples of everyday abolitionist practice.

The Extent of Carceral Control

"The fallacy is in believing the function of police and prisons is to mete out punishment and justice in an equitable manner and not to first and foremost serve as a means of maintaining the race, gender, and class hierarchy of an oppressive society."

BREE NEWSOME BASS

About **1 in 40** US adult residents is currently under some form of correctional control.

1,430,800
people in prisons

3,540,000
on probation

738,400
in local jails

878,000
on parole[1]

Ending mass incarceration does not end carceral control. The majority of people under carceral control are those under community supervision, such as probation or parole, numbering around **4.4 million**, or **1 in 58** US adult residents. Black people are more likely to be subjected to the continued surveillance and control of parole and less likely to be granted probation as an alternative to incarceration.

■ Black or African American ☐ White ▨ Other

ADULT ON PROBATION

ADULTS ON PAROLE[2]

TOTAL OF POPULATION[3]

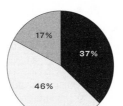

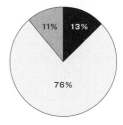

Diversion programs allow people to avoid a conviction or incarceration if they abide by certain terms—but **the threat of incarceration looms**.

A recent survey of participants of Alabama diversion programs found about **1 in 5** were dropped from diversion programs because they **could not afford costs**.[4]

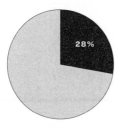

risked being fired because
court appearances related to a diversion
program made them miss work

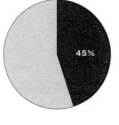

used payday or title loans
to meet costs

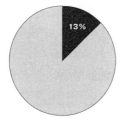

were fired because of court
appearances

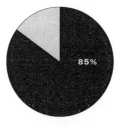

borrowed money from
friends or family

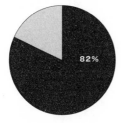

sacrificed rent, food, or prescribed
medication to pay for diversion programs

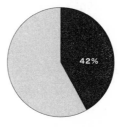

admitted to committing a crime to pay
diversion costs and fees

Data stories researched and conceptualized by Tamara K. Nopper

Three Traps
of Police Reform

By Naomi Murakawa

A bolitionists are practiced in fielding questions asked with raised
eyebrows and a hint of ridicule. *You want to build a better world—
one that values people over profits and functions without police,
prisons, and borders? Sounds utopian. How would that work?*

These are fair questions. But the parallel line of interrogation is
rarely thrown at reformists. *You want to build better police and prisons?
Sounds practical, meaning we can reform now because we have before. How
has that worked out?*

Decades of reform have built an agile, deadly police force and
the largest prison system in the world. This is not because previous
generations slept on the job. The call to shrink, dismantle, or abolish

police and prisons—not improve them—reverberates through the Civil Rights Congress and *We Charge Genocide*; through Bayard Rustin and the Journey of Reconciliation; through the Black Panthers and the Young Lords; through Marsha P. Johnson, Sylvia Rivera, and queer liberation movements, to the creation of Critical Resistance in the late 1990s.[1] Today many are new to abolition, but abolition is not new. I say this to remember some simple lessons. Abolitionist lineages run deep. The fight is long. And, finally, I say this to remember that—given that brilliant abolitionists are here and have been here—it would be foolish to underestimate the allure of reformism. Abolitionists are called dreamers, but it is the promise of reform that works as fantasy.

The first trap of reform is that *reform the police* usually means *reward the police*. As a supposed concession to the first wave of Black Lives Matter protests in 2014 through 2016, the Obama administration gave police a gift basket: $43 million for body cameras. Body cameras have not delivered on early promises to reduce force and increase accountability, but they have expanded police surveillance powers, especially when equipped with facial-recognition software. As police patrolled Black Lives Matter protests in 2020, they captured images of protesters[2]—by using the very technology that elites promised would contain some of the police powers that had sparked the protests just a few years ago.

Even larger rewards for police departments come under the guise of feel-good cop-speak labels like "community policing," "guardian policing," or "procedurally just policing."[3] After mass uprisings against policing in the mid-1960s, the Johnson administration created the Law Enforcement Assistance Administration,[4] which dispensed $10 billion mostly to local police, often in the name of improving racial fairness and police-community relations.

The more police brutalize and kill, the greater their budgets for training, hiring, and hardware. The Los Angeles Police Department exemplifies this cruel exchange rate, as Max Felker-Kantor documents in *Policing Los Angeles*.[5] Between January 1964 and July 1965—the eighteen months before the people of Watts rebelled—the LAPD killed sixty-four people. Despite the fact that twenty-seven of them were shot in the back, the police's internal affairs department ruled that sixty-two of the sixty-four were justifiable homicides. During the Watts rebellion, the LAPD and the National Guard killed another twenty-three Angelenos, most of whom were Black. Many concluded that the LAPD must be professionalized, given better training and equipment to "fight crime" without provoking protests that cost millions in property damage. As federal, state, and county budgets ciphoned more into policing, LAPD chief Thomas Reddin did not sound like a leader chagrined, chastened by the onus of reform. He felt triumphant, lavished in loot. It was "The Year of the Cop," he said of 1968, adding, "Everything you want, you get. And I say I want more, and I should be getting it."[6]

The protests of 2020 have popularized key abolitionist demands to defund police[7] and abolish the prison industrial complex.[8] But federal elites have instead doubled down on rewarding police, particularly through the Community Oriented Policing Services (the COPS Office), a 1994 Clinton administration creation that has already given $14 billion to local police. In June 2020—as total unemployment reached 18 million people, one in five families was food insecure, and Black, Latino, and Indigenous mortality rates for coronavirus were as much as double those of whites—federal lawmakers prioritized hiring over three thousand more cops through the COPS Office, and President Biden promises to give another $300 million to community-oriented policing.[9]

This history suggests that police, like banks, are too big to fail. When market crashes or mass protests stop business as usual, elites deliver a bailout—for the authors of the devastation, not the people they left broke and broken.

Policing is intrinsically predatory[10] and violent.[11] Police push millions of people into the carceral state, where racial disparity and other inequities rise through each circle of hell. Black people comprise 13 percent of the US population but roughly 30 percent of the arrested, 35 percent of the imprisoned, 42 percent of those on death row, and 56 percent of those serving life sentences.[12] Nearly half of people murdered by police have disabilities. Sexual violence is a routine but invisible form[13] of police brutality used especially against LGBTQ youth, sex workers, undocumented women, and Black women and women of color.

Here we see the second trap of reform: Because police *seem* lawless, reformers hope that new laws will rein in their power. But the premise is wrong. Policing is not law's absence; it is law's essence in a system of racial capitalism.[14] In this system, laws affirmatively protect the police's right to target the poor, to lie, and to kill.

Racism is not a contaminant that seeps into policing as if lawmakers left some loophole that dutiful reformers could close. Police saturate working-class, Black, and Brown neighborhoods with explicit legal permission. Courts validate endless police stops. Stopping someone for walking in a "high-crime area"? Perfectly legal.[15] Searching a car for drugs because the Black driver paused too long at a stop sign? Perfectly reasonable.[16] As police commonly joke about racial profiling, "It never happens—and it works."[17]

Reformers try to enhance people's procedural rights as if arming individuals with legal protections might slow the churn of criminalization. But consider the crowning glory of the procedural rights revolution, the 1966 *Miranda v. Arizona* Supreme Court decision requiring cops to recite the speech that begins "You have the right to remain silent." Outraged conservatives griped about liberal courts handcuffing the cops. But police simply adapted to a new protocol. After reading Miranda rights during an arrest, police secure incriminating statements in more than half of all interrogations—rates comparable to those pre-*Miranda*.[18] Police routinely use lies, intimidation, and confinement to coerce confessions, but simply saying the magic words became proof of professionalism. In short, *Miranda* offers good protection— for police, not the people they interrogate.

Reformers try to regulate police use of force, but regulations are also instructions. In the 1985 *Tennessee v. Garner* decision, for example, the Supreme Court held that Memphis police wrongfully killed Edward Garner, a Black child in the eighth grade. It was wrong to shoot the child in the back, the Court found; such violence was justifiable only *if* the cop feared deadly injury to bystanders or themself. With this conditional clause, the Court gave police instructions on how to kill legally. Police learned the script, "I feared for my life." If cops forget their lines, then internal investigators help them remember. After Chicago police killed a child—identified in a Department of Justice report only as an "unarmed teenager"—the police internal investigator steered the cop toward exoneration with this question: "You were in fear for your life, so you fired how many times?"[19]

Reform orbits around bad "incidents," as if police *brutality* and police *profiling* are somehow discrete moments when police do something wrong. But brutality and racism are woven into policing. This becomes clear when we name the core police function: to use coercive power to preserve the status quo. And what is the status quo? Put simply by Ruth Wilson Gilmore, "capitalism requires inequality and racism enshrines it. Thus, criminalization and mass incarceration are class war ... Police killings are the most dramatic events in a contemporary landscape thick with preventable, premature deaths."[20] Police protect private property, enforce the color line, patrol the gender binary, and hold national borders for everyone except the corporations. No amount of reform can erase these core functions.

With each new video of cops brutalizing and killing, there are new expressions of horrified disbelief. Then come announcements of police non-indictment or exoneration, and more statements of disappointment and shock.

Here, in this sea of disbelief, we see the third trap of reform: perpetual reform exploits and feeds the fantasy that violence is a technical glitch of policing. Because reformers refuse abolition, they can only tinker with the style of police violence.

Chokehold bans, for example, prohibit a technique of killing but not the fact of killing. The bans are nonetheless hailed as victories, and New York City just celebrated its recent chokehold prohibition. But the New York Police Department prohibited chokeholds once before, in November 1993. It was hailed as a victory then, too. From 2006 to 2013, nearly 2,000 New Yorkers came forward with chokehold complaints. Just weeks after cops killed Eric Garner in 2014, the NYPD used the chokehold on Rosann Miller, a Black woman who was seven months pregnant, after they confronted her for barbequing in front of her house.[21] The departmental ban was in full effect.

What trajectory of progress is this, to ban the chokehold—again— but allow police to kill with flashlights, vans, stun guns, handguns, and chokeholds by another name? An analogy can be made to death penalty reformers who replaced the noose with the electric chair and then replaced the electric chair with chemical cocktails. Reformers witnessed the horror of electrocutions that set heads aflame, and so they came up with a better way.

But better for whom? The technique of execution does not comfort the dead. It comforts the executioners—and all their supporters.

Chokehold bans are typical of a certain type of reform—reforms to the arsenal of police weaponry. In the words of one activist, the chokehold ban is "useless." Such reforms are useful, however, if the goal of reform is to rescue police from a legitimacy crisis of their own making. Reform becomes an elegant solution: let one particular weapon or tactic absorb the blame, while policing goes on as usual. Same terror, different tools.

We have seen this before. For a textbook lesson in police reshuffling of weaponry, we can turn again to the Los Angeles Police Department. Between 1977 and 1982, Los Angeles police killed sixteen people with the chokehold; fourteen of the murder victims were Black.[22] LAPD Chief Daryl Gates defended the categorically "non-lethal" chokehold by blaming Black people for their peculiar "veins or arteries," slower to open than those of "normal people."[23] Facing lawsuits from Black Angelinos, in 1982 LAPD banned the "bar-arm" chokehold and restricted use of the carotid chokehold.[24]

Apparently it was the chokehold—and not the police—that killed Black people.

After the world watched LAPD beat Rodney King with fifty-six baton swings in 1991, Chief Gates commissioned a study to formally reintroduce the chokehold. Chokeholds would be less bone crushing and "more humane" than the baton, Gates suggested.[25] "After the video played that night," said an LAPD Deputy Chief about the beating of Rodney King, cops "hardly ever used the baton. It was banished." Some evidence suggests that the weapon did indeed cycle out of favor with LAPD, with a reported 741 baton "force incidents" in 1990 compared to "just" fifty-four in 2015.[26] The baton, Chief Gates said, had become a "symbol of police oppression."[27]

Apparently it was the baton—and not the police—that got a bad reputation for brutalizing Black people.

Tasers then became a police favorite. In Los Angeles in 2015, with baton use at historic lows, LAPD used the Taser 519 times.[28]

In that same year across the US, police killed forty-eight people with Tasers. One was Natasha McKenna, a thirty-seven-year-old Black woman who, despite being handcuffed and leg-shackled, so overpowered six specially trained Emergency Response Team officers that they felt compelled to tase her four times. She stopped breathing and died several days later. Before officers tased her to death, Natasha McKenna pleaded with them, saying, "You promised . . . you wouldn't kill me."[29]

And in the eyes of the law, police did *not* kill her. Tasers are technically non-lethal weapons. This designation holds regardless of the death toll, because "normal" bodies do not die when tased.

Apparently the problem is not that police use Tasers to terrorize and kill Black people. The problem is that too many Black people have "non-normal bodies." They die when the appropriate response is to suffer.

Given the reformers' tendency to blame the machinery, we should be able to predict what will follow from this latest round of chokehold bans. "By simply banning all chokeholds," warns *Police1* magazine, well-meaning people "are forcing officers to move to a higher level of physical control (strikes) or an intermediate weapon (chemical spray, baton, or Taser), which can be more harmful to the subject."[30] Police have warned us. Ban the chokehold and suffer the consequences of more brutal weapons.

We pursue reform on the premise that the system is broken. But as Mariame Kaba tells us, the system isn't broken but highly functioning just as the powers that be intended.[31] I agree and will add this: Police reform does not fail. It works—for the police. ◼

READER'S GUIDE

- According to Naomi Murakawa, what are the three traps of reform? How does each trap reinforce the others? And why do these traps ultimately reward the police?

- How have police been "rewarded" since (and in response to) the 2020 protests? Provide three to four examples.

- What does the author mean by "Policing is not law's absence; it is law's essence in a system of racial capitalism"? Do you agree or disagree? Explain.

- What suggestions does the author offer for avoiding reformist traps and for pursuing abolitionist futures? What are your own suggestions for pursuing abolitionist futures?

Putting a Black Face on Police Agendas

BLACK COPS DON'T MAKE POLICING ANY LESS ANTI-BLACK

By Bree Newsome Bass

A mid growing calls throughout summer 2020 to defund police, a series of billboards appeared in Dallas, Atlanta, and New York City. Each had the words "No Police, No Peace" printed in large, bold letters next to an image of a Black police officer. Funded by a conservative right-wing think tank,[1] the billboards captured all the hallmarks of modern pro-policing propaganda. The jarring choice of language, a deliberate corruption of the protest chant "no justice, no peace," follows a pattern we see frequently from proponents of the police state. Any word or phrase—for example "woke" and "Black lives matter"—made popular by the modern movement is quickly co-opted and repurposed until it's rendered virtually meaningless. But perhaps the most insidious aspect of modern pro-police propaganda is reflected in the choice to make the officer on the billboard the face of a Black man.

This is in keeping with a narrative that pro-police advocates seek to push on a regular basis in mass media—that policing can't be racist when there are Black officers on the force and that the police force itself is an integral part of Black communities. When Freddie Gray died in police custody, police defenders quickly pointed out that three of the officers involved were Black,[2] implying that racism couldn't be a factor in a case where the offending officers were the same race as the victim.

When I scaled the flagpole at South Carolina's Capitol[3] in 2015 and lowered the Confederate flag, many noted that it was a Black officer who was tasked with raising the flag to the top of its pole again. When an incident of brutality brings a city to its brink, Black police chiefs are paraded to podiums and cameras to serve as the face of the United States' racist police state and to symbolically restore a sense of order. One of the most frequent recommendations from police reformists is to recruit and promote more Black officers. This is based on an argument that's gained enormous popularity in recent years in direct response to protests that the primary problem with policing centers on a "breakdown of trust" between police forces and communities they have terrorized for decades; the solution, then, is to "restore trust" between the two parties by recruiting officers who resemble the communities they police. Images of police officers dancing or playing basketball with Black children in economically deprived neighborhoods are often published as local news items to help drive this narrative home—even as some of the officers featured in such photos are later discovered to have their own records of brutality and misconduct. Bobby White was one such officer in Gainesville, Florida. Hailed as the "basketball cop"[4] he appeared on news programs promoting his nonprofit that claimed to ease tensions between police and Black youth until video emerged of him slamming a Black teen against the hood of his patrol car. The idea gained traction in the aftermath of numerous urban rebellions in the 1960s and has seen a resurgence in the wake of the 2014 Ferguson uprising.

When protests broke out in Atlanta in summer 2020 in response to the killings of George Floyd, Breonna Taylor, and Ahmaud Arbery, the city's Black mayor, Keisha Lance Bottoms, held a press conference flanked by some of Atlanta's most famous and wealthy Black residents.

Together they pleaded for protesters to go home and leave property alone. Soon after, Rayshard Brooks was killed by white police officers in Atlanta. The moment exposed a class divide that exists in cities all over the nation: a chasm between the image of Black affluence promoted by Black politicians and the Black middle class and the lived realities of the majority of Black residents in those cities, many of whom still face disproportionate unemployment, displacement by rapid gentrification, and policies that cater to white corporate interests. If the solution to racism were simply a matter of a few select Black people gaining entry to anti-Black institutions, we would see different outcomes than what we're witnessing now. But the idea that we can resolve racism by integrating what is perhaps the most fundamentally anti-Black institution in the US—its policing and prison industry—is the most absurd notion of all.

Part of the reason why calls to defund police have sent such shock waves through the nation, prompting placement of pro-police billboards and pushback from figures of the Black establishment, is because it cuts right to the heart of how structural racism operates in the United States. At a time when the Black elite would prefer to measure progress by their own tokenized positions of power and symbolic gestures like murals, the push to defund police would require direct confrontation with how the white supremacist system has been organized since the end of chattel slavery—when the prisons replaced plantations as the primary tool of racial control. Actions that may have been widely seen as adequate responses to injustice just a couple of decades ago now ring hollow to many observers who see that Black people continue to be killed by a system that remains largely unchanged.

Police forces represent some of the oldest white fraternal organizations[5] in the United States. The rules of who is empowered to police and who is subject to policing are fundamental to the organization of the racial caste system. Even in the earliest days of integrating police forces, Black officers were often told they couldn't arrest white people.[6] The integration of police forces does nothing to alter their basic function as the primary enforcers of structural racism on a daily basis, and the presence of Black officers only serves as an attempt to mask this fact.

Police forces in America began as slave patrols, and their primary function has always been to act in service of the white ownership class[7] and its capitalist production. In one century, that meant policing and controlling enslaved Black people, with the purview to use violence against free Black people as well; in another, it involved cracking down on organized labor, for the benefit of white capitalists.[8] Receiving a badge and joining the force has been an entryway to white manhood for many European immigrants—providing them a sense of citizenship and superiority[9] when they would have traditionally been part of the peasantry rather than the white owner class.

That spirit of white fraternity remains deeply entrenched in the culture of policing and its unions today, regardless of this new wave of Black police chiefs and media spokespeople. Police forces became unionized[10] around the same time various other public employees sought collective bargaining rights—however, under capitalism, their role as maintainers of race-property relations remains the same. The most fundamental rule of race established under chattel slavery was that Black people were the equivalent of white property (if not counted as less than property). This relationship between race and property is most overt during periods of open rebellion against the police state, where officers are deployed to use lethal force in the interest of protecting inanimate property. We see swifter and harsher punishments handed out to those who vandalize police cars than to police who assault and kill Black people. (This is a major reason why the press conference in Atlanta with T.I. and Killer Mike struck people as classist and out of touch with the majority Black experience.)

This same pattern extends throughout the carceral state. Roughly a quarter of all bailiffs, correctional officers, and jailers are Black,[11] yet there's no indication that diversifying the staff of a racist institution results in less violence and death for those who are held within it. That's because the institution continues to operate as designed. It is not "broken," as reformists are fond of saying. The fallacy is in believing the function of police and prisons is to mete out punishment and justice in an equitable manner and not to first and foremost serve as a means of maintaining the race, gender, and class hierarchy of an oppressive society.

Believing that the system is "broken" rather than functioning exactly as intended requires a certain adherence to white supremacist and anti-Black beliefs. One has to ignore the rampant amount of violence, fraud, and theft being committed by some of the most powerful figures in society with little to no legal consequence while massive amounts of resources are devoted to the hyper-policing of the poor for infractions as minor as trespassing, shoplifting, and turnstile jumping at subway stations.

The Trump era has provided some of the starkest examples of this dynamic. Throughout the Trump presidency, Trump and his associates were able to break the law and violate the Constitution—including documented crimes against humanity—in full view of the public while he proclaimed himself the upholder of law and order. Wealthy celebrities involved in the college admissions bribery scandal have gotten away with a slap on the wrist for orchestrating a multimillion-dollar scheme while a dozen NYPD officers surrounded a Black teenager, guns drawn, for the "crime" of failing to pay $2.75[12] for a subway ride.

The propaganda that depicts this type of policing as being essential to public safety and order is fundamentally classist and anti-Black. It traces its roots to the Black Codes[13] that were passed immediately after the Civil War to control the movements of newly freed Black people. It relies on the racist assumption that Black people would run amok and pose a threat to the larger society if not kept under the constant surveillance of a police force that has authority to kill them if deemed necessary, and with virtual impunity. That's why we are inundated with a narrative that depicts the police officer who regularly patrols predominantly Black communities as being an essential part of maintaining order in society.

One of the primary talking points against calls to defund and abolish police is that Black communities would have no way to maintain peace and order, and that a state of chaos would ensue. In wealthier neighborhoods, if an officer is present at all, they're most likely positioned by a gate at the top of the neighborhood to monitor who enters. Meanwhile, the officer assigned to the predominantly Black community is there to keep a watchful eye on the residents themselves, and to ensure they are contained in their designated place within the larger city or town.

The current political divide on this issue falls exactly along these lines, separating those who think the system is simply in need of reform and those who correctly define the problem as the system itself. The reality is that Black people fall on both sides of this divide, which is why we find so many Black officers in uniform arguing for a reformist agenda even as every reform they propose is vociferously opposed by the powerful, majority-white police unions and most of the rank and file. Reformists remain committed to preserving the existing system even though the idea of reforming it to be the opposite of what it was designed to be is an unproven theory that's no more realistic than the idea of abolishing police altogether.

The most pressing question remains: Why are we seeking to integrate and reform modern manifestations of the slave patrols and plantations in the first place? In Mississippi and Louisiana, state penitentiaries are converted plantations. What is a reformed plantation—and what is its purpose?

We must remember that many of these so-called "reforms" are not new. For as long as the plantation and chattel slavery systems existed, there also existed Black slaveowners, Black overseers, and Black slave catchers who participated in and profited from the daily operations of white supremacy. The presence of these few Black people in elevated positions of power did nothing to change the material conditions of the millions of enslaved people back then. And it makes no greater amount of sense to believe they indicate a shift in material conditions for Black people now. ▲

READER'S GUIDE

- "The idea that we can resolve racism by integrating what is perhaps the most fundamentally anti-Black institution in the US—its policing and prison industry—is the most absurd notion of all," writes Bree Newsome Bass. What makes this wrong-headed assumption so powerful?

- What is the author's criticism of the argument that police violence is based on a "breakdown in trust" between police and communities? How has this argument served to promote reform and challenge abolitionist movements?

- What is the author's analysis of the role that class plays in police reform and, relatedly, police violence? Do you agree or disagree? Explain.

- The author demonstrates that "police forces in America began as slave patrols." Do you believe this history is important to understand integrationist/reformist impulses to policing today? Please explain your answer.

The New Jim Code

THE SHINY, HIGH-TECH
WOLF IN SHEEP'S CLOTHING

By Ruha Benjamin

From everyday apps to complex algorithms, technology has the potential to hide, speed, and deepen discrimination, all while appearing neutral and even benevolent when compared to overtly racist practices of a previous era. Predictive policing programs,[1] criminal risk assessment tools,[2] and electronic ankle[3] shackles are a few of the tools that perpetuate the injustices of the US criminal legal system, or what I call the New Jim Code. The good news is that with the rise of the New Jim Code, many individuals and organizations are developing abolitionist tools as part of a larger data justice movement—challenging surveillance technologies that harm communities and designing interventions that foster collective well-being. Struggles over abolitionist futures are being waged not just in the streets, but on our phones, apps, and platforms.

For example, Appolition is an app that converts your daily change into bail money to free Black people from jail. (Calls for abolition are never simply about bringing harmful systems to an end, but also envisioning new ones.) When Appolition co-founder Kortney Ziegler and I sat on a panel together at the 2018 Allied Media Conference, he pointed out the existence of similar technologies that present themselves as liberatory but whose creators do not share an abolitionist commitment. At the time, Jay-Z's Roc Nation had invested in a "decarceration startup" called Promise, which aims to address the problem of pretrial detention for people who cannot afford bail. But among its other features, Promise is also in the business of digitally tracking individuals [4] to ensure they meet court appointments, show up for drug tests, and other forms of supervision as part of individual "Care Plans"—a euphemism if there ever was one.

In a piece on the website for BYP100 (Black Youth Project 100), an organization focused on transformative leadership development, direct action organizing, advocacy, and education, writer Alyxandra Goodwin described Promise as a harbinger of the Prison Industrial Complex's next iteration. "The digital sphere and tech world of the 2000s is the next sector to have a stronghold around incarceration," she wrote, "and will mold what incarceration looks like and determine the terrain on which prison abolitionists have to fight as a result."

If both Appolition and Promise help people who cannot afford bail get out of cages, why is Promise a problem for those who support prison abolition? Because it creates a powerful mechanism that makes it easier to lock people back up—and because, rather than turning away from the carceral apparatus, it extends that apparatus into everyday life.

Whereas the money crowdfunded for Appolition operates like an endowment that is used to bail people out, Promise is an investment in and collaboration with law enforcement. The company, which received $3 million in venture capital, is not in the business of decarceration but is part of the "technocorrections" industry, which seeks to capitalize on very real concerns about mass incarceration and the political momentum of social justice organizing. Products like Promise make it easier and more cost-effective to track and reimprison people for technical violations like missing a court appointment or a drug test.

Promise, in this way, is exemplary of the New Jim Code; it is dangerous and insidious precisely because it is packaged as social betterment. For-profit prison conglomerates such as the Geo Group and CoreCivic (formerly Corrections Corporation of America, or CCA) are proving especially adept at reconfiguring their business investments to create similar misdirection, leaving prisons and detention centers and turning to tech alternatives like ankle shackles and other digital tracking devices. In some cases, the companies that hold lucrative government contracts to imprison asylum seekers are the same ones that ICE hires[5] to provide social services to these very people, even as they continue to be monitored remotely. While not being locked in a cage is an improvement, the alternative is a form of coded inequity and carceral control, and it is vital that the people committed to social justice look beyond the shiny exterior of organizations that peddle such reforms.

A key tenet of prison abolition is that caging people works directly against the safety and well-being of communities because jails and prisons do not address the underlying reasons why people harm themselves and others—in fact, they exacerbate the problem by making it even more difficult to obtain any of the support needed to live, work, and make amends for harms committed. But in the age of the New Jim Code, and as abolitionists have long argued, our vision must extend beyond the problem of caging to our consideration of technological innovations marketed as supporting prison reform.

It is vital to divert money away from imprisonment to schools and public housing if we really want to make communities stronger, safer, and more supportive for all their members. But, as abolitionist organization Critical Resistance[6] has argued, simply diverting resources in this way is no panacea because schools and public housing as they currently function are an extension of the Prison Industrial Complex:

many operate with a logic of carcerality and on policies that discriminate against those who have been convicted of crimes—like "blanket ban[7] policies maintained by many private landlords and public housing authorities." Pouring money into them as they are will only make them more effective in their current function as institutions of social control.

We have to look beyond the surface of what they say they do to what they actually do, in the same way in which I am calling on all of us to question the tech industry's "do good" rhetoric. This requires us to consider not only the ends but also the means. How we get to the end matters. If the path is that private companies, celebrities, and tech innovators should cash in on the momentum of communities and organizations that challenge mass incarceration, the likelihood is that the end achieved will replicate the current social order.

"To see things as they really are, you must imagine them for what they might be," said the late legal and critical race scholar Derrick A. Bell, urging a radical assessment of reality through creative methods and racial reversals. Take, for instance, a parody project that begins by subverting the anti-Black logics embedded in new high-tech approaches to "crime prevention." Instead of using predictive policing techniques to forecast what some might call "street crime," the White Collar Early Warning System[8] flips the script by creating a heat map that flags city blocks where financial crimes are likely to occur. The system not only brings into view the hidden—but no less deadly—crimes of capitalism and the wealthy's hoarding of resources, but also includes an app that alerts users when they enter high-risk areas to encourage "citizen policing and awareness."[9]

Taking it one step further, the development team for the White Collar Crime Early Warning System is working on a facial recognition program meant to flag individuals who are likely perpetrators, and the training set used to design the algorithm includes the profile photos of 7,000 corporate executives downloaded from the popular professional networking site LinkedIn—subverting the documented racism of AI algorithms[10] and predictive policing by using a corpus of data that is largely white and male. By deliberately and inventively upsetting the status quo, analysts can better understand and expose the many forms of discrimination embedded in and enabled by technology. Together, we must critically examine the progressive narratives that surround technology, shining a light on how technical fixes for social problems can both perpetuate racism and resist it, as we continue to seed an abolitionist world that may, at times, entail developing tools that resist and reimagine the carceral status quo. ◪

READER'S GUIDE

- Ruha Benjamin introduces the term "the New Jim Code" to discussions about reform and abolition. Define the term. Please provide three to four examples of the New Jim Code from your own life.

- How does the New Jim Code build upon historical forms of incarceration? What, in your opinion, may be some of the dangers or concerns with these forms of technology?

- What is the technocorrections industry? Provide an example from the essay.

- The author argues that technology can be deployed both as a form of oppression and as a tool of resistance and liberation. Please provide three to four examples of both oppression and resistance/liberation from the essay. Identify contemporary technologies that can be used to build a world beyond policing and prisons.

PART

IV

Abolition
Now

Change from the Roots

WHAT ABOLITION LOOKS LIKE, FROM THE PANTHERS TO THE PEOPLE

By Robin D. G. Kelley

"What if Trayvon Martin was offered a ride home instead?"
—Dream Defenders, "Defund Police and Rebuild Our Communities"

The slogan "Defund the Police" has become a political lightning rod. To former President Donald Trump and his people, it is a terrorist plot hatched by socialists (read: Democrats) and thugs (read: Black people). President Joe Biden and most of his party stalwarts run from the idea, proposing instead to increase funding for law enforcement for better equipment and training. Abolition also has its share of critics on the left[1] who think it is utopian fantasy and a political dead end. All sides share two things in common: they believe police keep us safe, and they fundamentally misunderstand the demand to defund or abolish the police.

For Black, Brown, Indigenous, and other communities of color, especially the poor, women, and LGBTQ folx, the police are often a threat to safety and security—alongside a racist and sexist "criminal justice" system, inadequate income, housing, health care, and schools, and neighborhoods divested of services and subject to environmental and health hazards. They are more likely to live near toxic waste dumps, freeways, bus barns, and oil and gas production facilities, and lack access to healthy food, clean drinking water, and safe affordable housing, among other things. This is why abolition is necessary. Abolition works to dismantle systems that have caused harm, namely police and prisons, and reallocate funds to social and economic resources, and to develop new systems of community-controlled public safety and restorative justice. The Movement for Black Lives (M4BL), a coalition made up of over 150 organizations, came up with such a plan to divest billions of dollars from prisons,[2] policing, and the Pentagon, and invest in education, universal health care, housing, living wage jobs, restorative justice, food justice, and green energy.

For example, since 9/11, the Department of Homeland Security (DHS) gave over $30 billion in direct grants to state and local law enforcement, and the Department of Defense's (DOD) 1033 Program issued some $7 billion worth of surplus military equipment to police departments as well law enforcement units to select colleges and school districts. The federal government doles out billions with little oversight and no accountability, and no evidence that we are safer as a result of militarized policing. The M4BL policy platform proposes reallocating these funds to "long-term safety strategies such as education, community restorative justice, and employment programs." The data is clear: Children in a Chicago study[3] who did not participate in preschool programs were 70 percent more likely to be arrested by age eighteen; in another study,[4] youth who participated in summer job programs in Chicago saw a 43 percent decrease in arrests over a sixteen-month period. Shifting $37 billion from policing to education and restorative justice initiatives will not only strengthen communities—it will make them safer.

Abolition is neither new nor hopelessly utopian. On the contrary, after over a half century of "reforms," police and prisons continue to enact irreparable harm to vulnerable populations. None of the police reforms currently proposed are new: civilian review boards, better training, altering use of force policy, more Tasers, more transparency, diversifying the force[5] (especially by hiring more Black cops),[6] residency requirements (officers must live in the city where they work), better data to flag patterns of misconduct, body cams, and banning chokeholds. These reforms have not stopped the wanton killing and beating of civilians or made communities that are consistently policed any safer. Before George Floyd's execution in Minneapolis, the city's police department was a poster child of reform. Minneapolis's diverse force was well-trained in mental health crisis intervention,[7] implicit bias, de-escalation,[8] and praised for being exceptionally compassionate.[9]

A decade of unremitting police violence followed by non-indictments has inspired new movements to embrace abolitionist principles. Those organizations include: #BlackLivesMatter, Dream Defenders, Black Youth Project 100, We Charge Genocide, BOLD (Black Organizing for Leadership and Dignity), Million Hoodies Movement for Justice, Dignity and Power Now, Ella's Daughters, Assata's Daughters, Black Feminist Future, Know Your Rights Camp, Leaders of a Beautiful Struggle, and the #LetUsBreathe Collective, to name just a few. Before Black Lives Matter became a hashtag, Oakland's Black Organizing Project[10] and the Community Rights Campaign[11] in Los Angeles were fighting to demilitarize schools, decriminalize tardiness and truancy, and abolish school police. In Ferguson, Missouri, in the wake of Michael Brown's death, Black youth in Hands Up United,[12] Lost Voices, and Millennial Activists United gave us a model of a sustained revolt dedicated to police abolition that inspired a group of anarchists to publish a pamphlet A World Without Police[13] and launch a companion website.[14]

Abolishing the police is not the brainchild of some extreme left-wing think tank but a product of grassroots social movements fighting police violence and racially biased laws while simultaneously trying to make their own communities safer. We have been taught that fear of rising crime and urban rebellions ensured Richard Nixon's election in 1968 because he promised to restore "law and order." But the wave of urban rebellions were responses to *police violence*, exacerbated by the violence of disinvestment, segregation, and poverty.

The Black Panther Party (BPP) was formed in 1966 in Oakland, California, precisely to monitor police violence, to create community-based models of public safety, and to provide for the social needs of Black communities where the state failed. Panthers around the country patrolled the streets, held know-your-rights workshops, exposed the names of brutal cops, and in various places provided free medical care, free clothing and groceries, free breakfast and lunch programs, liberation schools for children,[15] food banks, community gardens, drug rehab centers, ambulance services, and housing cooperatives. These efforts at mutual aid were deemed so dangerous to national security that FBI director J. Edgar Hoover dubbed the Panthers as "the greatest threat to internal security of the country." BPP members, along with other liberation movement activists, sought to reimagine criminal justice at the Revolutionary People's Constitutional Convention held in Philadelphia in 1970. They proposed reorganizing the police[16] as "a rotating volunteer nonprofessional body coordinated by the Police Control Board from a (weekly) list of volunteers from each community section." Board members would be elected, its policies approved by popular vote, and "community rehabilitation programs" would replace jails and prisons. However, through systematic raids on Panther headquarters,[17] surveillance, agent provocateurs, targeted assassinations, and harassment, the police and FBI[18] actually created a dangerous and insecure environment. The assassinations of Fred Hampton, head of the Illinois chapter of the BPP, and Mark Clark,[19] leader of the Peoria chapter, on December 4, 1969, are the best known examples of the government's war on the Panthers.

Today's vision of abolition, rooted in anti-prison movements, can be traced to the long 1990s (roughly 1989–2003), to opposition to Bush- and Clinton-era neoliberalism, the war on drugs, the war on terror, prison expansion, the movement to free political prisoners, police violence, anti-Black and anti-immigrant racism, Islamophobia, and violence against women of color and the LGBTQ community. That vision is present in movements like Mothers ROC (Reclaiming Our Children), the Malcolm X Grassroots Movement, the National Jericho Movement, Prison Activist Resource Center, the Prison Moratorium Project, Critical Resistance, All of Us or None, Labor/Community Strategy Center, Project South, Southerners on New Ground (SONG), INCITE! Women of Color Against Violence, Sista 2 Sista, the Los Angeles Community Action Network, the Praxis Project, Safe OUTside the System (SOS), Project NIA, FIERCE (Fabulous Independent Educated Radicals for Community Empowerment), Queers for Economic Justice, the Sylvia Rivera Law Project (SRLP), Bay Area Transformative Justice Collective (BATJC), and UBUNTU!, to name only a few.

The founders and forces behind many of these movements were key theorists of abolition, community organizers, survivors of gender-based violence, formerly incarcerated, and scholar-activists whose writings—even if not promoting an abolitionist agenda—profoundly shaped the current generation of activists. The current movement is unimaginable without the writings of my colleagues and compatriots who have also contributed to this project, as well many others.

It is not an accident that gender-based violence (physical, sexual, and psychological violence directed at women, girls, femmes, and queer and gender-nonconforming people meant to subjugate and maintain gender inequalities) emerged as a key abolitionist issue. Women of color as well as queer and trans folx are simultaneously criminalized and rendered disposable. It is not enough to say the names of those killed by police but also the tens of thousands whose deaths, disappearances, and abuse go unresolved. Legal scholar and activist Kimberlé Crenshaw, co-founder of the African American Policy Forum, launched #SayHerName[20] not only to draw attention to Black women killed by police but to expose how the state and the law make them more vulnerable to other forms of violence by failing to ensure adequate income, affordable housing, effective protections from domestic violence, and persistent race and gender discrimination. Economic precarity, social marginalization, and criminalization render them more susceptible to harm. Police not only enact harm through direct violence in the course of their daily operations—arresting, beating, intimidating, threatening those deemed "suspicious"—but as perpetrators of sexual assault on and off duty. The CATO Institute revealed that sexual misconduct was the highest category of complaints filed against police,[21] second only to excessive use of force. These connections were on display when Oklahoma City police officer Daniel Holtzclaw[22] was charged in August 2014 for sexually assaulting at least eight Black women during traffic stops while on duty.

The criminal justice system is simply incapable of addressing gender-based and intimate violence. Carceral feminists[23] believe that police, prosecution, and prison are the best way to address gender and sexual violence; abolition feminists[24] argue that locking perpetrators up in cages reinforces violent behavior and never addresses the problem of gender-based violence and its survivors. Instead, the carceral state criminalizes and locks up women, transgender, and gender-nonconforming people in jails, prisons, and detentions centers where they are frequently subjected to gendered violence.

In 2001, INCITE! Women of Color Against Violence and Critical Resistance[25] issued a statement calling for "strategies and analyses that address both state and interpersonal violence, particularly violence against women," and the development of safe, community-based responses to violence independent of the criminal justice system and accountable to survivors of sexual and domestic violence. Following the police killing of two teenaged women of color in 2000, the Brooklyn-based collective Sista 2 Sista,[26] created "Sistas Liberated Ground" as an alternative to calling the police to deal with gendered violence. To protect Sistas Liberated Ground, women were trained in self-defense and conflict resolution. Through street performances, video screenings, discussions, and direct interventions they dealt with violence as a community issue. As a result, they succeeded in making their community safer without police. In 2008, INCITE! published a 117-page tool kit[27] offering an array of strategies and resources designed to reduce violence and build caring communities without police.

The abolition of police and prisons is not only possible—it is necessary if we are serious about preserving Black life, reducing trauma, creating safer communities, and investing municipal funds in social needs rather than settling wrongful death and excessive force cases. But it will not happen without a political struggle. Because, truth be told, the role of police in the US was never to keep our communities safe, but to protect property and its owners, to function as an occupying force in America's impoverished ghettoes, barrios, and reservations, to use coercive force to oversee "criminalized" populations. And as protesters know firsthand, police are the first line of defense against strikes, demonstrations, and dissident social movements. Abolitionists know it's not enough just to win the argument, and that abolition is not an event but a process, a struggle. Abolitionists expose the system's oppressive character while also fighting to ultimately end state and interpersonal violence, end policing, end mass spying and the surveillance state, create structures of accountability, demilitarize law enforcement, end solitary confinement, the death penalty, cash bail, resist police and prison expansion, roll back punitive measures, and find ways to interrupt violence and create safety so the police would not have to be called. ◼

Resources:

#BlackLivesMatter:
blacklivesmatter.com
Dream Defenders:
dreamdefenders.org
Black Youth Project 100:
byp100.org
We Charge Genocide:
wechargegenocide.org
BOLD (Black Organizing for Leadership
and Dignity):
boldorganizing.org
Million Hoodies Movement for Justice:
olbios.org/the-million-hoodies
-movement-for-justice
Dignity and Power Now:
dignityandpowernow.org
Ella's Daughters:
ellasdaughters.blogspot.com
Assata's Daughters:
assatasdaughters.org
Black Feminist Future:
blackfeministfuture.org/our-vision
Know Your Rights Camp:
knowyourrightscamp.com
Leaders of a Beautiful Struggle:
lbsbaltimore.com
The #LetUsBreathe Collective:
letusbreathecollective.com
Malcolm X Grassroots Movement:
facebook.com/MXGMnational
National Jericho Movement:
thejerichomovement.com
Prison Activist Resource Center:
prisonactivist.org
Prison Moratorium Project:
nomoreprisons.org
Critical Resistance:
criticalresistance.org
All of Us or None:
prisonerswithchildren.org/about
-aouon
Labor/Community Strategy Center:
fightforthesoulofthecities.com

Project South, Southerners on
New Ground (SONG):
southernersonnewground.org
INCITE! Women of Color Against Violence:
incite-national.org
Sista 2 Sista:
facebook.com
/sista2sistaempowerment
Los Angeles Community Action Network:
cangress.org
The Praxis Project:
thepraxisproject.org
Safe OUTside the System (SOS):
alp.org/programs/sos
Project NIA:
project-nia.org/tools-for-action
FIERCE (Fabulous Independent
Educated Radicals for Community
Empowerment):
gethealthyheights.org/service/fierce
-fabulous-independent-educated
-radicals-community-empowerment
Queers for Economic Justice:
facebook.com/Q4EJ.org
Sylvia Rivera Law Project (SRLP):
srlp.org
Bay Area Transformative Justice Collective
(BATJC):
batjc.wordpress.com
UBUNTU!:
iambecauseweare.wordpress.com
Abolitionist Futures:
abolitionistfutures.com/full-reading
-list
The African American Intellectual Society
(AAIHS):
aaihs.org/prison-abolition
-syllabus-2-0
Radical History Review:
radicalhistoryreview.org/abusablepast
/reading-towards-abolition-a-reading
-list-on-policing-rebellion-and-the
-criminalization-of-blackness

READER'S GUIDE

- Robin D. G. Kelley writes that "abolition is neither new nor hopelessly utopian" and that "abolition works to dismantle systems that have caused harm, namely police and prisons, and reallocate funds to social and economic resources, and to develop new systems of community-controlled public safety and restorative justice." Provide an example of a program/practice/policy in your community that is based on 1) reallocating funds to social and economic resources, 2) developing new systems of community-controlled public safety, and 3) restorative justice.

- What is carceral feminism and how does it stand at cross-purposes with abolition?

- The author references over twenty-five organizations that currently embrace abolitionist principles and support the larger movement toward abolition. Identify one you're interested in researching and report your findings. Which organization did you choose? What did you learn?

- The author argues that the gender-based violence movement is integral to the abolitionist movement. Why do you think there is a connection between the two?

Casting Off the Shadows of Slavery

LESSONS FROM THE
FIRST ABOLITION MOVEMENT

By Mumia Abu-Jamal

I n 1981, veteran Black Panther Party member and award-winning radio
journalist Mumia Abu-Jamal was wrongfully sentenced to death by a
"hanging judge" for the killing of a white police officer in Philadelphia. In 2000, Amnesty International found that the case "was irredeem-
ably tainted by politics and race and failed to meet international fair trial
standards." Mumia forms part of the generation of Black radicals on whom
the state tested law-and-order propaganda and lockdown in the '60s—a
prelude to the carceral repression it would deploy against poor Black and
Brown urban communities in the 1980s and 1990s. On death row, Mumia
became a writer of great literary power, and we are pleased to present his
piece as part of this collection.

* * *

When one thinks of the term "abolition," there is a tendency to see it as a threat emerging from the left. Another perspective understands, however, that abolition is a natural response to a situation that has become untenable.

What condition lay before the nation in its founding days? Slavery: human bondage, which sat like an incubus upon the new nation's foundation and transformed its stated aims and ideals into lies. After some reflection, perhaps, we will see that the notion of abolition has deep historical roots.

Consider summer, 1776, when delegates from the Continental Congress gathered in a sweltering room in Philadelphia. These men, some of the country's intellectual elite, were scientists, writers, doctors, and thinkers, yet their claims of the new nation's ideals were thick with contradiction. They wrote and adopted a document that said, among other things, the following:

> "We hold these Truths to be self-evident, that all Men are created equal, that they are endowed by their Creator with certain unalienable Rights, that among these are Life, Liberty and the Pursuit of Happiness. That to secure these Rights, Governments are instituted among Men, deriving their just Powers from the Consent of the Governed, that whenever any Form of Government becomes destructive of these Ends, it is the Right of the People to alter or abolish it."

These words emerge from the Declaration of Independence, adopted July 4, 1776, and celebrated throughout the US annually on Independence Day today.

When people came together in the nineteenth century to oppose the expanding chattel slave system, they were called abolitionists. Among both the rulers and the press, such people were regarded as oddballs at best and nuts at worst. Despite present popular opinion, slavery was the air that people breathed. The nation was so deeply and openly ne-grophobic and racist that the idea of a multiracial group opposed to slavery was considered both aberrant and abhorrent.

Furthermore, the document, signed by such luminaries as Ben Franklin, Thomas Jefferson, Dr. Benjamin Rush, and John Adams, included platitudes like "all men are created equal" while dark men, propertyless white men, and all women were neither able to vote nor receive votes for posts of political power. Indigenous people were seen as part of a distant "wilderness" and not part of the nation that was being contemplated.

In October 1859, white abolitionist leader John Brown, joined by a multiracial group of twenty-one men, raided the US Armory at Harpers Ferry, Virginia (now West Virginia), in an attempt to arm African captives in neighboring plantations and across the South so they could strike out for freedom. Such an attempt had to face fierce logistical challenges, given the communications needed to gain the ear and trust of a largely illiterate and deeply repressed enslaved community, constantly subjected to white armed militia surveillance.

Abraham Lincoln, one of the most admired presidents in history, would describe the raid and the raiders as little better than lunatics and regicides, less than a year after the attack failed. In February, 1860,[1] Lincoln spoke before a crowd at New York's Cooper Institute (now known as Cooper Union) to distance himself and his party (Republicans) from the Harpers Ferry raid. Lincoln told his audience that Brown wasn't a Republican, and that Republicans had nothing to do with the raid. Indeed, Lincoln assured his northern audience that neither he nor his party supported abolition. And, truth be told, this is far from a remarkable perspective, for the fact of chattel slavery was one deeply normalized in American experience and history.

Indeed, abolition was the exception, not the rule.

What this means, of course, is that abolitionists were truly remarkable people who saw beyond the present into a time not yet born. Spurred often by religious convictions, abolitionists supported attacks against the slave system, which they saw as an unnecessary evil.

In 1858, a year before the Harpers Ferry raid, Lincoln opined that slavery would last for at least 100 more years—or at least until 1958 or the 1960s. It is important to note that Lincoln's prognostication was meant to appease the slavocracy. It was not an assessment of the counterrevolutionary dynamic that would detonate *after* the war.

Despite this observation, what that means to us writing from the twenty-first century is that people we now regard as successful African American leaders and entrepreneurs like Oprah Winfrey, Rev. Dr. Martin Luther King Jr., Thurgood Marshall, Rev. Jesse Jackson, Duke Ellington, Lena Horne, Muhammad Ali, Dr. Maya Angelou, Debbie Allen, Toni Morrison, Malcolm X, Bessie Smith, Maxine Waters, Alex Haley, Lerone Bennett Jr., Hank Aaron, and, yes, even Supreme Court Justice Clarence Thomas, would have been born into captivity if Lincoln's opinion had prevailed.

Abolitionists brought forth another vision, and hence, another future. Harpers Ferry, Virginia, was a step in the fateful march to war that, after earth-shaking sacrifice, led to the abolition of slavery. Thus, abolition was not a skip in the park. It is a deep, committed movement of social transformation that seeks to bring down institutions that needlessly inflict pain upon the People.

Prison abolitionists are today's freedom dreamers who seek to expand the experience of liberty for all. Close analyses of their proposals make good sense. They want to build a society in which social problems are solved not by police and prison guards but by medical and mental health specialists, social workers, domestic violence experts, educators, and community-based organizers and problem solvers charged with addressing crises in the communities where they live. Because they are radicals, they seek solutions that address the root causes of social problems. They posit that if we build society anew to meet the human needs of education, health care, housing, meaningful and well-remunerated employment, and community togetherness and cohesion, many of the challenges historically oppressed and exploited communities face today will dissipate.

Abolitionists like Frederick Douglass, Harriet Tubman, and John Brown forged a new America, one unimaginable to earlier generations. They saw further than their contemporaries, and even warned them of problems threatening from the periphery.

In May 1865, a month after the Confederacy surrendered to Union forces, Douglass delivered a potent warning for his fellow abolitionists about the counterrevolutionary threats that emerged from the ruins of the Civil War:

"Slavery has been fruitful in giving itself names. It has been called 'the peculiar institution,' 'the social system,' and the 'impediment'. . . It has been called by a great many names, and it will call itself by yet another name; and you and I and all of us had better wait and see what new form this old monster will assume, in what new skin this old snake will come forth next."[2]

Douglass's warning about the mutability of that old racist snake was not heeded. The dreams and short-lived achievements of Reconstruction—land redistribution for the descendants of enslaved Africans as reparations for slavery, greater representation in local government, greater access to education, health care, and the franchise, and greater control over the conditions of their labor on the part of the "freedmen"—were drowned in a sea of terror and blood.

Abolitionists tried to make the nation live up to its promises of equal justice, of freedom, and the rights enshrined in the Reconstruction Amendments set forth in the 13th, 14th, and 15th Amendments to the Constitution, which were designed to enshrine and protect the rights of Black citizens.

The Reconstruction Era marked the brief period of Black postwar freedom until the US Supreme Court overturned the 1875 Civil Rights Act and the federal government removed the Union army from southern territory in 1877. In that era, white supremacists waged a terror war against Black people and maintained it for the better part of a century, until the emergence and rise of the Civil Rights Movement, first in the era of World War II, and then again during the 1950s and 1960s. The lessons of the noble antislavery Abolition Movement are before us. The lessons to struggle and struggle, from generation to generation, until the People are finally free, and that "old snake" has no more masks behind which to hide.

The 13th Amendment ensured the continuation of slavery by another name—in the guise of the carceral state. Today, prisons are the third-largest employer[3] in the nation according to sociologist Loïc Wacquant—and Black people are, once again, its currency. The consequences of this barbarity are suffered in incalculable ways by the disproportionately Black American and Latino people housed in these cages and their families. Ironically, the consequences are also suffered by the managers and employees of this gargantuan apparatus, who ostensibly benefit from it. The daily duties of the foot soldiers of the prison industrial complex are to control and contain, with repressive violence, other human beings—those at the bottom of society. Not surprisingly, higher incidences of suicide, domestic violence, and substance abuse are reported among prison guards and police officers.

In the final analysis, can a country that professes to be the land of the free, but which holds 25 percent of the world's prisoners and only 4 percent of the world's population, truly reflect its promise of happiness and democracy?

Although we have drawn from the text of the Declaration of Independence to cite "the Right of the People . . . to abolish" unjust systems that threaten the Life, Liberty, and Pursuit of Happiness of the People, that right doesn't arise from the document. It comes from the hearts, minds, and urgings of the People—the living People who today breathe the air that sustains us all. Is that not the same energy that calls us to support today's abolition movement, that works to tear down the system that deprives millions of people—entombed in prison cells and solitary confinement and in this prison house of nations—of their Life, Liberty, and the Pursuit of Happiness? Like the revolutionary struggles of 1776 and 1860 and those of 1917 and 1959, among others, today's abolitionist movement dares to dream up the world anew to replace carceral repression with compassionate practices and structures that meet basic social and economic needs, so that we might flourish individually and collectively as humanity in an ecologically protected planet.

We need not historicize questions, nor cast them into the hoary days of the past. They live within us, in our hopes, our dreams, our visions of a world free of such repressive systems that are but the shadows of slavery. Abolition now! ◼

* * *

As this publication went to press, Mumia Abu-Jamal was diagnosed with COVID-19 and congestive heart failure. He is also suffering from a flare-up of an intractable, severe, and debilitating chronic skin condition, secondary to his Hepatitis C diagnosis five years ago for which the Pennsylvania Department of Corrections delayed treatment. This delay in treatment produced cirrhosis of the liver as well as the skin condition described here. The movement to Bring Mumia Home joins abolitionists in their call for decarceration now, through the release of all aging people in prison over the age of fifty and all those with medical conditions.

—Dr. Johanna Fernández

After coming close to execution twice in the 1990s, Mumia's life was saved when a mass international movement mobilized in the streets on his behalf. In 2011, after more than twenty-eight years on death row, a federal court ruled that Mumia's death sentence had been obtained unconstitutionally; his sentence was commuted to life in prison without parole. Make no mistake: this is not enough. Freeing political prisoners is the moral assignment of every emerging generation of revolutionaries and freedom fighters. It's time to bring Mumia—and all political prisoners—home.

— The Editors, Kaepernick Publishing

READER'S GUIDE

- Who is Mumia Abu-Jamal? Share three facts that you have learned about him.

- Describe the link Mumia Abu-Jamal draws between the institution of enslavement and today's carceral state—what he calls "the shadow of slavery."

- Who is John Brown and what is Brown's relationship to abolition? Do you believe he can serve as an example for the contemporary movement for abolition? Explain.

- The author writes, "Abolition was not a skip in the park. It is a deep, committed movement of social transformation that seeks to bring down institutions that needlessly inflict pain upon the People." What, in your opinion, are reasons for why abolition requires a deep, committed movement?

Survivors at the Forefront of the Abolitionist Movement

By Connie Wun

We seek to build movements that not only end violence, but that create a society based on radical freedom, mutual accountability, and passionate reciprocity. In this society, safety and security will not be premised on violence or the threat of violence; it will be based on a collective commitment to guaranteeing the survival and care of all peoples.
   —INCITE! Critical Resistance Statement[1]

In 1998, more than 3,500 participants attended the first Critical Resistance[2] conference held at the University of California, Berkeley. The conference—initially created by scholars and organizers including Drs. Angela Davis, Julia Chinyere Oparah, and Ruth Wilson

Gilmore; Dylan Rodríguez; and other community organizers and formerly incarcerated community members—was the first event to highlight the need and demands for prison abolition.

Over a span of a weekend in September, all of us in attendance learned, shared ideas, and organized around the violence of the criminal justice system through hundreds of workshops and performances taught by youth organizers, formerly incarcerated political prisoners, university professors, community educators, high-school teachers, students, policy analysts, lobbyists, anti-gender violence organizers, artists, and so many more.

In 2000, another monumental event, the Color of Violence: Violence Against Women of Color conference, took place at the University of California, Santa Cruz. The network, INCITE!,[3] was formed directly out of the convening. Initiated by scholars and organizers including Drs. Beth Richie, Mimi Kim, Andrea Smith, Nadine Naber, and so many more, the conference provided a framework for the thousands of feminists—mainly those of color—to understand the intersections of state and interpersonal violence. Dr. Haunani-Kay Trask reminded the attendees of, and provided a feminist framework for, understanding colonial violence and illegal occupation of Hawai'i by the United States.[4] Colonialism and its violence was a feminist of color issue. We, the attendees, were also reminded of the violence that incarcerated women and LGBTQI communities experienced through the prison system. It was the first time in my life where I heard women of color unapologetically claim their space. White women or other non-BIPOC attendees were asked to defer their space in workshops to women of color attendees. In other words, they were asked to leave and to make room for Black, Indigenous, women of color. *We were the priorities.*

One year later, the two organizations issued a joint statement[5] to address the challenges of each siloed movement—the abolitionist movement and that of the anti-gender-based violence movement. Those of us who wrote and signed onto the letter, including Marilyn Buck, a white political prisoner, community organizer, and poet who passed away in August 2010, understood the connections between state violence and gender violence. We wanted both organizations and movements to not only be accountable to one another, but to focus on ending all of the violence against our BIPOC communities. We wanted the survival of all of our communities. And we knew that we needed to center our most vulnerable in both our analysis and political organizing.

Arguing that the nascent but growing abolitionist movement had too often left out the experiences and political analyses of women and LBTQI prisoners as well as those susceptible to police violence, the statement argued that we also needed to, "Put poor/working-class women of color in the center of their analysis, organizing practices, and leadership development" and "center stories of state violence committed against women of color in our organizing efforts."

Unfortunately, as mainstream society continues to develop a critique of the criminal justice system, there is still a need to center the leadership and analyses of Black, Indigenous, and other women of color abolitionists.[6]

Instead, popular discourses around abolition are appropriated for reformist strategies and white-male-led think tanks.[7] Meanwhile, BIPOC women and LBTQI community organizers, such as current and former sex workers and formerly incarcerated survivors of color, continue to work despite being underesourced, underrecognized, and susceptible to state violence. Their experiences and political analyses continue to be marginalized.

As an example, Kate D'Adamo[8] has been a longtime community organizer in New York and Baltimore. She has worked as an advocate and organizer with sex-worker-led organizations. She shares that those most impacted by the intersections of criminalization and the policing of the sex industry are cis and trans BIWOC—many of whom are providers for their families. In particular, according to a recent study,[9] transgender sex workers of color are more than twice as likely (46.8%) than their white counterparts (18.3%) to report being "arrested for being trans." Importantly, these disturbing numbers do not account for the harassment and terror that sex workers, particularly BIPOC transgender sex workers, experience in the form of state surveillance and harassment. Their lives and vulnerabilities are shaped by the need to perpetually navigate through conditions of state terror.[10]

In D'Adamo's work, she explains, "people would rather risk the potential violence perpetrated by a client than risk being subject to the police." That is, sex workers are often forced to "mitigate one risk over another," with a consistent recognition that the police would more than likely be a greater perpetrator of harm than their clients. In addition to being subject to harassment and surveillance, sex workers are also vulnerable to physical and sexual assault by police officers. In a study on the impacts of criminalization on sex workers' vulnerability to HIV and violence, researchers identified that:

"Sex workers are disproportionately affected by violence. The perpetrators of violence include law enforcement, clients, those posing as clients, institutional representatives such as medical personnel, and peers. While prevalence research on violence against sex workers is scant, some regional studies estimate that 40 to 70 percent of sex workers experience violence in a given year."[11]

In the past decade, there has been a growth in attention around the sex trades, including sex workers' needs and organizing for sex worker rights. These international advocacy[12] and local community organizing[13] efforts are in large response to the state violence that sex workers experience. They are also in response to the vulnerable conditions that state violence has helped to create. As a criminalized population, sex workers are not only subject to violence, they are also denied protections,[14] including that of labor protections, access to resources such as the COVID-19 stimulus payments,[15] and general safety.

Sex workers, particularly those that are BIPOC, are some of the most vulnerable populations who understand and experience the vulnerabilities of state and interpersonal violence. Many of them (myself included), who are working towards abolition, recognize that the interpersonal violence that we experience by clients is made possible through the state—which has not only failed to protect us but has directly subjected us to harm. We also know that the stigmatization and

ridicule that we experience by society writ large works in tandem with
the ongoing criminalization of our communities to enable the physical
and emotional violence that we have experienced.

D'Adamo reminds us that there is a long-term vision. One that is
"rooted in collective liberation." She imagines a world where "those
who trade sex are able to access holistic health and wellness resources."
Similarly, many of us who are former sex workers in the abolitionist
movement also imagine and work towards creating a world in which
those who trade sex have viable immediate and long-term options for
their entire well-being.

Ny Nourn,[16] a formerly incarcerated survivor, organizes with Advancing Justice, Survived & Punished, and California Coalition for
Women Prisoners as well as the Asian Prisoners Support Committee.
She has been working alongside and at the forefront of numerous criminal justice reform and abolitionist campaigns including the work to end
deportations and to free incarcerated survivors. Nourn draws from her
experiences as a Cambodian refugee, formerly incarcerated survivor
who served fifteen and a half years in prison, including six months in
ICE detention, to organize at the intersections of anti-gender violence
and abolition. Through the help of community organizers across the
US, Nourn was granted a pardon in 2020.[17] Through her experiences
and political analyses, she has worked across sectors with incarcerated
communities, legal teams, and elected officials to create and demand
legislation to help end the deportation[18] of criminalized immigrant
communities, including that of 16,000 Southeast Asians[19] from Laos,
Cambodia, and Vietnam who have been issued orders of deportation
since 1998 due to anti-immigrant policies.

This work is a part of her commitment to abolish all carceral
institutions. These carceral institutions, including prisons, policing,
and ICE detention centers, target and criminalize impoverished communities that "lack resources, are survivors of war and genocide,
intergenerational trauma." Nourn argues that many incarcerated
community members are survivors of these violent conditions. She

also shares that nearly 90 percent of the incarcerated women that she works with are domestic violence survivors. This means that they were "already victims themselves" before they were incarcerated.

According to community organizers and the ACLU, "nearly 60 percent of people in women's prison nationwide, and as many as 94 percent of some women's prison populations, have a history of physical or sexual abuse before being incarcerated."[20] Additionally, "Women of color and low-income women are disproportionately affected by mandatory arrest policies[21] for domestic violence. Of survivors in a New York City study who had been arrested along with their abusers (dual arrest cases) or arrested as a result of a complaint lodged by their abuser (retaliatory arrest cases), 66 percent were African American or Latina, 43 percent were living below the poverty line, and 19 percent were receiving public assistance at the time."

Carceral institutions further this violence by punishing community members who are already survivors of racial colonial wars, genocide, poverty, systemic violence, white supremacy, anti-Blackness, and gender-based violence.

Prisons, Nourn, reminds us, "don't make anybody safe, especially with over one million people locked up and people dying in prison." She shares that while she was incarcerated it was not prisons or the policing that helped her but rather the relationships inside—the friendships, communities, and support groups for survivors—that helped her.

Her work and that of D'Adamo reminds us that we must create and provide resources for historically marginalized communities so that everyone is able to build community-based structures and systems of accountability and joint responsibility.[22] Nourn explains that we need to help "communities to heal from their traumas" and to create conditions in which people are "not desperate for financial resources or temporary relief." We must end the systems and cultures that do not only create conditions of harm for BIPOC communities, but criminalizes and punishes the communities for how they survive.

An abolitionist project is one that addresses the systemic and immediate needs of communities, particularly the most marginalized, not only by demanding the end to carceral institutions that are violent but to create structures that are built upon mutual aid, transformative justice, community accountability, and collective liberation. Following the legacies of both Critical Resistance and INCITE!, contemporary abolitionists—including sex workers and formerly incarcerated survivors—are working for the *"survival and care of all peoples"* because our lives and our futures depend on it. ◢

Resources:

Advancing Justice:
    advancingjustice-aajc.org
Survived & Punished:
    survivedandpunished.org
California Coalition for Women Prisoners:
    womenprisoners.org
Asian Prisoner Support Committee:
    asianprisonersupport.com

READER'S GUIDE

- What were the purposes of the Critical Resistance and Color of Violence conferences? Where did they differ and overlap?

- There was a joint statement written by the two organizations. Why do you think it was written? And how do you think the statement applies to current abolitionist and anti-gender violence movements?

- What are your thoughts on the movements being led by sex workers and formerly incarcerated survivors?

- How do the experiences of sex workers, incarcerated survivors, and criminalized immigrants help you to understand the work to end carceral institutions?

Who Is Being Healed?

CREATING SOLUTIONS IS ABOUT
ANSWERING QUESTIONS PRISONS NEVER ASKED

By Marlon Peterson

The first and only time my name was mentioned in the *New York Times* was in connection with the 2001 headline "Man Found Guilty in Killings at Muffin Shop in Manhattan."[1] My name was buried in the sixth paragraph. The headline was meant for my co-defendant, but I was the nineteen-year-old villainous co-star in a cast of crooks who were hoping a savior like Viola Davis's[2] Anna Keating who could help us get away with (felony) murder. The same year of this headline, Critical Resistance,[3] an organization founded on the politics of abolition, held its second conference in Manhattan.

Critical Resistance was all about abolishing the prison industrial complex, back when only super leftists understood the word "abolition" in a context other than its association with Harriet Tubman, Frederick Douglass, and Sojourner Truth. I wonder what some of the founders of the organization—notables like Angela Davis, Rose Braz, and Ruth Wilson Gilmore—thought about those of us in that *New York Times* article. My co-defendants and I are the case studies that skeptics of abolition parade out as examples of its supposed impracticality.

If you abolish the police and prisons, what are you going to do about people like Marlon Peterson? What does accountability look like for him? Are you suggesting that he remain in the community, and possibly (felony) murder more people?

Referring to myself in the third person isn't my narcissism taking the wheel. It is me, a self-proclaimed abolitionist, asking aloud the questions I ask myself every time I attend a shooting response for a murdered baby, when I hear about a violent weekend in Chicago, and yes, even when I chant in the streets that I want the killers of Breonna Taylor to be arrested.

Abolition is more than politics evincing an end of prisons and police. "Abolition" is an action word. It is a daily practice, just like meditation, yoga, and veganism. Abolition is questioning ourselves first— why we believe that prison is the only form of justice (outside of the Old Testament axiom of "an eye for an eye") for people who live in the headlines like I once did. Who taught you that prison was justice for any human? Where did you learn that police equates to public safety? Where did you first hear that vengeance is what healing and accountability looks like?

Prisons and police did not always exist. The first American brick-and-mortar prison, the Walnut Street prison,[4] is barely older than the Declaration of Independence. The first modern police force was organized in Boston only in 1838.[5] Slave patrols in the South predated this Northern innovation of police reform, and guess who had no voice in the establishment of either? Black people, Brown people, Indigenous people, and poor whites. Rich white men dreamt of the idea of an armed group of white men who would protect the property of landowners, catching runaway slaves. In the spirit of reform, liberal whites, who were also champions of the abolition of slavery, conjured prisons as a form of penance for "unhappy creatures" (as the Philadelphia Society for Alleviating the Miseries of Public Prisons described them).[6] The idea of America coincided with the creation of incarceration.

In this historical moment of Breonna Taylor, George Floyd, Tony McDade, and others becoming involuntary martyrs of this racial revolution, we must also reconsider the conditioned belief that police and prisons are a panacea for the unhappiness demonstrated through everyday violence exhibited in the streets of places like Jackson, Mississippi, Englewood, Chicago, Los Angeles, Indian Country, and Appalachia.[7] Cages and cops for Black and Brown people were imagined and implemented without our input before it became our policy. At some point we were persuaded that some of us were innately bad, and that police and prisons were required to "correct" us.

White male landowners taught us that the most marginalized residents of the United States were bad while conveniently omitting the flaws of the American idea, which is that democracy can thrive with a few determining what is best for all, that the induced despair of the poor and Black can be solved by their confinement.

Modern abolition work requires that we ask different, better, more difficult, more unpopular questions.

Does incarceration make the community safer?

Will a prison cell address the hurt, loss, and sense of insecurity felt by the real victims of the headline—the people harmed by Marlon and his co-defendants?

Do prisons really heal victims of crime?

Do prisons address the root causes of crime generative factors[8] of working class Black people, Brown people, Indigenous people, Asian and Pacific Islander people, and poor whites?

During the three years that my co-defendants and I went back and forth to court, without bail, praying for an Anna Keating to free us, no one but the district attorneys and the NYPD—default coconspirators of a violent system—were allowed to make suggestions regarding how we were to be held accountable. My attorney, a fidgety Black man from Compton, relayed their options of justice to me. First, it was forty years, then thirty-five years to life, then fifteen, then up to twenty-five, then twelve years. None of the aforementioned questions were asked in court, during my legal visits from my attorney, and not once during the ten years I eventually served. No one asked about healing, they only doled out punishment, and prisons are not centers of human healing. We have a litany of books[9] and reports[10] about prison abuse; sexual abuse has become synonymous with incarceration. How many prison rape jokes have you laughed at in your lifetime? Those jokes are based on the reality that harm *is* prison harm, which is incompatible with healing, and accountability is just revenge when cyclical hurt is state-sponsored vigilante justice, aka prison.

Now, I have already accepted the standard of accountability offered to me. I served my time. My co-defendants are serving their time: fifty years and forty-five years. The keys to their cells have been thrown away—keys I hope to help recover one day.

Is society better for it? Have we solved the reasons for their despondency as twenty-year-olds who shot up a café? What will fifty years of incarceration prove, other than that vengeance is the preferred elixir of justice?

Did prison and punishment "fix" me?

Conversely, I have never given prison credit for who I am today. Educators like Dr. Larry Mamiya[11] and Dr. Nadia Lopez[12] have been sources of happiness and healing for me. People have supported me in growing beyond the trauma of my youth. Not prison. Not the police. Educators.

Through people like them, I have been able to realize that abolition is more than closing prisons and ending policing as we know it. It is about the everyday questions and creation of solutions to the underlying reasons why people cause harm and are harmed. It is identifying and working to dismantle policies like redlining and the war on drugs so the police could bother me[13] and to remove those in power who created these mandates. It is about closing the prisons and defunding the police. It is mainstreaming and resourcing the imagination of working-class and poor Black, Brown, Indigenous, and white people to create community options that value our happiness. It is about freeing and centering the needs of those in prisons, jails, and immigrant detention centers, and those walking the streets with and without ankle bracelets.

Through my education, I have come to understand that gun violence is the visible display of underlying trauma. No baby is born wanting to kill another baby. At some point the child learns that harming another is a viable option. The conditions that made these lessons possible must be undone.

I want us to commit to politics that pushes us to believe that a country that is the world's largest jailer, a world leader in firearm-related deaths,[14] is wholly unhealthy and is in need of a remedy that prioritizes creating a society not defined by guns, prisons, and police. If a few privileged white people can conjure up an incarceration nation, then let the mass of working-class and poor Black, Brown, Indigenous, and white people imagine and create a new nation—one that can lead the world in policies of happiness for many and not just the few.

Abolition must be accepted as a realistic option in the realm of justice if we are to believe in the possibilities of humans to be better than they were yesterday. ◼

READER'S GUIDE

- Marlon Peterson poses several important questions to readers: Who taught you that prison was justice for any human? Where did you learn that police equates to public safety? Where did you first hear that vengeance is what healing and accountability looks like? Does incarceration make the community safer? Please answer them here.

- If "prison isn't what healed" the author, then what does the author share that did help or support them?

- The author argues that "abolition is more than closing prisons and ending policing as we know it." What do you think the author means by this?

- Do you agree or disagree that there is a need for a new nation? Explain. And if applicable, what might it look like?

Ending the War on Black Women

BUILDING A WORLD WHERE
BREONNA TAYLOR COULD LIVE

By Andrea J. Ritchie

T he outcry in response to Breonna Taylor's murder by the Louisville Metropolitan Police Department is indisputably unprecedented—I have never, in my two and a half decades of organizing to end police violence against Black women, queer and trans people, seen billboards,[1] mainstream magazine issues,[2] celebrities, or an entire basketball season[3] dedicated to demanding justice on behalf of a Black woman killed by police. Police violence against Black women, is, at least to some degree, indeed invisible no more.[4]

The thing is, visibility is only the starting point, not the endgame.

The goal is a world where Breonna Taylor would still be with us. A world where Black women aren't the group most likely to be killed by police when unarmed,[5] the women most likely to experience arrest or use of force during a traffic stop,[6] the fastest-growing arrest, prison, and jail populations.[7] The goal is a world where cops like Daniel Holtzclaw don't target Black women, queer and trans people for sexual violence.[8] The goal is a world where Black women, queer and trans people don't face the highest levels of domestic, sexual, and community violence[9] alongside Native women and Two Spirit people.

Black women, queer and trans people's experiences of policing and safety teach us that abolition is the path that leads us there.[10]

Yet, overwhelmingly, the primary call of the chorus demanding #JusticeforBreonna is for arrests and prosecutions of the cops who killed her. And, as shown by the state's decision not to indict anyone for her murder, accountability won't come from the system that sent them to her door.

As Mariame Kaba and I wrote in July 2020 for *Essence*, "We want far more than what the system that killed Breonna Taylor can offer— because the system that killed her is not set up to provide justice for her family and loved ones. . . . Families and communities deserve more than heartbreak over and over again each time the system declines to hold itself accountable."[11]

Beyond leading to dead ends, calls for prosecutions legitimize the criminal punishment system by promoting the idea that it can do justice in individual cases, including against cops, a premise that directly undermines our wholesale challenges to its legitimacy on the grounds that it systematically defines justice as killing, maiming, raping, caging, and deporting Black people. As longtime abolitionists Rachel Herzing and Isaac Ontiveros taught me:[12]

> If we apply the same logic to the state that we do to ourselves, however, the same questions remain: How does putting an agent of the state in a cage hold the state accountable? How does prosecuting an agent of the state highlight the systemic nature of repression and genocide of Black communities and not simply exceptionalise this situation as the result of one bad cop . . . ? Appealing to the same system that engineers and executes repression and genocide

of poor people, youth, queer communities, and communities of color for remedies only strengthens that system's hold over us.

Calls for police prosecutions offer an illusion of justice while reinforcing the *status quo*. That's why they garner widespread support among people invested in upholding it. Arresting individual cops leaves the conditions that make their violence possible unchanged, and injustices multiply in the absence of effective accountability.

Of course, I share deep and fierce outrage at the blatant unfairness of a system that refuses to sanction an officer for killing a Black woman in her home but will imprison a man for life for attempted theft of lawn shears,[13] lay charges on a pregnant Black woman that could put her in prison for three years simply for voting while on probation,[14] or incarcerate Black women and queer and trans people for decades for defending themselves when society won't.[15] But doubling down on trying to make a violent system "work for us" comes at tremendous costs—of fueling the system, and of what we could be doing instead.

Abolition—dismantling systems of surveillance, policing, and punishment rather than trying to "fix" them—invites us to stop investing our faith, time, energy, and resources into seeking justice from a system that has consistently failed to recognize harm against Black women, queer and trans people—and has consistently perpetrated, and then justified it.

Imagine what would be possible if all the energy and resources directed toward demanding arrests and prosecutions of the officers who killed Breonna Taylor were instead focused on making a world where she would still be here. As Kaba, author of the *New York Times* bestseller *We Do This 'Til We Free Us*, powerfully put it, "People are tweeting every day about Breonna Taylor, about her death and what are they saying? When are you going to arrest these people, when are they going to prison? People don't put the question as when are we going to dismantle that police department?" What if, instead of acting from a futile hope of justice from the system that killed her, we sought broader and more lasting accountability by working to #DefundPolice[16] and build community-based safety strategies[17] that prioritize the safety of

Black women like Breonna—and hundreds of others killed[18] by police or state-sanctioned violence?

What if we committed our energies instead to creating a world where we don't entrust the safety of Black women and trans and gender-nonconforming people to institutions that report that nobody was injured[19] in a home invasion that left Breonna bleeding to death, or to people who describe the events of that night as "legal, moral, and ethical."[20] A world where the police department that killed her is no longer looting resources from the health care system[21] she was proud to be an essential part of[22] while violating and killing people who demand justice in her name. In other words, a world without police.

What if the national days of action, billboards, sports team tributes, and celebrity statements, instead of demanding prosecutions that won't get us there, called for an end to the "war on drugs"—which is really a thinly veiled war on Black and Brown communities like Breonna's. That would bring us closer to a world where women like Breonna Taylor, Tarika Wilson,[23] Kathryn Johnston,[24] and Alberta Spruill[25] would no longer be continuing casualties of militarized police drug raids, a world where women like Frankie Ann Perkins would no longer be choked to death by police in broad daylight—like George Floyd—on the suspicion that they swallowed drugs, a world where Shelly Treasure Hilliard[26] wouldn't have been killed after police disclosed her identity to a dealer she helped them arrest. A world where we invest in strategies around drug use and sales that save lives instead of taking them—like voluntary, accessible, and universally available harm-reduction programs that don't mobilize the threat of punishment, but instead offer support in all the forms it is needed, for as long as it is needed.

What if our outrage at Breonna's murder extended to demanding a world where officers like Brett Hankison aren't empowered by their position[27] to engage in sexual harassment and assault, whether in the context of the war on drugs, traffic stops, and "broken windows"[28] policing like Holtzclaw, or under the pretext of offering assistance,[29] like Hankison. A world where women like Charnesia Corley aren't subjected to state-sanctioned rape[30] through an eleven-minute forcible body cavity search in full public view because an officer claimed to have caught a whiff of marijuana during a traffic stop for rolling through a stop sign on the way to the store to pick up medicine for her grandmother. Where Black women can travel safely without fear that they will be strip-searched, their breasts groped, or their genitals probed when they land.[31]

What if our indignation at the state's failure to hold the officers who killed Breonna Taylor accountable led to demands—like those enshrined in the Movement for Black Lives' BREATHE Act,[32] launched in the wake of the summer 2020 uprisings to elevate the demands of the streets into federal legislation—to defund police[33] as a systemic form of accountability for what is in fact a systemic problem. Defunding police[34] offers more expansive and more effective accountability—ensuring that neither cops who kill, nor those who come after them, will be able to do harm in the future. It also points us toward a world where the $100 billion we currently invest[35] in policing every year would be diverted to quality, affordable, accessible, sustainable, and affirming housing, public spaces, health care, education, jobs, and community-based violence prevention and intervention strategies.

The BREATHE Act also calls for accountability in the form of reparations[36] for survivors of police violence, families of people killed by police, and communities, inviting us to apply the framework of the historic struggle for justice for survivors of police violence in Chicago[37] to current demands for accountability, and seek holistic repair of individual and collective harms of police violence. Beyond Chicago's victories, a reparations framework would provide for immediate cessation of harm through termination of all cops involved in perpetrating it, and non-repetition through termination of the policing that requires it.

What about violence against Black women, queer and trans people in a world without police? Our calculus when answering this question must include all forms of violence—recognizing that Black women, queer and trans people currently experience significant violence at the hands of police, and very little protection. Black women's safety requires us to build a world where Black women are not killed, violently arrested, sexually assaulted, or deported by police—or abandoned to be killed or harmed by someone else. A world where women like Aura

Rosser,[38] Janisha Fonville,[39] and Kiwi Herring[40] aren't killed by police responding to calls for assistance, and where Mia Green,[41] a Black trans woman allegedly killed by a man she was in a relationship with, would still be with us. A world where survivors like Kassandra Jackson—a Black woman violently arrested, manhandled, handcuffed to a chair, placed in restraints, and incarcerated away from her children for days for simply expressing frustration that she was unable to obtain an order of protection against a man who was abusing her—aren't subjected to more violence from the very institutions looting resources from the things they desperately need to prevent, escape, and avoid violence.

What if our demands to protect, defend, and value Black women did not call for more policing and prosecutions, fueling a system we cannot and do not trust with our safety because it targets us? Over 40 percent of domestic violence survivors[42] and 75 percent of rape and sexual assault survivors[43] don't call the police.[44] For every Black woman who reports her rape, at least fifteen do not.[45] Two-thirds of Black trans respondents to the US Transgender Survey said they would be uncomfortable asking for help from the police[46] if they needed it—in spite of epidemic levels of physical, sexual, and fatal violence targeting trans women. Both groups cite fears that they will not be believed, or will experience further violence and criminalization by cops. Almost a third of respondents to a national survey[47] of survivors, advocates and service providers reported that police used force and threatened to arrest or arrested survivors, noting that these tactics were disproportionately mobilized against Black women. None of this can be reformed away[48]—in fact, reforms attempted to date, like mandatory arrest policies requiring officers to arrest someone when they respond to domestic violence calls, have resulted in increased arrests of Black women[49] and girls[50] who are survivors, because the system operates through controlling narratives[51] that frame us as deserving of and contributing to violence against us, and unworthy of protection.

We can end this war on Black women.[52] But that victory will not be achieved through prosecutions or police reform. It requires us to invest in the things survivors need to prevent, avoid, escape, and transform conditions of violence.

Black Lives Matter Louisville's demands for justice in Breonna Taylor's name[53] have shifted over time to reflect these realities—from focusing on arrests of officers involved and elimination of no-knock warrants to tackling systemic forces of gentrification that contributed to Breonna's killing, defunding the police department that took her life, and securing investments in institutions that would make her community safer[54] like ecosystems of health care workers, universally accessible and affordable housing, universal basic income, and community conflict resolution training. They mirror a similar evolution across the country in the context of the ongoing uprising against police violence in calls to #DefundPolice.[55]

The In Our Names Network, made up of over twenty organizations and individuals working to end police violence against Black women and girls and trans and gender nonconforming people has followed a similar path, from demanding justice in individual cases of police violence to simultaneously working toward systemic responses that would have prevented them from happening in the first place. For instance, EveryBlackGirl, founded in the wake of the #AssaultatSpringValleyHigh,[56] is creating safety for Black girls in and out of the classroom, including fighting for #PoliceFreeSchools. Along with other network members, they will train Black youth as researchers to document sexual harassment and violence by cops stationed in and around schools to show that police presence in schools makes students less safe,[57] not more.

Oakland's Anti-Police Terror Project, which organized around police killings of Yuvette Henderson[58] and Jessica Williams,[59] is building Black-led prevention and intervention responses to unmet mental health needs through the Mental Health First program that prioritize avoiding police involvement and psychiatric incarceration.[60] Programs like this could prevent up to half of police killings[61] of Black people who are—or are perceived to be—in a mental health crisis. Network member Maria Moore is fighting for justice on behalf of her sister Kayla Moore, a Black trans woman killed by police,[62] by working toward a twenty-four-hour non-police mental health crisis response in Berkeley, CA. Network members Solutions Not Punishment Collaborative (SNaPCo), Tamika Spellman[63] of HIPS, Monica Jones of the Outlaw Project, BYP100, and

Black LGBTQIA+ Migrant Project are working to build safety for Black trans women—from police, migration-related, and community violence.

Organizations like INCITE! teach us that expanding the lens through which we examine police violence and gender-based violence[64] to include Black women, and trans and gender-nonconforming people's experiences leads us much more quickly to abolition. It helps us to see how policing Black women, queer and trans people whose labor is deemed essential, but whose lives and safety are not, is at the core of the criminal punishment system, whether we are targets of police or seeking protection. It also helps us see how other institutions offered as "alternatives" to police—like the family court and foster system, medical industrial complex,[65] and social services—can operate as "soft police," controlling and criminalizing Black women and queer and trans people through denial of care, benefits, resources, and protection.

The Interrupting Criminalization initiative I cofounded with Mariame Kaba is identifying women and LGBTQ people's points of contact with all forms of policing[66] so as to interrupt and eliminate them. We work collaboratively with groups across the country to document the criminalization of Black women and girls and trans and gender-nonconforming people, decriminalize, divert, decarcerate, divest, and dismantle, and dream a world without policing,[67] in which everything we need to be safe is universally and accessibly available. The goal is to reduce police contact and, as Kaba often puts it, to multiply the options available to survivors to access safety and transform harm.

That is what #SayHerName means to me: Not just making sure we know Breonna Taylor's name, but understanding the forces that converged to kill her; divesting financially, ideologically, and emotionally from the systems that perpetrated and justify her death; and directing our energies toward building a world where Black women, queer and trans people are safe, in her name and in honor of her life. It means understanding that the value of our lives is not set by the amount of time a person does in a cage for hurting us, but by the ways in which we organize to keep each other safe. Kaba and Herzing teach us that the tools for abolition are in our hands,[68] and we can practice them every day, in every interaction, institution, and imagining we engage in. We each have a role[69] in bringing us closer to a world where Breonna would still be with us—let's put all of our collective energies into getting there. ◾

Resources:

Survived & Punished:
survivedandpunished.org

In Our Names Network:
inournamesnetwork.com

Every Black Girl Inc.:
facebook.com/EveryBlackGirl

Anti-Police Terror Project:
antipoliceterrorproject.org

Mental Health First:
antipoliceterrorproject.org
/mental-health-first

Solutions Not Punishment:
snap4freedom.org/home

The Outlaw Project:
theoutlawproject.org

BYP100:
byp100.org

Black LGBTQIA + Migrant Project:
transgenderlawcenter.org
/programs/blmp

INCITE!:
incite-national.org

Movement for Family Power:
movementforfamilypower.org

Transform Harm:
transformharm.org

Interrupting Criminalization:
interruptingcriminalization.com

One Million Experiments:
millionexperiments.com

Defund the Police:
defundpolice.org

M4BL:
m4bl.org/policy-platforms/end-the-
war-black-women

m4bl.org/policy-platforms/end-the-
war-trans

m4bl.org/policy-platforms/end-the-
war-black-health

The Breathe Act:
breatheact.org

READER'S GUIDE

- Andrea J. Ritchie argues that "calls for police prosecutions offer an illusion of justice while reinforcing the status quo" and will not "end police violence against Black women." According to the author, why is this the case? What examples does the author cite?

- The author lists a number of "what if" questions to push readers to imagine a different world. What are your thoughts around these questions, including, "What if our demands to protect, defend, and value Black women did not call for more policing and prosecutions, fueling a system we cannot and do not trust with our safety because it targets us?" How do they make you feel? And what world is the author trying to get the reader to imagine?

- What do you believe #SayHerName means to the author? And given the author's arguments in this essay, what does it mean to you?

- Please list at least three community-based safety strategies that would prioritize the safety of Black women.

Bankrolling the Carceral State

"Improvements become investments, and investments become expanded state capacity to arrest, process, and punish." [1]

POLICE SPENDING [2]

1980

$47B

2015

$143B

% change   **204%**

On a local level
Police spending accounted for roughly:
- **$1 of every $10** spent by counties, municipalities, and townships and
- **$1 of every $100** spent by states. [3]

On a federal level
Two Department of Justice programs—COPS and Byrne JAG, enacted by Clinton in 1994—boost police budgets further:
- In 2019, COPS provided **$304 million** to state and local policing and
- JAG usually funds about **$435 million** annually. [4]

Since the creation of the Department of Homeland Security, the budgets of both Customs and Border Protection (CBP) and Immigration and Customs Enforcement (ICE) have **almost tripled.** [5]

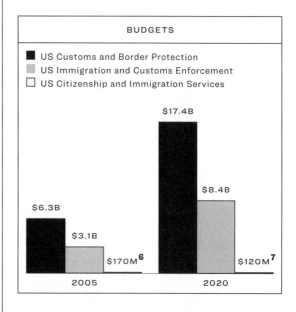

BUDGETS

- ■ US Customs and Border Protection
- ▨ US Immigration and Customs Enforcement
- ☐ US Citizenship and Immigration Services

$17.4B

$8.4B

$6.3B

$3.1B

$170M [6]

$120M [7]

2005   2020

Per capita spending on the criminal justice system overall (police, corrections, and judicial systems) has also increased. [8]

$388

per capita in 1982

$937

per capita in 2015

Homicide has decreased sharply since the 1990s, but police funding has not.[9]

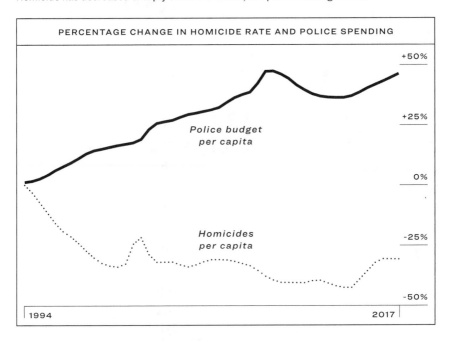

PERCENTAGE CHANGE IN HOMICIDE RATE AND POLICE SPENDING

Police budget
per capita

Homicides
per capita

+50%

+25%

0%

-25%

-50%

1994   2017

Cities and counties must take on the cost of lawsuits filed for police violence and murder. Often this debt is in the form of bond borrowing: **a transfer of wealth from communities to Wall Street**. A few examples from across the country: [10]

City/County	Total estimated Police Brutality Bonds 2008–2017	Interest paid to investors	Total cost to taxpayers
Chicago (2010–2017)	$709.3M	$860M	$1.57B
Cleveland	$12.9M	$7.4M	$20.3M
Lake County	$18.1M	$1.8M	$19.9M
Los Angeles	$71.4M	$18M	$89.4M
Milwaukee	$26.1M	$3.7M	$29.8M
Total	**$837.8M**	**$891M**	**$1.73B**

Data stories researched and conceptualized by Tamara K. Nopper

We Can Dismantle the System at the Polls, Too

By Rukia Lumumba

I
magine a society in which prisons, police, and all other institutions that inflict violence on Black people are abolished. Now imagine the money previously funding those institutions being used to create housing and mental health investments that actually prevent harm from happening in the first place.

Imagine these funds are used to create opportunities for under-resourced and under-invested communities.

Imagine these funds are used to create effective systems of accountability and to strengthen voting rights so that voting is a system not anchored in anti-Blackness.

Close your eyes for twenty seconds and really visualize it.

You've just reimagined public safety. This is what abolition can look like.

I stand firmly in the belief that the American carceral, criminal, legal, and electoral systems are rooted in racism, patriarchy, and capitalism. These systems must be abolished in order to build a new system of justice that ensures that the basic needs of all people are met. To achieve this goal, we must engage in abolitionist visioning while participating in political processes that help us gain power and control of the resources necessary to build the new institutions that replace the harmful ones that exist today.

My father, the late mayor of Jackson, Mississippi, and human rights icon Chokwe Lumumba, once said, "Mass incarceration is a symptom of a rotting system." I agree. The carceral and criminalizing systems represent a tremendous symptom of government-sanctioned violence and oppression.

When you have 59 people die in Mississippi prisons over the course of the first 8 months of 2020, that is a symptom of a rotting system. When you have women serving life sentences for drug use, being criminalized for addiction, that is a symptom of a rotten system. When you have children sentenced to life without the possibility of parole, that is a symptom of a rotting system. When you have parents arrested at work and detained in ICE prisons while their children are attending their first day of school, that is a symptom of a rotting system. When you have more than 200,000 formerly incarcerated people denied the right to vote in one state, that is a symptom of a rotting system.

We see these symptoms most evidently in prisons like the notorious Parchman Penitentiary in Mississippi and Angola Prison in Louisiana, where people have died due to torture and inhumane living conditions. We more readily see these symptoms in the murders of Breonna Taylor, George Floyd, Tony McDade, Ricky Ball, Jonathan Sanders, George Robinson, and countless others killed by police.

Since America's inception, our communities have been denied our right to our full humanity. Our Black bodies have been subjected to violence in the form of chattel slavery, lynchings, police terrorism, state neglect, inadequate health care, inadequate housing, toxic living conditions, mass incarceration, and state-sanctioned theft of Black-owned land. As a consequence of this violence, as Black, Brown, and poor people, we are consistently making the case against racism, yet we are still suffering under white supremacy and white fear. While our protests are necessary and have resulted in us seeing some policy changes, it is time to redouble our efforts to gain control of all of the political processes that govern our lives and thus the resources to support a system overhaul.

Current conditions and many of the failed punitive approaches to "criminal justice reform" have clearly demonstrated it's time to take a new approach to dismantling the system—one that combines abolition with electoral justice. If we want to intervene to reduce and eventually end the murders of our loved ones, part of our strategy must be to remove from office the sheriffs, district attorneys, and judges that are allowing this violence to occur.

Engaging in the electoral process is about unseating over 400 years of white supremacy that still plagues the US system in very real and systemic ways. It is about creating a system of justice that values Black, Brown, trans, gender-nonconforming, gay, lesbian, and disabled lives and does not condone modern-day lynchings as we have seen in the murders of Korryn Gaines and Alton Sterling, or the deaths of Sandra Bland, Rexdale Henry, and Andre Jones that took place behind jail walls. It's about government representation that protects the lives of our children and their children.

It's not about a particular party. Instead, as Jessica Byrd, co-founder of the Electoral Justice Project of the Movement for Black Lives teaches us, it's about "the process of making change—in politics, policies and social practices." Electing judges, district attorneys (DAs), mayors, senators, state legislators, city council members, county commissioners/supervisors, and sheriffs who not only have experiences in common with their communities but are delegates from their communities that understand the need for a system overhaul is critically important.

Participating in the electoral process is about creating policies such as decarceration for marijuana and other drug use, ending pretrial detention and cash money bail, stopping rent hikes to prevent homelessness, and the BREATHE Act[1] to end police violence and invest in a new vision of public safety. It is also the creation of programs that prevent violence through community-led efforts of violence intervention like the Credible Messenger[2] and Cure Violence[3] models. It is the creation of community-based services that tackle the effects of poverty and its criminalization by creating community land trusts and housing cooperatives, worker-owned and cooperatively led businesses that get at the root cause of economic injustice, instead of building more prison and jails to lock up poor, Black, and mentally ill people for profit and to legitimize the need for warlike city police. It is beautifully about a Vision for Black Lives,[4] a comprehensive and visionary policy agenda endorsed by over fifty Black-led organizations.

The merger of electoral justice and abolition allows for a return of politics to the people. Community should be central and not peripheral to system change. Individuals as well as grassroots, faith, and neighborhood organizations in local communities are most effective in doing work that is transformational and liberating. Seizing electoral justice for the sake of abolishing prisons and jails allows us to use community co-governance tools, such as people's assemblies, toward the long-term practice of educating, motivating, and organizing our people to be prepared and committed to designing new systems of accountability that do not rely on our current systems of oppression. People's Assemblies are instituted around the world as well-facilitated gatherings of community members to determine solutions to common problems to then be implemented by their city or state governments.

So, as we dive into the visioning and implementation work of abolition, let us also engage in the politics of it. A politics that encourages full participation in the process of achieving abolition and puts frontline community members in positions of power. That includes mothers who are separated from their children because they can't afford bail, children who have to navigate decisions without the benefit of their incarcerated loved one's support, and grandmothers who are forced to take on the full financial burden that incarceration causes the entire family.

As municipalist Debbie Bookchin encourages, let us re-envision what society could be if we developed a program of abolition that includes a "caring economy," equal access to technology, and the opportunity for "every human being to live in freedom and exercise their civic rights as members of flourishing, truly democratic communities."

* * *

This article is dedicated to all of our political prisoners that stood on the front lines of protest and movement for Black lives in the 1970s and 1980s and have remained incarcerated or in exile for several decades as a result. It is past time for them to come home. Free our elders—Mutulu Shakur, Sundiata Acoli, Russell "Maroon" Shoatz, Mumia Abu-Jamal, and David Gilbert, and allow Assata Shakur to come home free! Free 'Em All! ◢

Resources:

M4BL, "The BREATHE Act":
    breatheact.org
Credible Messenger Justice Center:
    cmjcenter.org

Cure Violence:
    cvg.org
M4BL, Vision for Black Lives:
    m4bl.org/policy-platforms

READER'S GUIDE

- How does Rukia Lumumba imagine public safety?

- Please cite two to three examples the author uses to explain this statement: "Since America's inception, our communities have been denied our right to our full humanity."

- The author argues, "Current conditions and many of the failed punitive approaches to 'criminal justice reform' have clearly demonstrated it's time to take a new approach to dismantling the system—one that combines abolition with electoral justice." In the author's view, how can engaging the electoral process be used to usher in an abolitionist future?

- What do you imagine is included in a "caring economy" and how would this relate to the author's concept of abolition?

What Is & What Could Be

THE POLICIES OF ABOLITION

By Dan Berger *and* David Stein

T he far-reaching vision of abolition is enacted daily in political struggles over spending priorities—a key measure of whose lives matter and how. Abolitionists have picked up the torch of twentieth-century Black labor radicals[1] and other racial and economic justice organizers who have insisted that public budgets have moral implications.

The call to defund the police is a deeply rooted strategy that to some entered the 2020 landscape as if from nowhere. Yet the demand has been shaped by more than five decades of organizing against police and prisons. It has been molded by what historian Barbara Ransby has described as movements filled with leaders:[2] from the 1960s-era freedom movement foot soldiers in the Student Nonviolent Coordinating Committee (SNCC) and the Black Panther Party, to activists like James Yaki Sayles[3] in the 1980s, to Ransby's own work building the Black Radical Congress[4] in the 1990s, to that of Eddie Ellis[5] and the New York–based Prison Moratorium Project[6] in the 1990s and 2000s, to the ascent of the broader Movement for Black Lives and both the ephemeral and durable formations that have sprung up over the past six years since the Ferguson protests gripped the world's attention. The uprisings in the summer of 2020—the largest sustained protest in US history—renewed these freedom dreams.

The call to defund is best understood as an effort to revoke the political and economic power of police—and of the larger criminal legal system it upholds. Indeed, before the protests against the murders of George Floyd and Breonna Taylor in 2020 popularized the demand to defund the police, abolitionists around the country initiated campaigns for clemency[7] and to decarcerate jails, prisons, and detention centers due to COVID-19. These struggles could be found in prison, too. Incarcerated people have staged dozens of rebellions[8] against institutional medical neglect in the face of a deadly pandemic, building on ten years of labor and hunger strikes[9] inside US prisons.

While Republicans and Democrats may use different talking points, state spending demonstrates their shared commitment to preserving racist social control through police and prisons. Whether speaking the language of authoritarianism[10] or professionalism,[11] both Donald Trump and Joe Biden responded to the summer 2020 uprisings by pledging additional funding and support to police. That is why abolitionist campaigns to defund the police and decarcerate prisons are so transformative: they approach local and national budgets with necessary urgency as a venue in which the status quo can be either reinforced or remade. It is both a defensive posture and a visionary one. It's a three-pronged strategy that the abolitionist organization Critical Resistance has summarized as Dismantle, Change, Build.

Abolitionists have long operated at this intersection of opposing what is and fighting for what could be. The battle against Jim Crow spoke the language of abolition. "The black South wants equality now," Hampton Institute professor J. Saunders Redding wrote in 1944, "The black South wants segregation laws abolished now." By the 1960s, Black activists applied this abolitionist ethos to the police and prisons. Civil Rights activists hoisted signs during the 1963 March on Washington reading "We Demand: An End to Police Brutality Now!" SNCC militants filled Southern jails demanding "freedom now" not only from incarceration but from the racist system that produced it. And the Black Panther Party, which began in Oakland in 1966 and soon spread globally, inaugurated a novel abolitionist praxis.

Known for their bold armed patrols of police, the Black Panthers grounded their far-reaching vision in practical organizing through their "survival pending revolution programs." These efforts notably included community schools and health clinics, and different chapters also had food and clothing giveaways, bus programs to help community members visit their incarcerated loved ones, and more. In *To Die for the People*, BPP co-founder Huey Newton wrote of these programs, "We recognized that in order to bring the people to the level of consciousness where they would seize the time, it would be necessary to serve their interests in survival by developing programs which would help them meet their daily needs."

Resisting criminalization was a core, if underappreciated, constant of the twentieth-century Black freedom struggle. The government's punitive response to the radical upsurge of the late 1960s expanded to a full-throated embrace of mass incarceration as a way to discipline Black and Latinx working-class communities in the 1970s. In response, several progressive national organizations—operating both independently and in tandem—tried to stop the government's expanded criminalization and the construction of new prisons. Though they failed to stem the tide of get-tough policies, their thinking informs modern abolitionism.

After Black Marxist scholar and abolitionist Angela Davis was acquitted of federal charges[12] in 1972, her defense committee transformed into a broader effort to stem the tide of criminalization. Among its priorities, the National Alliance Against Racist and Political Repression (NAARPR) protested "repressive legislation" and "police crimes," both of which were abetted by massive funding grants enabled through the Law Enforcement Assistance Administration and the Nixon administration's open hostility to communities of color and the left.

The NAARPR was one of several national coalitions to contest this increasingly repressive turn under the Nixon administration. As historian Elizabeth Hinton has shown in her book *From the War on Poverty to the War on Crime*, Nixon and Bureau of Prison officials hoped to increase federal prison capacity by 20 percent between 1972 and 1982. This project entailed both making existing prisons bigger and building new prisons. By the end of the decade, Hinton reports, 500,000 Americans were incarcerated across federal and local jurisdictions—"reflecting an increase of more than 25 percent, or an additional 120,000 incarcerated men and women." The National Moratorium on Prison Construction (NMPC),[13] however, had gathered faith-based and secular progressives to challenge the federal government's plan to construct additional prisons in the 1970s. One of the most colorful efforts in this era, the Stop the Olympic Prison (STOP) campaign, worked to block turning the 1980 Olympic village living quarters for athletes into a prison.[14] The US Olympic Committee sued STOP for its poster,[15] which featured the Olympic rings locked in a cage. A judge sided with NMPC on 1st Amendment grounds, though the prison was ultimately built.

These and similar campaigns sought not only to stop new construction but to support currently incarcerated people, who continued to publish newspapers, form labor unions, support defense campaigns, and otherwise organize against their captivity. And while they could not stop the onslaught of repression that sacrificed millions of people to police and prisons, groups like the Southern Coalition on Jails and Prisons[16] and the Committee to End the Marion Lockdown,[17] formed in the 1970s and 1980s, helped seed new abolitionist efforts in the 1990s and 2000s that began to have greater success.

While the federal government set the tone, the biggest changes were evident at the state level. California was instructive:[18] From 1980 to

2000, the state witnessed a nearly 500 percent rise in its prison population, complete with a two-decade prison building spree that saw twenty-three new prisons open. At its height, the California prison system held 160,000 people—well over half the entire country's prison population in 1970. To stem that tide, organizations and coalitions like Critical Resistance, California Prison Moratorium Project, California Coalition for Women Prisoners, Justice Now, Californians United for a Responsible Budget, and the Prison Activist Resource Center thwarted plans to open additional facilities in the state. More recently, these and other organizations have stopped jail expansion and pressured the governor to grant several large-scale clemencies. Together, these and other organizations comprising Californians United for a Responsible Budget have helped ensure that more than 140,000 new prison and jail beds were never built. As a result of this organizing, including the emergency clemency campaigns[19] in response to the pandemic, the state's prison population[20] has dropped below 100,000 people for the first time in thirty years.

The upheaval and crackdown of the 2020 protests prompts the question of the last half-century and earlier: What type of protest movements could be built if communities were freed from the violence of policing and incarceration? Contests over budget priorities are about what the state can be and should be. Many abolitionists[21] root this work in W. E. B. Du Bois's classic analysis of abolition democracy[22]— the political struggle led by formerly enslaved people in the wake of the Civil War to construct new institutions while also eradicating violent ones. A similar fight is underway today, where currently and formerly incarcerated people and their allies work to change the world by abolishing the prison-industrial complex. Scholar-activist Ruth Wilson Gilmore has similarly stressed that "abolition is a theory of change, it's a theory of social life. It's about making things."[23]

Abolition is and has always been a slate of affirmative demands for the world we need. The struggles to defund the police and decarcerate prisons are wholly intertwined with other efforts to transform society. Medicare for All, a job guarantee, and a homes guarantee are battles for a humane and ecologically just budget, as are efforts to release aging people in prison and close detention centers. The Green New Deal[24] is or could be an abolitionist project; the Red New Deal[25] certainly is. While many of those policy goals can only be fully achieved at the federal level,[26] that spirit animates local and state battles, which is where most spending on police and prisons takes place. For example, while federal spending on prisons accounts for about 10 percent of all prison spending,[27] only the federal government[28] can thoroughly cushion against economic recessions and depressions.

But with the jackboots of local police off the necks of activists across the country, movements against austerity will have greater chances to flourish. Combating inequality will still be an uphill climb, particularly as municipalities try to co-opt or dilute abolitionist demands by affirming that "Black Lives Matter" while continuing or even expanding the funding for local police, sheriffs, and jails. By reducing the number of police and prisons—by eliminating the state's capacity for repression—the defund struggles work to enlarge broader movement capacity. Abolitionists remain resolute on the larger goal of freedom.

From the civil rights movement to Occupy Wall Street, criminalization has been a key tactic to undermine protest and roll back or exclude access to[29] public housing, education, and other social provisions offered by the government. Neoliberal[30] austerity was imposed via a police officer's pistol and the bars of prison cells. In response, abolitionists pursue what anthropologist Hannah Appel has called "reparative public goods"[31] like housing, education, and health care for all. Entering the realm of public policy, abolition rejects the political obstinacy and technocratic fixes[32] that have seen many major cities actually increase their funding[33] for police departments this year, and most states continue to use conviction status to deny voting rights to most currently and formerly incarcerated people. According to the Sentencing Project, one out of every forty-four adults is disenfranchised by the carceral system—just one of many ways that policing and imprisonment constrain political participation.[34]

Police and prisons uphold the world that is. Abolition fights for the world that should be. Abolition unites struggles across time and space.

Abolitionist causes like ending cash bail, decarcerating and closing prisons, freeing elderly and vulnerable incarcerated people, providing humanitarian aid to migrants, decriminalizing sex work, halting evictions, supporting incarcerated survivors of domestic violence, blocking deportations, expanding health care—these reforms have revolutionary implications,[35] which is why they have been resisted so bitterly. When united together, they form a comprehensive agenda. It is a platform to eliminate austerity and create what Black radical scholars Ruth Wilson Gilmore and Paul Gilroy have discussed as a universal future for humanity.[36] These practices are both the abolitionist horizon and its route.[37] ◼

Resources:

Chicago Community Bond Fund:
    chicagobond.org
Decarcerate PA:
    decarceratepa.info
RAPP:
    rappcampaign.com
No More Deaths:
    nomoredeaths.org/about-no-more
    -deaths
DecrimNY:
    decrimny.org
Survived & Punished:
    survivedandpunished.org
Mijente:
    mijente.net
California Prison Moratorium Project,
    Bay View:
    freedomarchives.org/tag/committee
    -to-end-the-marion-lockdown
California Coalition for People in
    Women's Prisons:
    womenprisoners.org

Californians United for
    a Responsible Budget:
    curbprisonspending.org
Prison Activist Resource Center:
    prisonactivist.org
Movement for Black Lives:
    m4bl.org
Critical Resistance:
    criticalresistance.org
National Alliance Against Racist and
    Political Repression:
    naarpr.org
Justice Now:
    prisonactivist.org/resources
    /justice-now
Medicare For All:
    medicare4all.org
Jobs for All:
    jobguaranteenow.org
Homes Guarantee:
    homesguarantee.com

READER'S GUIDE

- Dan Berger and David Stein reference several abolitionist campaigns over the last forty years. Please list one and describe why it is important.

- The authors cite W. E. B. Du Bois's analysis of abolition democracy. What is abolition democracy and how does it relate to the abolition of prisons and policing?

- "The struggles to defund the police and decarcerate prisons are wholly intertwined with other efforts to transform society," write the authors. Please list three additional contemporary abolitionist demands on the policy-level beyond the abolition of prisons and policing.

- The authors write, "Abolitionists have long operated at this intersection of opposing what is and fighting for what could be." Please provide an example of each—"opposing what is" and "fighting for what could be"—from the essay, and cite three to four examples from your own life.

The Journey Continues

SO YOU'RE THINKING
ABOUT BECOMING AN ABOLITIONIST

By Mariame Kaba

T oday, more people are discussing and contemplating prison abolition than ever before. Decades of collective organizing have
brought us to this moment: some are newly aware that prisons,
policing, and the criminal punishment system in general are racist, oppressive, and ineffective.

However, some might be wondering: Is abolition too drastic? Can we
really get rid of prisons and policing all together? The short answer: We
can. We must. We are.

Prison industrial complex (PIC) abolition is a political vision, a
structural analysis of oppression, and a practical organizing strategy.
While some people might think of abolition as primarily a negative

project—"Let's tear everything down tomorrow and hope for the best"—PIC abolition is a vision of a restructured society[1] in a world where we have everything we need: food, shelter, education, health, art, beauty, clean water, and more. Things that are foundational to our personal and community safety.

Every vision is also a map. As freedom fighter Kwame Ture taught us,[2] "When you see people call themselves revolutionary always talking about destroying, destroying, destroying but never talking about building or creating, they're not revolutionary. They do not understand the first thing about revolution. It's creating." PIC abolition is a positive project that focuses, in part, on building a society where it is possible to address harm without relying on structural forms of oppression or the violent systems that increase it.

Some people may ask, "Does this mean that I can never call the cops if my life is in serious danger?" Abolition does not center that question. Instead, abolition challenges us to ask, "Why do we have no other well-resourced options?" and pushes us to creatively consider how we can grow, build, and try other avenues to reduce harm. Repeated attempts to improve the sole option offered by the state, despite how consistently corrupt and injurious it has proven itself, will neither reduce nor address the harm that actually required the call. We need more and effective options[3] for the greatest number of people.

An abolitionist journey ignites other questions capable of meaningful and transformative pathways: What work do prisons and policing actually do?[4] Most people assume that incarceration helps to reduce violence and crime, thinking, "The criminal punishment system might be racist, sexist, classist, ableist, and unfair, but it at least keeps me safe from violence and crime."

Facts and history tell a different story: Increasing rates of incarceration have a minimal impact[5] on crime rates. Research[6] and common sense suggest that economic precarity is correlated with higher crime rates. Moreover, crime and harm are not synonymous. All that is criminalized[7] isn't harmful, and all harm isn't necessarily criminalized. For example, wage theft by employers isn't generally criminalized, but it is definitely harmful.

Even if the criminal punishment system were free of racism, classism, sexism, and other -isms, it would not be capable of effectively addressing harm. For example, if we want to reduce (or end) sexual and gendered violence, putting a few perpetrators in prison does little to stop the many other perpetrators. It does nothing to change a culture that makes this harm imaginable, to hold the individual perpetrator accountable, to support their transformation, or to meet the needs of the survivors.

A Black, Indigenous, and people of color survivor-led transformative justice movement[8] has emerged in the past two decades to offer a different vision for ending violence and transforming our communities.

A world without harm isn't possible and isn't what an abolitionist vision purports to achieve. Rather, abolitionist politics and practice contend that disposing of people, by locking them away in jails and prisons, does nothing significant to prevent, reduce, or transform harm in the aggregate. It rarely, if ever, encourages people to take accountability for their actions. Instead, our adversarial court system discourages people from ever acknowledging, let alone taking responsibility, for the harm they have caused. At the same time, it allows us to avoid our own responsibilities to hold each other accountable, instead delegating it to a third party—one that has been built to hide away social and political failures. An abolitionist imagination takes us along a different path than if we try to simply replace the PIC with similar structures.

None of us has all of the answers, or we would have ended oppression already. But if we keep building the world we want, trying new things, and learning from our mistakes, new possibilities emerge.

Here's how to begin.

First, when we set about trying to transform society, we must remember that we ourselves will also need to transform. Our imagination of what a different world can be is limited. We are deeply entangled in the very systems we are organizing to change. White supremacy, misogyny, ableism, classism, homophobia, and transphobia exist everywhere. We have all so thoroughly internalized these logics of oppression that if oppression were to end tomorrow, we would be likely to reproduce previous structures. Being intentionally in relation to one another, a part of a collective, helps to not only imagine new worlds but also to imagine ourselves differently. Join some of the many organizations,[9] faith groups, and ad hoc collectives that are working to learn and unlearn—for example, what it feels like to actually be safe, or those that are naming and challenging white supremacy and racial capitalism.

Second, we must imagine and experiment with new collective structures that enable us to take more principled action, such as embracing collective responsibility to resolve conflicts. We can learn lessons from revolutionary movements, like Brazil's Landless Rural Workers Movement[10] (Movimento dos Trabalhadores Rurais Sem Terra), that have noted that when we create social structures that are less hierarchical and more transparent, we reduce violence and harms.

Third, we must simultaneously engage in strategies that reduce contact between people and the criminal legal system. Abolitionists regularly engage in organizing campaigns and mutual aid efforts[11] that move us closer to our goals. We must remember that the goal is not to create a gentler prison and policing system, because, as I have noted, a gentler prison and policing system cannot adequately address harm. Instead, we want to divest from these systems as we create the world in which we want to live.

Fourth, as scholar and activist Ruth Wilson Gilmore notes, building a different world requires that we not only change how we address harm, but that we change everything.[12] The PIC is linked in its logics and operation with all other systems—from how students are pushed out of schools when they don't perform as expected to how people with disabilities are excluded from our communities to the ways in which workers are treated as expendable in our capitalist system.

Changing everything might sound daunting, but it also means there are many places to start, infinite opportunities to collaborate, and endless imaginative interventions and experiments to create.

Let's begin our abolitionist journey not with the question "What do we have now and how can we make it better?" Instead, let's ask, "What can we imagine for ourselves and the world?" If we do that, then boundless possibilities of a more just world await us. ◼

READER'S GUIDE

- Mariame Kaba writes, "Prison industrial complex (PIC) abolition is a political vision, a structural analysis of oppression, and a practical organizing strategy." Why is such a framework integral to the political project of abolition?

- The author writes that over the past two decades "a Black, Indigenous, and people of color survivor-led transformative justice movement has emerged . . . to offer a different vision for ending violence and transforming our communities." Please describe some features of transformative justice. Describe the relationship of transformative justice to abolition.

- The author explains that abolition does not center the question: "Does this mean that I can never call the cops if my life is in serious danger?" But it instead asks: "Why do we have no other well-resourced options?" Have you asked yourself and others the latter question? What has come up? And how have you addressed your responses or others' responses?

- The author writes that abolition means to "creatively consider how we can grow, build, and try other avenues to reduce harm." What are some strategies that you have employed to do these things? What have been some of the challenges and successes?

Notes

Editors' Preface

A Journey to Safer Futures

1   Dylan Rodríguez, "Abolition as Praxis of Human Being: A Foreword," *Harvard Law Review* 132, no. 6 (April 10, 2019), https://harvardlawreview.org/2019/04/abolition-as-praxis-of-human-being-a-foreword/.

2   Quoted in Micah Herskind, "Some Reflections on Prison Abolition," Medium, December 7, 2019, https://micahherskind.medium.com/some-reflections-on-prison-abolition-after-mumi-5197a4c3cf98.

Foreword

Believe in New Possibilities

1   Stephen Lurie, "There's No Such Thing as a Dangerous Neighborhood," *Bloomberg CityLab,* February 25, 2019, https://www.bloomberg.com/news/articles/2019-02-25/beyond-broken-windows-what-really-drives-urban-crime.

2   The Combahee River Collective Statement, April 1977, http://circuitous.org/scraps/combahee.html.

3   Robin D. G. Kelley, "What Did Cedric Robinson Mean by Racial Capitalism?" *Boston Review,* January 12, 2017, http://bostonreview.net/race/robin-d-g-kelley-what-did-cedric-robinson-mean-racial-capitalism.

Introduction

A Future Worth Building

1   Joy James, ed., *Imprisoned Intellectuals: America's Political Prisoners Write on Life, Liberation, and Rebellion* (Lanham, MD: Rowman & Littlefield Publishers, 2003).

2   L. H. Roper, "The 1701 'Act for the Better Ordering of Slaves': Reconsidering the History of Slavery in Proprietary South Carolina," *The William and Mary Quarterly* 64, no. 2 (April, 2007): 395–418.

3   Huey Newton, "Huey Newton Speaking on Police in the Black Community," YouTube video, 1:09, September 26, 2017, https://www.youtube.com/watch?v=OtwX_PjkjfQ.

4 100 Suits for 100 Men, https://www.facebook.com/100SUITS.

5 Khristopher J. Brooks, "Redlining's Legacy: Maps Are Gone, but the Problem Hasn't Disappeared," CBS News, CBS Interactive, February 19, 2020, https://www.cbsnews.com /news/redlining-what-is-history -mike-bloomberg-comments.

6 Ruth Wilson Gilmore, interview by Chenjerai Kumanyika, *The Intercept,* podcast transcript, June 10, 2020, https://theintercept.com/2020/06/10 /ruth-wilson-gilmore-makes-the -case-for-abolition.

7 Angela Davis, "Masked Racism: Reflections on the Prison Industrial Complex," History Is a Weapon, http://www.historyisaweapon.com /defcon1/davisprison.html.

8 Angela Y. Davis, *Are Prisons Obsolete?* (New York: Seven Stories Press, 2003).

9 Colin Kaepernick, "Colin Kaepernick Explains Why He Won't Stand during National Anthem," YouTube video, 18:23, August 29, 2016, https://www .youtube.com/watch?v=ka0446tibig.

10 Ruth Wilson Gilmore, "Geographies of Racial Capitalism with Ruth Wilson Gilmore," Antipode Foundation, YouTube video, 16:18, June 1, 2020, https://www.youtube.com /watch?v=2CS627aKrJI.

11 Michel Foucault, *Discipline & Punish: The Birth of the Prison* (New York: Vintage Books, 1995).

Police & Policing

The Feds Are Watching

1 James Forman to E. William Henry, August 2, 1964, telegram, Civil Rights Movement Archive, San Francisco, https://www.crmvet.org/docs/wats /wats64-0802_sncc.pdf.

2 Ibid.

3 Gathering News Information (WATS Reports), Atlanta SNCC Office, June 24, 1964, Civil Rights Movement Archive, San Francisco, https://www.crmvet.org/docs/wats/.

4 *Caution!! Colored people of Boston, one & all, you are hereby respectfully cautioned and advised, to avoid conversing with the watchmen and police officers of Boston, for since the recent order of the mayor & aldermen, they are empowered to act.* Boston, 1851, https://www.loc.gov /item/rbpe.06002200/.

5 Harriet Ann Jacobs, *Incidents in the Life of a Slave Girl* (Boston, 1861).

6 Eve Tuck and K. Wayne Yang, "Decolonization Is Not a Metaphor," *Decolonization: Indigeneity, Education & Society* 1, no. 1 (2012): 1–40.

7 Lila Boswell, "Getting Pulled Over? Siri Can Secretly Record It," Medium, June 17, 2020, https://medium.com/@ lilalilaboswell/getting-pulled-over-siri -can-secretly-record-it-2f58b02d63e0.

8 Ring, "End-to-End Encryption" (white paper), January 2021, https:// assets.ctfassets.net/a3peezndovsu /7bwgu7ybi1XoyH61pDraYT/94e4bab 9347d4abe07f8d843fdfd4bd4 /Ring_Encryption_Whitepaper _FINAL.pdf.

9 Edward Ongweso Jr., "Amazon's Ring Announces an Entire Line of Dystopian Surveillance Devices," *Vice,* September 24, 2020, https://www .vice.com/en/article/bv8qjq/amazons -ring-announces-an-entire-line-of -dystopian-surveillance-devices.

10 "Organizing Resources," Survived & Punished, https://survivedandpunished.org /organizing-resources.

11 Dean Spade, *Mutual Aid: Building Solidarity During This Crisis (and the Next)* (Brooklyn, NY: Verso Books, 2020).

The Myth of the Good Cop

1   Raymond Nelson, "Domestic Harlem: The Detective Fiction of Chester Himes," *The Virginia Quarterly Review* 48, no. 2 (Spring, 1972): 260–76.

The Truth About "Officer Friendly"

1   "Normalizing Injustice: The Dangerous Misrepresentations that Define Television's Scripted Crime Genre," Color of Change, January 2020, https://hollywood.colorofchange.org /crime-tv-report/.

2   Ibid.

3   "Contacts Between Police and the Public, 2015" Bureau of Justice Statistics, US Department of Justice, October 2018, https://www.bjs.gov /content/pub/pdf/cpp15_sum.pdf.

4   "Fatal Force," infographic, *Washington Post,* https://www.washingtonpost.com /graphics/investigations/police -shootings-database/.

SWAT's Paramilitary Fever Dream

1   Daryl Gates, *Chief: My Life in the L.A.P.D.* (New York: Bantam, 1992).

2   Mike Davis and Jon Wiener, *Set the Night on Fire: L.A. in the Sixties* (Brooklyn, NY: Verso Books, 2020).

3   Matthew Fleischer, "50 Years Ago Raided Teams Have Been Targeting Communities Ever Since," *Los Angeles Times,* December 8, 2019, https://www.latimes.com/opinion /story/2019-12-08/50-years-swat -black-panthers-militarized -policinglos-angeles.

4   Radley Balko, *Rise of the Warrior Cop: The Militarization of America's Police Forces* (New York: Public Affairs, 2013).

5   Stuart Schrader, *Badges Without Borders: How Global Counterinsurgency Transformed American Policing* (Oakland: University of California Press, 2019).

6   Brian Barrett, "The Pentagon's Hand-Me-Downs Helped Militarize Police. Here's How," *Wired,* June 2, 2020, https://www.wired.com/story /pentagon-hand-me-downs-militarize -police-1033-program.

7   Michael Leo Owens, Tom Clark, and Adam Glynn, "Where Do Police Departments Get Their Military-Style Gear? Here's What We Don't Know," *Washington Post,* July 20, 2020, https://www.washingtonpost.com /politics/2020/07/20/where -do-police-departments-get-their -military-style-gear-heres-what -we-dont-know.

8   Stuart Schrader, "Yes, American Police Act Like Occupying Armies. They Literally Studied Their Tactics," *Guardian,* June 8, 2020, https://www.theguardian.com /commentisfree/2020/jun/08/yes -american-police-act-like-occupying -armies-they-literally-studied-their -tactics.

9   Julian Go, "The Imperial Origins of American Policing: Militarization and Imperial Feedback in the Early 20th Century," *American Journal of Sociology* 125, no. 5 (March 2020): 1193–1254.

10 Paul McLeary, "Pentagon Says It Doesn't Want Active Duty Troops Facing Protesters," *Breaking Defense,* June 2, 2020, https://breakingdefense .com/2020/06/pentagon-says-it -doesnt-want-active-duty-troops -putting-down-protests.

11 Stuart Schrader, "When Police Treat Protesters Like Insurgents, Sending in Troops Seems Logical," *Washington Post,* June 4, 2020, https://www .washingtonpost.com/outlook /militarized-police-troops-protest /2020/06/04/94b5ed3e-a610 -11ea-b619-3f9133bbb482_story.html.

12 Stuart Schrader, "What Defunding the Police Can Mean for US Foreign Policy,"

Responsible Statecraft, June 26, 2020, https://responsiblestatecraft.org/2020/06/26/what-defunding-the-police-can-mean-for-us-foreign-policy.

Disability Justice Is an Essential Part of Abolishing Police & Ending Incarceration

1   Abigail Abrams, "Black, Disabled and at Risk: The Overlooked Problem of Police Violence Against Americans with Disabilities," *Time,* June 25, 2020, https://time.com/5857438/police-violence-black-disabled/.

2   Talila A. Lewis, "January 2021 Working Definition of Ableism," *Talila A. Lewis* (blog), January 1, 2021, https://www.talilalewis.com/blog.

3   Talila Lewis, "Emmett Till & the Pervasive Erasure of Disability in Conversations about White Supremacy & Police Violence," Medium, January 28, 2017, https://medium.com/@talewis/emmett-till-the-pervasive-erasure-of-disability-in-conversations-about-white-supremacy-police-5eb9ad595ba2.

4   Dustin P. Gibson, "Grounding Movements in Disability Justice," webinar, May 2, 2020, https://www.dustinpgibson.com/offerings/groundingmovementsindj.

5   Sarah Blahovec, "Confronting the Whitewashing of Disability: Interview with #DisabilityTooWhite Creator Vilissa Thompson," *HuffPost,* updated December 6, 2017, https://www.huffpost.com/entry/confronting-the-whitewash_b_10574994.

6   Talila A. Lewis, "Longmore Lecture: Context, Clarity & Grounding," *Talila A. Lewis* (blog), March 5, 2019, https://www.talilalewis.com/blog/longmore-lecture-context-clarity-grounding.

7   Talila A. Lewis, "January 2021 Working Definition of Ableism," *Talila A. Lewis* (blog), January 1, 2021, https://www.talilalewis.com/blog.

8   Talila A. Lewis, "Trump's Rule Attacking Disabled and Low-Income Migrants Has Violent History," *Truthout,* August 27, 2019, https://truthout.org/articles/trumps-rule-attacking-disabled-and-low-income-migrants-has-violent-history.

9   Talila A. Lewis, "Why I Don't Use 'Anti-Black Ableism' (& Language Longings)," *Talila A. Lewis* (blog), August 17, 2020, https://www.talilalewis.com/blog/why-i-dont-use-anti-black-ableism.

10 Harald Schmidt, "The Way We Ration Ventilators Is Biased," *New York Times,* April 15, 2020, https://www.nytimes.com/2020/04/15/opinion/covid-ventilator-rationing-blacks.html.

11 Talila A. Lewis, "Honoring Arnaldo Rios-Soto & Charles Kinsey: Achieving Liberation Through Disability Solidarity," *Talila A. Lewis* (blog), July 22, 2016, https://www.talilalewis.com/blog/achieving-liberation-through-disability-solidarity.

12 Patty Berne, "Disability Justice—a Working Draft by Patty Berne," *Sins Invalid* (blog), June 9, 2015, https://www.sinsinvalid.org/blog/disability-justice-a-working-draft-by-patty-berne.

13 Mariame Kaba, "Yes, We Mean Literally Abolish the Police," *New York Times,* June 12, 2020, https://www.nytimes.com/2020/06/12/opinion/sunday/floyd-abolish-defund-police.html.

14 Jessica Benham and Dustin Gibson, "No Cages, High Wages: A Renewed Call for Cross-Movement Solidarity Between Unions and Disabled People," *Pittsburgh Current,* October 22, 2019, https://www.pittsburghcurrent.com/polk-state-centers.

15 "Disability Impacts All of Us," infographic, Centers for Disease Control and Prevention, US Department

of Health and Human Services, September 16, 2020, https://www.cdc.gov/ncbddd/disabilityandhealth/infographic-disability-impacts-all.html.

16 Dominic Bradley and Sarah Katz, "Sandra Bland, Eric Garner, Freddie Gray: The Toll of Police Violence on Disabled Americans," *Guardian,* June 9, 2020, https://www.theguardian.com/commentisfree/2020/jun/09/sandra-bland-eric-garner-freddie-gray-the-toll-of-police-violence-on-disabled-americans.

17 Doris J. James and Lauren E. Glaze, "Mental Health Problems of Prison and Jail Inmates," Bureau of Justice Statistics, US Department of Justice, revised December 14, 2006, https://www.bjs.gov/content/pub/pdf/mhppji.pdf.

18 "Supporting Youth with Disabilities in Juvenile Corrections," Office of Special Education and Rehabilitative Services, US Department of Education, May 23, 2017, https://sites.ed.gov/osers/2017/05/supporting-youth-with-disabilities-in-juvenile-corrections.

19 Stella Akua Mensah, "Abolition Must Include Psychiatry," Disability Visibility Project, July 22, 2020, https://disabilityvisibilityproject.com/2020/07/22/abolition-must-include-psychiatry.

20 Kraig McNutt, "I Appear This Evening as a Thief and a Robber," *The Civil War Gazette,* https://civilwargazette.wordpress.com/2006/12/05/i-appear-this-evening-as-a-thief-and-a-robber.

21 "Diseases and Peculiarities of the Negro Race" (*De Bow's Review,* New Orleans, 1851), *Africans in America,* part 4, PBS, https://www.pbs.org/wgbh/aia/part4/4h3106t.html.

22 Ibid.

23 "1880 Census: Volume 1. Statistics of the Population of the United States," US Census Bureau, https://www2.census.gov/library/publications/decennial/1880/vol-01-population/1880_v1-22.pdf.

24 "Report on the Defective, Dependent, and Delinquent Classes of the Population of the United States," US Census Bureau, 1888, https://www2.census.gov/prod2/decennial/documents/1880a_v21-01.pdf.

25 Craig Swenson, "Seeking Asylum: A Story of Reconstruction, Race, and Mental Health," Clara Barton Missing Soldiers Office Museum, May 17, 2017, https://www.clarabartonmuseum.org/asylum.

26 Lisa Ko, "Unwanted Sterilization and Eugenics Programs in the United States," *Independent Lens,* PBS, January 29, 2016, https://www.pbs.org/independentlens/blog/unwanted-sterilization-and-eugenics-programs-in-the-united-states.

27 "Belly of the Beast: Survivors of Forced Sterilizations in California's Prisons Fight for Justice," *Democracy Now!,* September 22, 2020, https://www.democracynow.org/2020/9/22/belly_of_the_beast_documentary.

28 Marc Meredith and Michael Morse, "The Politics of the Restoration of Ex-Felon Voting Rights: The Case of Iowa," *Quarterly Journal of Political Science* 10, no. 1 (May 2015): 41–100.

29 "Civil Disabilities of Convicted Felons," US Department of Justice, October 1996, https://www.ojp.gov/pdffiles1/pr/195110.pdf.

30 "Certificate of Relief from Disabilities," New York State Unified Court System, updated August 13, 2020, https://www.nycourts.gov/courthelp/Criminal/CRD.shtml.

31 "Coronavirus Criminalization: A Curated Collection of Links," The Marshall Project, February 9, 2021, https://www.themarshallproject.org

/records/8830-coronavirus
-criminalization.

32 Talila A. Lewis, "Freeing Black Fates &
Capturing Black Freedom: Reclaiming
Our Humanity, Contextualizing Our
Trauma and Honoring Our Resistance,"
Talila A. Lewis (blog), July 4, 2020,
https://www.talilalewis.com
/blog/freeing-black-fates-capturing
-black-freedom.

33 Jamelia Morgan, "Rethinking
Disorderly Conduct" (2020), *California
Law Review,* https://ssrn.com
/abstract=3552620.

34 Méabh O'Hare, Joshua Budhu,
and Altaf Saadi, "Police Keep Using
'Excited Delirium' to Justify Brutality.
It's Junk Science," *Washington
Post,* July 17, 2020, https://www.
washingtonpost.com/outlook
/chokehold-police-excited-delirium
/2020/07/17/fe907ec8-c6bc-11ea
-b037-f9711f89ee46_story.html.

35 "Civil Disabilities of Convicted Felons."

36 "A Guide to Disability Rights Laws,"
US Department of Justice,
February 2020, https://www.ada.gov
/cguide.htm.

37 Talila A. Lewis, "Response: Concerns
re Disability/Deaf Rights Communities'
Responses to Policing Systems'
Violence," Google doc, June 2019,
https://tinyurl.com/3s9ut3ae.

38 Equitable Education, "Beyond
Access: Mia Mingus on Disability
Justice," video interview by Greg
Macdougall, November 30, 2013,
https://equitableeducation.ca/2013
/mia-mingus-disability-justice.

39 Katie Tastrom, "Disability Justice and
Abolition," National Lawyers Guild,
June 27, 2020, https://www.nlg.org
/disability-justice-and-abolition.

40 Patty Berne, "Disability Justice—
a Working Draft by Patty Berne,"
Sins Invalid (blog), June 9, 2015,
https://www.sinsinvalid.org/blog
/disability-justice-a-working-draft-by
-patty-berne.

41 Talila A. Lewis, "Honoring Arnaldo
Rios-Soto & Charles Kinsey: Achieving
Liberation Through Disability
Solidarity," *Talila A. Lewis* (blog), July
22, 2016, https://www.talilalewis
.com/blog/achieving-liberation
-through-disability-solidarity.

42 Talila A. Lewis and Dustin Gibson,
"The Prison Strike Challenges Ableism
and Defends Disability Rights,"
Truthout, September 5, 2018, https://
truthout.org/articles/the-prison-strike
-is-a-disability-rights-issue.

43 Mia Mingus, "Transformative Justice:
A Brief Description," *Leaving Evidence*
(blog), January 9, 2019, https://
leavingevidence.wordpress
.com/2019/01/09/transformative
-justice-a-brief-description.

44 Talila A. Lewis, "Freeing Black Fates &
Capturing Black Freedom: Reclaiming
Our Humanity, Contextualizing Our
Trauma and Honoring Our Resistance,"
Talila A. Lewis (blog), July 4, 2020,
https://www.talilalewis.com
/blog/freeing-black-fates-capturing
-black-freedom.

45 Mia Mingus, "'Disability Justice' Is
Simply Another Term for Love," *Leaving
Evidence* (blog), November 3, 2018,
https://leavingevidence.wordpress
.com/2018/11/03/disability-justice-is
-simply-another-term-for-love.

46 Alice Wong, ed., *Resistance & Hope:
Essays by Disabled People*
(Disability Visibility Project, 2018).

47 Leah Lakshmi Piepzna-Samarasinha
and Ejeris Dixon, interview by Laura
Flanders, "Mutual Aid Justice: Beyond
Survival," *The Laura Flanders Show,*
podcast transcript, April 7, 2020,
https://lauraflanders.org/2020/04
/mutual-aid-justice-beyond-survival.

48 Eve L. Ewing, "Mariame Kaba:
Everything Worthwhile Is Done With
Other People," *Adi Magazine*
(Fall 2019), https://adimagazine.com/
articles/mariame-kaba-everything
-worthwhile-is-done-with
-other-people.

Snaps!

1 Ashley Eisenmenger, "Ableism 101," Access Living, December 12, 2019, https://www.accessliving.org /newsroom/blog/ableism-101/.

2 Gloria Anzaldúa, *Borderlands— La Frontera* (San Francisco: Aunt Lute Books, 1987).

3 Joseph G. Kosciw et al., "The Effect of Negative School Climate on Academic Outcomes for LGBT Youth and the Role of In-School Supports," *Journal of School Violence* 12, no. 1 (December 5, 2012): 45–63.

4 Angela Irvine and Aisha Canfield, "Reflections on New National Data on LGBQ/GNCT Youth in the Justice System," *LGBTQ Policy Journal,* January 29, 2018.

5 Dorothy Roberts, "Abolishing Policing Also Means Abolishing Family Regulation," *The Imprint,* June 16, 2020.

6 Bianca D. M. Wilson et al., "Sexual and Gender Minority Youth in Foster Care," UCLA School of Law Williams Institute, August 2014.

7 Dara E. Purvis and Melissa Blanco, "Police Sexual Violence: Police Brutality, #MeToo, and Masculinities," *California Law Review* 108, no. 5 (October 2020).

8 Eric A. Stanley and Nat Smith, eds., *Captive Genders: Trans Embodiment and the Prison Industrial Complex* (Chico, CA: AK Press, 2015).

9 Marcus Brock, "Dynasty Young Sues School District after Being Expelled," GLAAD, September 5, 2012, https://www.glaad.org/blog/dynasty -young-sues-school-district-after -being-expelled.

10 J. Worley, "'Street Power' and the Claiming of Public Space: San Francisco's 'Vanguard' and Pre-Stonewall Queer Radicalism," in Stanley and Smith, *Captive Genders.*

11 BreakOUT!, https://www .youthbreakout.org/mission/.

12 https://www.urban.org/research /publication/locked-interactions -criminal-justice-and-child-welfare -systems-lgbtq-youth-ymsm-and -ywsw-who-engage-survival-sex.

13 Mihir Zaveri, "Body Camera Footage Shows Arrest by Orlando Police of 6-Year-Old at School," *New York Times,* February 27, 2020, https://www .nytimes.com/2020/02/27/us /orlando-6-year-old-arrested.html.

14 Phillip Atiba Goff et al., "The Essence of Innocence," *Journal of Personality and Social Psychology* 106, no. 4 (February 24, 2014): 526–545.

15 J. J. Arnett, "Emerging Adulthood: A Theory of Development from the Late Teens through the Twenties," *The American Psychologist* 55, no. 5 (May 2000): 469–80.

Schools as Carceral Spaces

1 "Violent Schools—Safe Schools, The Safe School Study Report to the Congress, Volume I," US Department of Health, Education and Welfare, January 1978, https://www.ncjrs.gov/pdffiles1 /Digitization/45988NCJRS.pdf.

2 "Crime, Violence, Discipline, and Safety in U.S. Public Schools," National Center for Education Statistics, US Department of Education, July 2019, https://nces.ed.gov/pubs2019 /2019061.pdf.

3 Melinda D. Anderson, "When Schooling Meets Policing," *The Atlantic,* September 21, 2015, https://www.theatlantic.com/ education/archive/2015/09/when -schooling-meets-policing/406348; Amir Whitaker et al., "Cops and No Counselors," ACLU, https://www.aclu .org/report/cops-and-no-counselors.

4 "School Climate and Safety," US Department of Education, revised May 2019,, https://www2.ed.gov /about/offices/list/ocr/docs/school -climate-and-safety.pdf.

5   Data collected from corrections departments across the country and analyzed by Phillips Black, a public interest law practice, https://www.phillipsblack.org/.

6   Syllabus, Jones v. Mississippi, Supreme Court of the United States, October term, 2020, https://www.supremecourt.gov/opinions/20pdf/18-1259_8njq.pdf; Adam Liptak, "Supreme Court Rejects Limits on Life Terms for Youths," *New York Times,* April 22, 2021, https://www.nytimes.com/2021/04/22/us/supreme-court-life-terms-youths.html.

7   "2019 Crime in the United States, Table 43: Arrests by Race and Ethnicity," US Department of Justice, 2019, https://ucr.fbi.gov/crime-in-the-u.s/2019/crime-in-the-u.s.-2019/tables/table-43/#overview.

8   US Census Bureau, https://www.census.gov.

How Abolition Makes Schools Safer

1   "The State of Racial Diversity in the Educator Workforce," US Department of Education, July 2016, https://www2.ed.gov/rschstat/eval/highered/racial-diversity/state-racial-diversity-workforce.pdf.

2   Holy Kurtz et al., "School Policing Results of a National Survey of School Resource Officers," Education Week Research Center, Editorial Projects in Education, 2018, https://epe.brightspotcdn.com/15/03/8b55a2594956a360fee8e0dd454c/school-resource-officer-survey-copyright-education-week.pdf.

3   Devin Anderson, "Disrupt the Preschool-to-Prison-Pipeline with Equitable Practices," National Women's Law Center, November 17, 2017, https://nwlc.org/blog/disrupt-the-preschool-to-prison-pipeline-with-equitable-practices/.

4   Luke Darby, "Florida Police Officer Arrested and Handcuffed a 6-Year-Old Black Girl for a Tantrum in Class," *GQ,* September 23, 2019, https://www.gq.com/story/six-year-old-black-girl-arrested-for-a-tantrum.

5   Jonathan Nakamoto, Rebeca Cerna, and Alexis Stern, "High School Students' Perceptions of Police Vary by Student Race and Ethnicity," WestEd, 2019, https://www.wested.org/wp-content/uploads/2019/05/resource-high-school-students-perceptions-of-police.pdf.

6   Frank B. Wilderson III, interview by Jared Ball, Todd Steven Burroughs and Dr. Hate, in *"We're Trying to Destroy the World": Anti-Blackness & Police Violence After Ferguson,* radio interview transcript (Ill Will Editions, 2014), https://illwilleditions.noblogs.org/files/2015/09/Wilderson-We-Are-Trying-to-Destroy-the-World-PRINT.pdf.

7   Patricia L. Brougham, "Criminalblackman," in *Encyclopedia of Race and Crime,* ed. Helen Taylor Greene and Shaun L. Gabbidon (Thousand Oaks, CA: SAGE Publications, 2009), http://dx.doi.org/10.4135/9781412971928.n67.

8   "Principles of Unity," Dignity in Schools, 2017, http://dignityinschools.org/about-us/principles-of-unity/.

9   Dave Stovall, "Are We Ready for 'School' Abolition?: Thoughts and Practices of Radical Imaginary in Education," *Taboo: The Journal of Culture and Education* 17, no. 1 (2018), https://doi.org/10.31390/taboo.17.1.06.

10 Angela Y. Davis, "Why Arguments Against Abolition Inevitably Fail," *Level,* Medium, October 6, 2020, https://level.medium.com/why-arguments-against-abolition-inevitably-fail-991342b8d042.

11 Amy Goodman and Angela Davis, "Angela Davis on Abolition, Calls to Defund Police, Toppled Racist Statues & Voting in 2020 Election," *Democracy Now!,* June 12, 2020, https://www

.democracynow.org/2020/6/12
/angela_davis_on_abolition_calls_to.

We Must Center Black Women

1   Rachel Treisman et al., "Kentucky Grand Jury Indicts 1 of 3 Officers in Breonna Taylor Case," NPR, September 23, 2020, https://www.npr.org/sections /live-updates-protests-for-racial -justice/2020/09/23/914250463 /breonna-taylor-charging-decision -to-be-announced-this-afternoon -lawyer-says.

2   Ibid.

3   Sam Johnson, "AP Was There: 2 Men Acquitted of Murder in Emmett Till Case," AP News, July 12, 2018, https://apnews.com/article /f6e82e2661424204b0f1920c313fa307.

4   "Jury Nullification," Legal Information Institute, Cornell Law School, https://www.law.cornell.edu/wex /jury_nullification.

5   Robyn Mowatt, "Hours of Body-Cam Footage Exposes Gaps in Investigation of Breonna Taylor's Death," *Okayplayer,* September 2020, https://www .okayplayer.com/news/body-camera -footage-breonna-taylor-death -investigation.html.

6   Simone Browne, *Dark Matters: On the Surveillance of Blackness* (Raleigh, NC: Duke University Press, 2015).

Prisons & Carcerality

Stolen Freedom

1   "Minnesota: Carceral Colonialism: Imprisonment in Indian Country," States of Incarceration, November 20, 2018–February 18, 2019, https:// statesofincarceration.org/states /minnesota-carceral-colonialism -imprisonment-indian-country.

2   United Nations, *United Nations Declaration on the Rights of Indigenous Peoples* (New York: United Nations,

2007).

3   United Nations, "Article 10," in *United Nations Declaration on the Rights of Indigenous Peoples.*

4   United Nations, *United Nations Declaration on the Rights of Indigenous Peoples.*

5   "Gold, Greed and Genocide," International Indian Treaty Council, https://www.iitc.org/gold-greed -genocide/#timeline.

6   "Tribal History," Redding Rancheria, http://www.redding-rancheria.com /tribal-history.

7   Beth Rose Middleton Manning, *Upstream: Trust Lands and Power on the Feather River* (Tucson: University of Arizona Press, 2018).

8   Benjamin Madley, "California's First Mass Incarceration System: Franciscan Missions, California Indians, and Penal Servitude, 1769–1836," *Pacific Historical Review* 88, no. 1 (2019): 14–47.

9   "California Missions Native History," California Indian Museum & Cultural Center, http://calindianmissions.org.

10 Candice Francis, "Gold Chains: The Hidden History of Slavery in California," ACLU, November 5, 2019, https://www.aclu.org/news/racial -justice/gold-chains-the-hidden -history-of-slavery-in-california.

11 Kimberly Johnston-Dodds, "Early California Laws and Policies Related to California Indians" (Sacramento: California Research Bureau, 2002).

12 "Gold Chains: The Hidden History of Slavery in California," ACLU of Northern California, https://www.aclunc.org /sites/goldchains.

13 Ben Kesslen, "Native Americans, the Census' Most Undercounted Racial Group, Fight for an Accurate 2020 Tally," NBC News, December 29, 2019, https://www.nbcnews.com/news /us-news/native-americans-census -most-undercounted-racial-group -fight-accurate-2020-n1105096.

14 Peter Burnett, "State of the State Address," The Governors' Gallery, January 6, 1851, https://governors .library.ca.gov/addresses/s_01 -Burnett2.html.

15 Kat Chow, "So What Exactly Is 'Blood Quantum?,'" *Code Switch,* podcast transcript, February 9, 2018, https://www.npr.org/sections /codeswitch/2018/02/09/583987261 /so-what-exactly-is-blood-quantum.

16 Jen Deerinwater, "Paper Genocide: The Barriers to an Accurate Count of Native People in 2020," *Truthout,* December 12, 2019, https://truthout .org/articles/paper-genocide-the -barriers-to-an-accurate-count-of -native-people-in-2020.

17 "Finding Government Documents: Treaties," Library of Congress Research Guides, https://guides.loc.gov/finding -government-documents/treaties.

18 Larisa K. Miller, "The Secret Treaties with California's Indians," *Prologue* (Fall/Winter 2013): 38–45.

19 Roxanne Daniel, "Since You Asked What Data Exists about Native American Peoplein the Criminal Justice System?," Prison Policy Initiative, April 22, 2020, https://www.prisonpolicy .org/blog/2020/04/22/native.

20 Vision Maker Media, "'Two Spirit' – Injunuity," YouTube video, 4:19, November 11, 2013, https://www .youtube.com/watch?v=iDyaknNmg28.

21 "Family Seeks Justice for Slain Indigenous Mother," *El Tecolote,* April 25, 2019, http://eltecolote.org/content/ en/family-seeks-justice-for-slain -indigenous-mother.

22 "Gender Based Violence and Intersecting Challenges Impacting Native American & Alaskan Village Communities," VAWnet, September 1, 2016, https://vawnet.org/sc/gender -based-violence-and-intersecting -challenges-impacting-native -american-alaskan-village.

23 William Wood, "The Trajectory of Indian Country in California: Rancherias, Villages, Pueblos, Missions, Ranchos, Reservations, Colonies, and Rancherias," *Tulsa Law Review* 44, no. 2 (Winter 2008): 317–64.

24 "California Profile," Prison Policy Initiative, State Profiles, https://www .prisonpolicy.org/profiles/CA.html.

25 Ashley Gabbard et al., "Offender Data Points: Offender Demographics for the 24-Month Period Ending December 2018," California Department of Corrections and Rehabilitation, January 2020, https://www.cdcr.ca.gov /research/wp-content/uploads/sites /174/2020/01/201812_DataPoints.pdf.

26 Pamela A. Conners, *The Chico to Round Valley Trail of Tears* (Willows , CA: Mendocino National Forest, 1993).

27 "Tribal Territory Since Time Began," Round Valley Indian Tribes, https://www.rvit.org.

28 "Alcatraz Proclamation and Letter," History Is a Weapon, https://www .historyisaweapon.com/defcon1 /alcatrazproclamationandletter.html.

29 "Important Notice: IITC's Annual Day of Indigenous Peoples Sunrise Gathering on Alcatraz Island," International Indian Treaty Council, September 25, 2020, https://www.iitc.org/annual-sunrise -gathering-alcatraz-island.

30 George Snyder, "Obituary—Isidro Gali," SFGATE, June 8, 1995, https://www. sfgate.com/news/article /OBITUARY-Isidro-Gali-3030377.php.

31 Rebecca Clarren, "Judge Abby Abinanti Is Fighting for Her Tribe—and for a Better Justice System," *The Nation,* November 30, 2017, https://www .thenation.com/article/archive/judge -abby-abinanti-is-fighting-for-her -tribe-and-for-a-better-justice-system.

32 "Anti Police-Terror Project Sacramento," Anti Police-Terror Project, https://www.antipoliceterrorproject .org/sacramento.

33 "Restoring Justice for Indigenous Peoples," Restoring Justice for Indigenous Peoples, https://www.indigenousjustice.org.

34 Toronto Abolition Convergence, "An Indigenous Abolitionist Study Guide," Yellowhead Institute, August 10, 2020, https://yellowheadinstitute.org/2020/08/10/an-indigenous-abolitionist-study-group-guide.

35 "Yurok Tribe Wellness Coalition," Yurok Tribal Court, https://yuroktribalcourt.org.

36 Nadra Nittle, "Feeding an Indigenous Community and Rematriating Seeds in Minneapolis," *Civil Eats,* June 9, 2020, https://civileats.com/2020/06/09/feeding-an-indigenous-community-and-rematriating-seeds-in-minneapolis.

Queer & Trans Liberation Requires Abolition

1 Avianne Tan, "NYPD Unveils Rainbow-Themed Vehicle Before City's Gay Pride March," ABC News, June 23, 2016, https://abcnews.go.com/US/nypd-unveils-rainbow-themed-vehicle-ahead-citys-pride/story?id=40072112.

2 Alex Caprariello, "Austin Is the Latest City to Launch 'Safe Place' Program to Provide Refuge to LGBTQ+ Community," KXAN News, August 7, 2019, https://www.kxan.com/news/austin-is-the-latest-city-to-launch-safe-place-program-to-provide-refuge-to-lgbtq-community.

3 Garance Franke-Ruta, "An Amazing 1969 Account of the Stonewall Uprising," *The Atlantic,* January 24, 2013, https://www.theatlantic.com/politics/archive/2013/01/an-amazing-1969-account-of-the-stonewall-uprising/272467.

4 Sidney Fussell, "How Stonewall Reversed a Long History of Justifying Police Surveillance," *The Atlantic,* June 29, 2019, https://www.theatlantic.com/technology/archive/2019/06/how-police-surveillance-led-stonewall/593026.

5 *Democracy Now!,* "Angela Davis: Abolishing Police Is Not Just About Dismantling. It's Also About Building Up," YouTube video, 6:33, June 12, 2020, https://www.youtube.com/watch?v=8ebWFnGWOaA.

6 Ajamu Sankofa et al., "A Soldier's Story: Revolutionary Writings by a New Afrikan Anarchist," The Anarchist Library, 2001, https://theanarchistlibrary.org/library/kuwasi-balagoon-a-soldier-s-story.

7 Queers United in Support of Political Prisoners, *Dykes and Fags Want to Know . . . : A Written Interview with Lesbian Political Prisoners Laura Whitehorn, Linda Evans and Susan Rosenberg* (Toronto: Arm the Spirit, 1995).

8 Raquel Willis, "TransVisionaries: How Miss Major Helped Spark the Modern Trans Movement," *Them,* March 8, 2018, https://www.them.us/story/transvisionaries-miss-major.

9 Andrea J. Ritchie, https://www.andreajritchie.com/.

10 Walidah Imarisha et al., "The Fictions and Futures of Transformative Justice," TransformHarm.org, April 20, 2017, https://transformharm.org/the-fictions-and-futures-of-transformative-justice.

11 Roberto Sirvent, "BAR Abolition Spotlight: 'Mia Mingus,'" *Black Agenda Report,* January 9, 2019, https://www.blackagendareport.com/bar-abolition-spotlight-mia-mingus.

12 Dean Spade and Roberto Sirvent, "BAR Abolition & Mutual Aid Spotlight: Alisa Bierria," *Black Agenda Report,* May 13, 2020, https://www.blackagendareport.com/bar-abolition-mutual-aid-spotlight-alisa-bierria.

13 Tania Unzueta, Maru Mora Villalpando, and Angélica Cházaro, "We Fell in

Love in a Hopeless Place: A Grassroots History from #Not1More to Abolish ICE," Medium, June 29, 2018, https://medium.com/@LaTania /we-fell-in-love-in-a-hopeless-place -a-grassroots-history-from-not1more -to-abolish-ice-23089cf21711.

14 Tourmaline and Dean Spade, "No One Is Disposable: Everyday Practices of Prison Abolition" (online event), Barnard College, New York, February 7, 2014, http://bcrw.barnard.edu /event/no-one-is-disposable-everyday -practices-of-prison-abolition/.

15 Beth E. Richie, "How Anti-violence Activism Taught Me to Become a Prison Abolitionist," *The Feminist Wire,* January 21, 2014, https://www .thefeministwire.com/2014/01/how -anti-violence-activism-taught-me-to -become-a-prison-abolitionist/.

16 M. V. Lee Badgett, Soon Kyu Choi, and Bianca D. M. Wilson, "LGBT Poverty in the United States: A Study of the Differences Between Sexual Orientation and Gender Identity Groups" (Los Angeles: UCLA School of Law, 2019).

17 "LGBT Homelessness," National Coalition for the Homeless, https:// nationalhomeless.org/issues/lgbt.

18 Sejal Singh and Laura E. Durso, "Widespread Discrimination Continues to Shape LGBT People's Lives in Both Subtle and Significant Ways," Center for American Progress, LGBTQ Rights, May 2, 2017, https://www .americanprogress.org/issues/lgbtq -rights/news/2017/05/02/429529 /widespread-discrimination-continues -shape-lgbt-peoples-lives-subtle -significant-ways.

19 Emily Waters, "Lesbian, Gay, Bisexual, Transgender, Queer, and HIV-Affected Hate Violence in 2016" (New York: National Coalition of Anti-Violence Programs, 2017), https://avp.org /wp-content/uploads/2017/06/NCAVP _2016HateViolence_REPORT.pdf.

20 Ginia Bellafante, "Arrests by the Fashion Police," *New York Times,* April 5, 2013, https://www.nytimes .com/2013/04/07/nyregion/arrests -by-the-fashion-police.html.

21 MJ Eckhouse and Saxen MJ, "Police Brutality and Why It Is an LGBTQ Issue," *Fusion* (Spring 2017): 31–35.

22 National Center for Transgender Inequality, *LGBTQ People Behind Bars: A Guide to Understanding the Issues Facing Transgender Prisoners and their Legal Rights* (Washington, DC: National Center for Transgender Inequality, 2018).

23 Julie Moreau, "LGBTQ Migrants 97 Times More Likely to Be Sexually Assaulted in Detention, Report Says," NBC News, June 6, 2018, https://www .nbcnews.com/feature/nbc-out/lgbtq -migrants-97-times-more-likely-be -sexually-assaulted-detention-n880101.

24 Transgender Gender-Variant & Intersex Justice Project, "In Response to Increased Policing of Civic Center, Grand Marshals, Awardees Withdraw from Participation in Pride Parade," TGI Justice, June 24, 2016, http://www .tgijp.org/solidarity/in-response -to-increased-policing-of-civic-center -grand-marshals-awardees-withdraw -from-participation-in-pride-parade.

25 Sam Levin, "'Police Are a Force of Terror': The LGBT Activists Who Want Cops Out of Pride," *Guardian*, June 14, 2019, https://www.theguardian.com /world/2019/jun/13/cops-out-of -pride-lgbt-police.

26 "Why We March," Reclaim Pride Coalition, https://reclaimpridenyc.org /why-we-march.

27 "National Crime Victimization Survey," US Census Bureau, https://www. census.gov/programs-surveys /ncvs.html.

28 "Hate Violence Against Transgender Communities," National Coalition of Anti-Violence Programs, https://avp

.org/wp-content/uploads/2017/04/ncavp_transhvfactsheet.pdf.

29 National Center for Transgender Inequality, "Reforming Police and Ending Anti-Transgender Violence," in *Blueprint for Equality: A Transgender Federal Agenda* (Washington, DC: National Center for Transgender Inequality, 2016), 27–30.

30 Catherine Hanssens et al., *A Roadmap for Change: Federal Policy Recommendations for Addressing the Criminalization of LGBT People and People Living with HIV* (New York: Center for Gender & Sexuality Law at Columbia Law School, 2014).

31 Katelyn Burns, "Why Police Often Single Out Trans People for Violence," *Vox,* June 23, 2020, https://www.vox.com/identities/2020/6/23/21295432/police-black-trans-people-violence.

32 Ibid.

33 Nicole Pasulka, "How 4 Gay Black Women Fought Back Against Sexual Harassment—and Landed in Jail," NPR, Code Switch, June 30, 2015, https://www.npr.org/sections/codeswitch/2015/06/30/418634390/how-4-gay-black-women-fought-back-against-a-sexual-harasser-and-landed-in-jail.

34 Ibid.

35 Sabrina Ruben Erdely, "The Transgender Crucible," *Rolling Stone,* July 30, 2014, https://www.rollingstone.com/culture/culture-news/the-transgender-crucible-114095.

36 Barnard Center for Research on Women, "Ky Peterson—Survived and Punished," YouTube video, 2:15, August 9, 2017, https://www.youtube.com/watch?v=W7ySbCx_SwE.

37 Jack Herrera, "Why Are Trans Women Dying in ICE Detention?," *Pacific Standard,* June 4, 2019, https://psmag.com/social-justice/why-are-trans-women-dying-in-ice-detention.

38 Carla Green, "Transgender Honduran Woman Dies in ICE Custody" *Daily Beast,* May 31, 2018, https://www.thedailybeast.com/transgender-honduran-woman-dies-in-ice-custody.

39 Alex Caprariello, "Austin Is the Latest City to Launch 'Safe Place' Program to Provide Refuge to LGBTQ+ Community," KXAN News, August 7, 2019, https://www.kxan.com/news/austin-is-the-latest-city-to-launch-safe-place-program-to-provide-refuge-to-lgbtq-community.

40 Fern Renville, "The Shooting Death of John T. Williams," *Indian Country Today,* February 21, 2011, https://indiancountrytoday.com/archive/the-shooting-death-of-john-t-williams?redir=1.

41 "Justice Department Releases Investigative Findings on the Seattle Police Department," US Department of Justice, December 16, 2011, https://www.justice.gov/opa/pr/justice-department-releases-investigative-findings-seattle-police-department.

42 Fran Spielman, "CPD Unveils Rainbow-Bedecked Squad Car in Advance of Sunday's Pride Parade," *Chicago Sun Times,* June 24, 2019, https://chicago.suntimes.com/news/2019/6/24/18715819/pride-parade-chicago-police-vehicle-lgbtq-lightfoot.

43 Eckhouse and MJ, "Police Brutality and Why It Is an LGBTQ Issue."

44 Dean Spade, "Honor Our Stonewall Veterans by Being Your Most Queer Militant Self," *Out,* June 28, 2019, https://www.out.com/pride/2019/6/28/op-ed-honor-our-stonewall-veterans-being-your-queer-militant-self.

45 Emily Badger and Quoctrung Bui, "Cities Grew Safer. Police Budgets Kept Growing," *New York Times,* June 12, 2020, https://www.nytimes.com/interactive/2020/06/12/upshot

/cities-grew-safer-police-budgets -kept-growing.html.

46 Patrick Sisson, Jeff Andrews, and Alex Bazeley, "The Affordable Housing Crisis, Explained," *Curbed,* March 2, 2020, https://archive .curbed.com/2019/5/15/18617763 /affordable-housing-policy-rent-real -estate-apartment.

47 Sheryl Gay Stolberg, "Millions Have Lost Health Insurance in Pandemic-Driven Recession," *New York Times,* July 13, 2020, https://www.nytimes .com/2020/07/13/us/politics /coronavirus-health-insurance -trump.html.

48 Andrew Keshner, "America's Child-Care Crisis: 'The Entire System Is Experiencing Pressure from Every Angle and Something's Got to Blow,'" Market Watch, August 6, 2019, https://www.marketwatch .com/story/most-parents-to-be-are -clueless-about-the-career -and-money-costs-of-raising-a -child-2019-07-17.

49 "Trends in US Corrections," The Sentencing Project, updated May, 2021, https://www.sentencingproject.org /publications/trends-in-u-s-corrections/.

50 "Freedom to Thrive: Reimagining Safety & Security in Our Communities," Center for Popular Democracy, July 4, 2017, https://www.populardemocracy .org/news/publications/freedom-thrive -reimagining-safety-security-our -communities.

51 James Kilgore, "Let's Fight for Freedom from Electronic Monitors and E-Carceration," *Truthout,* September 4, 2019, https://truthout. org/articles/lets-fight-for-freedom -from-electronic-monitors-and -e-carceration.

52 Drug Policy Alliance, *Drug Courts Are Not the Answer: Toward a Health-Centered Approach to Drug Use* (New York: Drug Policy Alliance, 2017).

53 Erin Miles Cloud, "Toward the Abolition of the Foster System," *S&F Online* 15,

no. 3 (2019), https://sfonline.barnard .edu/unraveling-criminalizing-webs -building-police-free-futures/toward -the-abolition-of-the-foster-system.

54 Women's March (@womensmarch), "Why Support M4BL Demand to Defund the Police," June 6, 2020, https://www.instagram.com/p /CBGlwtdnzEL/?igshid=1qvdkigqprcbi.

55 Monica Luhar, "LGBT Behind Bars: Removal from General Population Causing Problems," KCET, November 11, 2014, https://www.kcet.org/agenda /lgbt-behind-bars-removal-from -general-population-causing-problems.

56 Mariame Kaba, "Yes, We Mean Literally Abolish the Police," *New York Times,* June 12, 2020, https://www.nytimes .com/2020/06/12/opinion/sunday /floyd-abolish-defund-police.html.

57 Bryan Stevenson, "Slavery Gave America a Fear of Black People and a Taste for Violent Punishment. Both Still Define Our Criminal-Justice System," *New York Times Magazine,* August 14, 2019, https://www.nytimes.com /interactive/2019/08/14/magazine /prison-industrial-complex-slavery -racism.html.

58 "#8toAbolition," 8toAbolition, 2020, https://www.8toabolition.com.

59 "Building Accountable Communities," Barnard Center for Research on Women, https://bcrw.barnard.edu /building-accountable-communities.

Challenging E-Carceration

1 Matt Masterson, "'We Reached That Limit': Cook County Sheriff Out of Electronic Monitoring Equipment," WTTW News, May 7, 2020, https:// news.wttw.com/2020/05/07/we -reached-limit-cook-county-sheriff -out-electronic-monitoring-equipment.

2 Jenifer B. McKim, "'Electronic Shackles': Use of GPS Monitors Skyrockets in Massachusetts Justice System," GBH, GBH News, August 10, 2020, https://www.wgbh.org/news

/local-news/2020/08/10/electronic-shackles-use-of-gps-monitors-skyrockets-in-massachusetts-justice-system.

3 Public Safety Performance Project, "Use of Electronic Offender-Tracking Devices Expands Sharply," PEW, September 7, 2016, https://www.pewtrusts.org/en/research-and-analysis/issue-briefs/2016/09/use-of-electronic-offender-tracking-devices-expands-sharply.

4 Lucas High, "Boulder's BI Incorporated Has Earned More than Half-Billion Dollars from ICE Contracts," *Daily Camera*, July 13, 2018, https://www.dailycamera.com/2018/07/13/boulders-bi-incorporated-has-earned-more-than-half-billion-dollars-from-ice-contracts/.

5 Johnny Page, Interview with the author, Chicago, Illinois, August 19, 2017.

6 Chrysse Haynes, "Lawsuit Confronts Extortion of Prisoners by Electronic Monitoring Firm," Equal Justice Under Law, August 6, 2018, https://equaljusticeunderlaw.org/thejusticereport/2018/8/6/lawsuit-confronts-extortion-of-prisoners-by-electronic-monitoring-firm.

7 MediaJustice, https://mediajustice.org/news-category/blog/?_sf_s=electronic%20monitoring.

8 "History in the Making: Illinois Bill to Eliminate Use of Electronic Monitoring Passes Vote in the House," MediaJustice, April 30, 2019, https://mediajustice.org/news/history-in-the-making-illinois-bill-to-eliminate-use-of-electronic-monitoring-passes-vote-in-the-house.

9 James Kilgore, "Monica Cosby Satellite Prison," YouTube video, 0:15, November 18, 2020, https://www.youtube.com/watch?v=j3qDx41wceM.

10 James Kilgore, "How to Improve Electronic Monitoring-Jean-Pierre Shackelford," YouTube video, 1:36, June 18, 2017, https://www.youtube.com/watch?v=4TJC69gresQ.

11 Afdhel Aziz, "The Power of Purpose: How Promise Is Using Technology to Solve the Epidemic of Mass Incarceration," *Forbes,* March 18, 2019, https://www.forbes.com/sites/afdhelaziz/2019/03/18/the-power-of-purpose-how-promise-is-using-technology-to-solve-the-epidemic-of-mass-incarceration/?sh=70875c611e19.

The Carceral State

1 Wendy Sawyer and Peter Wagner, "Mass Incarceration: The Whole Pie 2020, " Prison Policy Initiative, March 24, 2020, https://www.prisonpolicy.org/reports/pie2020.html.

2 Issa Kohler-Hausmann, "Misdemeanor Justice: Control without Conviction," *American Journal of Sociology* 119, no. 2 (September 2013), http://users.soc.umn.edu/~uggen/Kohler_Hausmann_.pdf.

3 Laura M. Maruschak and Todd D. Minton, "Correctional Populations in the United States, 2017–2018," Bureau of Justice Statistics, US Department of Justice, August 2020, https://www.bjs.gov/content/pub/pdf/cpus1718.pdf.

4 Naomi Murakawa, "Mass Incarceration Is Dead, Long Live the Carceral State!," *Tulsa Law Review* 55, no. 2 (Winter 2020), https://digitalcommons.law.utulsa.edu/cgi/viewcontent.cgi?article=3196&context=tlr&fbclid=IwAR3450Ixg09OVNMLE07M4nzu1Mc_SPEbJ4hkRMdjA8VD-LrQyf3HtICU6i0.

5 "Incarceration Rate in the United States, 1960–2012," infographic, The Hamilton Project, The Brookings Institution, May 1, 2014, https://www.hamiltonproject.org/charts/incarceration_rate_in_the_united_states_1960-2012.

6   Sawyer and Wagner, "Mass Incarceration."

7   E. Ann Carson, "Prisoners in 2019," Bureau of Justice Statistics, US Department of Justice, October 2020, https://www.bjs.gov/content/pub/pdf/p19.pdf; Maruschak and Minton, "Correctional Populations in the United States, 2017–2018"; Zhen Zeng, "Jail Inmates in 2018," Bureau of Justice Statistics, US Department of Justice, March 2020, https://www.bjs.gov/content/pub/pdf/ji18.pdf; and Danielle Kaeble and Mariel Alper, "Probation and Parole in the United States, 2017–2018," Bureau of Justice Statistics, US Department of Justice, August 2020, https://www.bjs.gov/content/pub/pdf/ppus1718.pdf.

8   Megan T. Stevenson and Sandra G. Mayson, "The Scale of Misdemeanor Justice," *Boston University Law Review* 98 (2018), https://digitalcommons.law.uga.edu/cgi/viewcontent.cgi?article=2210&context=fac_artchop.

9   "Aliens Apprehended by Program and Border Patrol Sector, Investigations Special Agent in Charge (SAC) Jurisdiction, and Area of Responsibility: Fiscal Years 2017 to 2019," 2019 Yearbook of Immigration Statistics, US Department of Homeland Security, updated October 28, 2020, https://www.dhs.gov/immigration-statistics/yearbook/2019/table35.

The Fight to Melt ICE

1   Jeffrey S. Passel, "Further Demographic Information Relating to the DREAM Act," The Urban Institute, October 21, 2003, https://www.nilc.org/wp-content/uploads/2015/11/dream_demographics.pdf.

2   "National Security Entry-Exit Registration System," ACLU, https://www.aclu.org/issues/immigrants-rights/immigrants-rights-and-detention/national-security-entry-exit-registration.

3   "The Cost of Immigration Enforcement and Border Security," American Immigration Council, January 20, 2021, https://www.americanimmigrationcouncil.org/research/the-cost-of-immigration-enforcement-and-border-security.

4   Ibid.

5   "Fatal Encounters with CBP Since 2010," Southern Border Communities Coalition, April 27, 2021, https://www.southernborder.org/deaths_by_border_patrol.

6   Lomi Kriel, "ICE Deported a Woman Who Accused Guards of Sexual Assault While the Feds Were Still Investigating the Incident," *ProPublica,* September 15, 2020, https://www.propublica.org/article/ice-has-deported-a-woman-who-said-guards-sexually-assaulted-her-while-the-investigation-is-ongoing.

7   Tina Vasquez, "Immigrants Allege Mistreatment by Georgia Doctor and Whistleblower," *Prism,* September 17, 2020, https://prismreports.org/2020/09/17/immigrants-allege-mistreatment-by-georgia-doctor-and-whistleblower.

8   Nick Miroff, "Immigrant Detainees Get Poor Medical Care, Face Retaliation for Speaking Out, According to Democrat-Led Report," *Washington Post,* September 21, 2020, https://www.washingtonpost.com/immigration/ice-detainees-health-care-report/2020/09/21/270a64f4-fc1e-11ea-830c-a160b331ca62_story.html.

9   "The Truth About ICE & CBP: A Comprehensive Analysis of the Devastating Human Impact of the Deportation Force by Immigrant Youth & Families Who Know It Best," United We Dream, 2019, https://unitedwedream.org/the-truth-about-ice-and-cbp/.

10 Tom Jawetz and Scott Shuchart, "Language Access Has Life-or-Death Consequences for Migrants," Center for American Progress, February 20, 2019, https://www.americanprogress

.org/issues/immigration
/reports/2019/02/20/466144
/language-access-life-death
-consequences-migrants.

11 Juliana Morgan-Trostle and Kexin
Zheng, "The State of Black Immigrants,
Part II: Black Immigrants in the
Mass Criminalization System,"
Black Alliance for Just Immigration,
NYU School of Law Immigrant Rights
Clinic, September 28, 2020,
https://nyf.issuelab.org/resource
/the-state-of-black-immigrants-part
-ii-black-immigrants-in-the-mass
-criminalization-system.html.

12 Doris Marie Provine, "Institutional
Racism in Enforcing Immigration Law,"
Norteamérica 8 (2013): 31–53.

The Hidden Pandemic

1   "United States COVID-19 Cases and
Deaths by State," Centers for Disease
Control and Prevention, COVID Data
Tracker, https://covid.cdc.gov/covid
-data-tracker/#cases
_casesinlast7days.

2   Mohammed Murad, "Biometrics Will
Enable Many COVID-19 Changes,"
Security, June 23, 2020, https://www
.securitymagazine.com
/articles/92665-biometrics-will
-enable-many-covid-19-changes.

3   "Bureau of Prisons COVID-19 Action
Plan: Phase Five," Federal Bureau of
Prisons, US Department of Justice,
March 31, 2020, https://www.bop.gov
/resources/news/pdfs/20200331
_press_release_action_plan_5.pdf.

4   Eileen Guo, "As Covid-19 Cases in
Prisons Climb, Data on Race Remain
Largely Obscured," *Stat,* August 20,
2020, https://www.statnews
.com/2020/08/20/covid19-prisons
-race-ethnicity-data.

5   "Coronavirus in the U.S.: Latest Map
and Case Count," *New York Times,* April
30, 2021, https://www.nytimes.com

/interactive/2020/us/coronavirus-us
-cases.html#clusters.

6   Laura M. Maruschak, Marcus Berzofsky,
and Jennifer Unangst, "Medical
Problems of State and Federal Prisoners
and Jail Inmates, 2011–12," Bureau of
Justice Statistics, US Department of
Justice, revised October 4, 2016,
https://bjs.ojp.gov/content/pub/pdf
/mpsfpji1112.pdf.

7   Haven Orecchio-Egresitz, "Women
at an ICE Facility in Georgia Accused
a Doctor of Performing Unwanted
Hysterectomies on Them. Lawyers
Say the Problems Run Even Deeper,"
Insider, September 18, 2020,
https://www.insider.com/allegations
-against-irwin-ice-facility-doctor
-mahendra-amin-2020-9.

8   Emily Shugerman, "ICE Hysterectomy
Doctor Wasn't Even a Board-Certified
OB-GYN," *Daily Beast,* September 18,
2020, https://www.thedailybeast.com
/ice-hysterectomy-doctor-wasnt-even
-a-board-certified-ob-gyn.

9   "A New Social Contract," Partners
for Dignity & Rights, https://
dignityandrights.org/initiative/a-new
-social-contract.

The Long Grip of Mass Incarceration

1   Peter K. Enns et al., "What Percentage
of Americans Have Ever Had a Family
Member Incarcerated?: Evidence from
the Family History of Incarceration
Survey (FamHIS)," *Socius* 5 (2019),
https://journals.sagepub.com/doi
/pdf/10.1177/2378023119829332;
and Lauren E. Glaze and Laura M.
Maruschak, "Parents in Prison and
Their Minor Children," Bureau of
Justice Statistics, US Department of
Justice, August 2008, https://www.bjs
.gov/content/pub/pdf/pptmc.pdf.

2   Beatrix Lockwood and Nicole Lewis,
"The Long Journey to Visit a Family
Member in Prison," The Marshall
Project, December 18, 2019,
https://www.themarshallproject

.org/2019/12/18/the-long-journey-to
-visit-a-family-member-in-prison.

3   Bernadette Rabuy and Daniel Kopf,
"Separation by Bars and Miles:
Visitation in State Prisons," Prison
Policy Initiative, October 20, 2015,
https://www.prisonpolicy.org/reports
/prisonvisits.html.

4   Weihua Li and Nicole Lewis, "This
Chart Shows Why the Prison Population
Is So Vulnerable to COVID-19,"
The Marshall Project, March 19, 2020,
https://www.themarshallproject
.org/2020/03/19/this-chart-shows
-why-the-prison-population-is-so
-vulnerable-to-covid-19.

My Father Deserves to Be Free

1   Russell Shoatz, "Who Is Russell Maroon
Shoatz?," Black Liberation Army,
http://rageuniversity.com
/PRISONESCAPE/ABC PRISONERS
/shoatz.pdf.

2   Frank B. Wilderson III, "The Black
Liberation Army & The Paradox
of Political Engagement," in
Postcoloniality-Decoloniality-Black
Critique: Joints and Fissures (Ill Will
Editions, 2014).

3   "Shoatz v. Wetzel," Abolitionist Law
Center, https://abolitionistlawcenter.org.

4   Jerome Coffey, "30 Years after the
Camp Hill Uprising: Repression in
Pennsylvania's Prison System," Workers
World, December 3, 2019, https://www
.workers.org/2019/12/44714.

5   "The History of Gracie Jiu-Jitsu,"
Gracie Jiu-Jitsu Youngsville, https://
gracieyoungsville.com/gracie-history.

6   "Freedom of Information and Privacy
Acts Subject: (COINTELPRO) Black
Extremist 100-448006 Section 1,
Federal Bureau of Investigation,
August 25, 1967, http://blackfreedom
.proquest.com/wp-content/uploads
/2020/09/nation1.pdf.

7   "Former Black Panther Wins
Settlement and Reprieve from Solitary
Confinement," Guardian, July 12, 2016,
https://www.theguardian
.com/news/2016/jul/12/solitary
-confinement-russell-shoatz
-pennsylvania-black-panthers.

8   Gali Katznelson and J. Wesley Boyd,
"Solitary Confinement: Torture, Pure
and Simple," Psychology Today, January
15, 2018, https://www
.psychologytoday.com/us/blog
/almost-addicted/201801/solitary
-confinement-torture-pure-and-simple.

We're All Living in a Future Created by Slavery

1   Kwame Nkrumah, Class Struggle in
Africa, 3rd ed. (New York: International
Publishers, 1973).

2   Malcom X, "Message to the Grass
Roots," speech, Northern Negro Grass
Roots Leadership Conference, Detroit,
November 10, 1963.

3   Achille Mbembe, On the Postcolony
(Oakland: University of California Press,
2001).

4   Marcus Buford Rediker,
The Slave Ship: A Human History
(New York: Viking, 2007).

5   "First Enslaved Africans Arrive in
Jamestown, Setting the Stage for
Slavery in North America," History, last
modified March 16, 2021, https://www
.history.com/this-day-in-history/first
-african-slave-ship-arrives-jamestown
-colony.

6   Allison Keyes, "The 'Clotilda,' the
Last Known Slave Ship to Arrive in
the U.S., Is Found," Smithsonian
Magazine, May 22, 2019, https://www
.smithsonianmag.com/smithsonian
-institution/clotilda-last-known-slave
-ship-arrive-us-found-180972177.

7   "Human Rights and Criminal Justice in
Brazil," Rede Justiça Criminal (Criminal
Justice Network), October 6, 2016,
https://www.upr-info.org/sites
/default/files/document/brazil
/session_27_-_may_2017/js17_upr27
_bra_e_main.pdf.

8 "Report of the Sentencing Project to the United Nations Special Rapporteur on Contemporary Forms of Racism, Racism Discrimination, Xenophobia, and Related Intolerance: Regarding Racial Disparities in the United States Criminal Justice System," The Sentencing Project, March 2018, https://www.sentencingproject .org/publications/un-report-on-racial -disparities/.

9 "Incarcerated Women and Girls" The Sentencing Project, November 24, 2020, https://www.sentencingproject .org/publications/incarcerated-women -and-girls/.

10 Wendy Sawyer, "Youth Confinement: The Whole Pie 2019," Prison Policy Initiative, December 19, 2019, https://www.prisonpolicy.org/reports /youth2019.html.

11 Jaime M. Grant, Lisa A. Motter, and Justin Tanis, "Injustice at Every Turn: A Report of the National Transgender Discrimination Survey," National Center for Transgender Equality and National Gay and Lesbian Task Force, 2011, https://transequality.org/sites/default /files/docs/resources/NTDS_Report.pdf.

12 Ana Ozuna, "Rebellion and Anti-colonial Struggle in Hispaniola: From Indigenous Agitators to African Rebels," *Africology: The Journal of Pan African Studies* 11, no. 7 (May 2018): 77–95.

13 J. Brent Morris, ed., *Yes, Lord, I Know the Road: A Documentary History of African Americans in South Carolina, 1526–2008* (Columbia: University of South Carolina Press, 2017).

14 Sultana Afroz, "The Manifestation of *Tawhid:* The Muslim Heritage of the Maroons in Jamaica," *Caribbean Quarterly* 45, no. 1 (1999): 27–40.

15 Sylviane A. Diouf, *Servants of Allah: African Muslims Enslaved in the Americas* (New York: NYU Press, 2013).

16 C. L. R. James, *The Black Jacobins: Toussaint L'Ouverture and the San Domingo Revolution* (New York: Random House, 1963).

17 Margarita Rosa, "Du'as of the Enslaved: The Malê Slave Rebellion in Bahía, Brazil," Yaqeen Institute for Islamic Research, April 5, 2018, https:// yaqeeninstitute.org/margarita-rosa /duas-of-the-enslaved-the-male-slave -rebellion-in-bahia-brazil.

18 Rebecca Hankins, "Sengbe Pieh (Cinque) and the Amistad Revolt," Poligon, February 27, 2017, https:// www.poligonnational.org/historical -action/sengbe-pieh-cinque-and-the -amistad-revolt.

19 National Jericho Movement, https:// thejerichomovement.com.

20 Fitzhugh Brundage, "American Slavery: A Look Back at the Peculiar Institution," *The Journal of Blacks in Higher Education,* no. 15 (Spring 1997): 118–20.

Fuck Reform

Reforms Are the Master's Tools

1 "Mental Health and Prisons," World Health Organization, https://www.who .int/mental_health/policy/mh_in _prison.pdf.

2 Maya Schenwar and Victoria Law, *Prison by Any Other Name: The Harmful Consequences of Popular Reforms* (New York: New Press, 2020).

3 "2017–18 Annual Report," Florida Department of Corrections, http://www.dc.state.fl.us/pub/annual /1718/FDC_AR2017-18.pdf.

4 Audre Lorde, "The Master's Tools Will Never Dismantle the Master's House" (1984), *Collective Liberation,* https:// collectiveliberation.org/wp-content /uploads/2013/01/Lorde_The _Masters_Tools.pdf.

5 Jodi S. Cohen, "A Teenager Didn't Do Her Online Schoolwork. So a Judge Sent Her to Juvenile Detention," *ProPublica,* July 14, 2020, https://www. propublica.org

/article/a-teenager-didnt-do-her-online-schoolwork-so-a-judge-sent-her-to-juvenile-detention.

6   Harry Belafonte, "Harry Belafonte Reflects on Working Toward Peace," Markkula Center for Applied Ethics, Santa Clara University, https://www.scu.edu/mcae/architects-of-peace/Belafonte/essay.html.

No Justice, No Freedom

1   Udi Ofer, "How the 1994 Crime Bill Fed the Mass Incarceration Crisis," ACLU, June 4, 2019, https://www.aclu.org/blog/smart-justice/mass-incarceration/how-1994-crime-bill-fed-mass-incarceration-crisis.

2   Alan Feuer, "Falsely Imprisoned for 23 Years: Now He's Received $7 Million," *New York Times,* November 19, 2019, https://www.nytimes.com/2019/11/19/nyregion/derrick-hamilton-louis-scarcella-exoneration.html.

3   Sean Piccoli, "A Former Detective Accused of Framing 8 People for Murder Is Confronted in Court," *New York Times,* April 1, 2019, https://www.nytimes.com/2019/04/01/nyregion/nypd-detective-louis-scarcella.html.

4   Scott Simon and Kenneth Thompson, "Brooklyn DS Works to Overturn His 'Legacy of Disgrace'," NPR, October 8, 2014, https://www.npr.org/2014/10/18/357153346/brooklyn-da-works-to-overturn-his-legacy-of-disgrace.

5   "NYPD 12," The Gathering for Justice, https://www.gatheringforjustice.org/nypd12.

6   Andrea Fenster, "New Data: Solitary Confinement Increases Risk of Premature Death after Release," Prison Policy Initiative, October 13, 2020, https://www.prisonpolicy.org/blog/2020/10/13/solitary_mortality_risk/.

7   J. C. Pan, "After Defunding the Police, Nationalize Their Benefits," *The New Republic,* June 5, 2020, https://newrepublic.com/article/158038

/defunding-police-nationalize-benefits.

8   Frances Robles and N. R. Kleinfield, "Review of 50 Brooklyn Murder Cases Ordered," *New York Times,* May 11, 2013, https://www.nytimes.com/2013/05/12/nyregion/doubts-about-detective-haunt-50-murder-cases.html.

Police Reform as Counterinsurgency

1   #8CantWait, https://8cantwait.org/.

2   DeRay McKesson et al., "Police Use of Force Policy Analysis," Campaign Zero, September 20, 2016, https://static1.squarespace.com/static/56996151cbced68b170389f4/t/57e1b5cc2994ca4ac1d97700/1474409936835/Police+Use+of+Force+Report.pdf

3   Olivia Murray, "Why 8 Won't Work: The Failings of The 8 Can't Wait Campaign and the Obstacle Police Reform Efforts Pose to Police Abolition," *Harvard Civil Rights–Civil Liberties Law Review,* June 17, 2020, https://harvardcrcl.org/why-8-wont-work/.

4   McKesson et al., "Police Use of Force."

5   William Earl, "Oprah, Ariana Grande and More Champion 8 Can't Wait, Project to Reduce Police Violence," *Variety,* June 4, 2020, https://variety.com/2020/biz/news/8-cant-wait-reduce-police-violence-oprah-ariana-grande-1234625314/.

6   Dylan Rodríguez, "The Political Logic of the Non-Profit Industrial Complex" (2009), *S&F Online* 13, no. 2 (2016), http://sfonline.barnard.edu/navigating-neoliberalism-in-the-academy-nonprofits-and-beyond/dylan-rodriguez-the-political-logic-of-the-non-profit-industrial-complex/.

7   Mariame Kaba, "Yes, We Mean Literally Abolish the Police," *New York Times,* June 12, 2020, https://www.nytimes.com/2020/06/12/opinion/sunday/floyd-abolish-defund-police.html.

8   Murray, "Why 8 Won't Work."

9   Survived & Punished,
     https://survivedandpunished.org/.

10   "Black Liberation and the Abolition of
     the Prison Industrial Complex:
     An Interview with Rachel Herzing,"
     Propter Nos (True Leap Press) 1, no. 1
     (Winter 2019) https://trueleappress
     .com/2016/08/30/black-liberation
     -and-the-abolition-of-the-prison
     -industrial-complex-an-interview-with
     -rachel-herzing/.

11   Alisa Bierria, "Racial Conflation:
     Rethinking Agency, Black Action, and
     Criminal Intent," *Journal of Social
     Philosophy,* January 2020, https://
     www.researchgate.net/publication
     /338671759_Racial_Conflation
     _Rethinking_Agency_Black_Action
     _and_Criminal_Intent.

12   Sarah Haley, *No Mercy Here: Gender,
     Punishment, and the Making of Jim Crow
     Modernity* (Durham: University of North
     Carolina Press, 2016).

13   Beth E. Richie, *Arrested Justice: Black
     Women, Violence, and America's Prison
     Nation* (New York: NYU Press, 2012).

14   Ruth Wilson Gilmore, *Change
     Everything: Racial Capitalism and the
     Case for Abolition* (Chicago: Haymarket
     Books, 2021).

15   H. L. T. Quan and Tiffany Willoughby-
     Herard, "Black Ontology, Radical
     Scholarship and Freedom, African
     Identities," *African Identities* 11,
     no. 2 (2013) https://www.tandfonline
     .com/doi/full/10.1080/14725843
     .2013.797281.

16   "Counterinsurgency," Field Manual
     No. 3-24, US Department of the Army,
     December 15, 2006, https://www.hsdl
     .org/?abstract&did=468442.

17   "If You're New to Abolition: Study
     Group Guide Week Four, Reformist
     Reforms vs. Abolition Steps," *Abolition,*
     June 25, 2020, https://abolitionjournal
     .org/studyguide/#weekfour.

18   Tiffany L. Green and Nao Hagiwara,
     "The Problem with Implicit Bias

Training," *Scientific American,*
     August 28, 2020, https://www
     .scientificamerican.com/article/the
     -problem-with-implicit-bias-training/.

19   Sylvia Wynter, *On Being Human
     as Praxis* (Durham, NC:
     Duke University Press, 2015).

20   Sylvia Wynter, "Unsettling the
     Coloniality of Being/Power/Truth/
     Freedom: Towards the Human, After
     Man, Its Overrepresentation—An
     Argument," *CR: The New Centennial
     Review* (Michigan State University
     Press) 3, no. 3 (Fall 2003): 257–337,
     https://law.unimelb.edu.au/__data
     /assets/pdf_file/0010/2432989
     /Wynter-2003-Unsettling-the
     -Coloniality-of-Being.pdf.

21   David E. Stannard, *American Holocaust:
     The Conquest of the New World*
     (Oxford: Oxford University Press, 1993).

22   Scott W. Murray ed., *Understanding
     Atrocities: Remembering,
     Representing and Teaching Genocide*
     (Calgary: University of Calgary Press,
     2017), https://prism.ucalgary.ca
     /bitstream/handle/1880/51806
     /9781552388860_chapter01
     .pdf;jsessionid=63ED09EA
     01EE210781BECACCB9CCAE17?
     sequence=4.

23   Glen Sean Coulthard, *Red Skin, White
     Masks: Rejecting the Colonial Politics of
     Recognition* (Minneapolis: University of
     Minnesota Press, 2014).

24   Dan Berger et al., "What Abolitionists
     Do," *Jacobin,* August 24, 2017, https://
     www.jacobinmag.com/2017/08/prison
     -abolition-reform-mass-incarceration.

25   #8toAbolition, https://
     www.8toabolition.com/.

26   George L. Jackson, *Blood in My Eye*
     (Baltimore, MD: Black Classic
     Press, 1996).

27   Dylan Rodríguez, "Abolition as Praxis
     of Human Being: A Foreword,"
     Harvard Law Review 132, no. 6 (April
     10, 2019), https://harvardlawreview.

org/2019/04/abolition-as-praxis-of
-human-being-a-foreword/.

28 Gaye Theresa Johnson and Alex Lubin,
Futures of Black Radicalism
(New York: Verso, 2017).

The Extent of Carceral Control

1 E. Ann Carson, "Prisoners in 2019,"
Bureau of Justice Statistics, US
Department of Justice, October 2020,
https://www.bjs.gov/content/pub/pdf
/p19.pdf; Laura M. Maruschak and Todd
D. Minton, "Correctional Populations in
the United States, 2017–2018," Bureau
of Justice Statistics, US Department of
Justice, August 2020, https://www.bjs
.gov/content/pub/pdf/cpus1718.pdf;
Zhen Zeng, "Jail Inmates in 2018,"
Bureau of Justice Statistics,
US Department of Justice, March 2020,
https://www.bjs.gov/content/pub/pdf
/ji18.pdf; Danielle Kaeble and Mariel
Alper, "Probation and Parole in the
United States, 2017–2018," Bureau of
Justice Statistics, US Department of
Justice, August 2020, https://www.bjs
.gov/content/pub/pdf/ppus1718.pdf.

2 Kaeble and Alper, "Probation and Parole
in the United States, 2017–2018."

3 "QuickFacts," US Census Bureau,
https://www.census.gov/quickfacts
/fact/table/US/PST045219.

4 "In Trouble: How the Promise of
Diversion Clashes with the
Reality of Poverty, Addiction, and
Structural Racism in Alabama's Justice
System," Fines & Fees Justice
Center, February 6, 2020,
https://finesandfeesjusticecenter.org
/articles/in-trouble-how-the-promise
-of-diversion-clashes-with-the-reality
-of-poverty-addiction-and-structural
-racism-in-alabamas-justice-system/.

Three Traps of Police Reform

1 Garrett Felber, "The Struggle to Abolish
the Police Is Not New," *Boston Review,*
June 9, 2020, http://bostonreview.
net/race/garrett-felber-struggle-
abolish-police-not-new; Regina
Kunzel, "Lessons in Being Gay: Queer
Encounters in Gay and Lesbian Prison
Activism," *Radical History Review*
(Winter 2008): 11–37.

2 Malkia Devich-Cyril, "Defund Facial
Recognition," *The Atlantic,* July 5,
2020, https://www.theatlantic.com
/technology/archive/2020/07/defund
-facial-recognition/613771/?gclid=EAI
aIQobChMIh4u58tbA7AIVjf7jBx1B3ge
cEAAYASAAEgJd1_D_BwE.

3 David Correia and Tyler Wall, *Police:
A Field Guide* (New York: Verso, 2018).

4 Elizabeth Hinton, *From the War
on Poverty to the War on Crime*
(Cambridge, MA: Harvard, 2017).

5 Max Felker-Kantor, *Policing Los Angeles*
(Chapel Hill: UNC Press, 2018).

6 Felker-Kantor, *Policing Los Angeles,* 43.

7 "The Time Has Come to Defund the
Police," M4BL, https://m4bl.org/defund
-the-police/.

8 Critical Resistance,
http://criticalresistance.org/.

9 Alice Speri, "As Calls to Defund the
Police Grow Louder, Joe Biden Wants
to Give Them More Money," *The
Intercept,* podcast transcript, June 11,
2020, https://theintercept
.com/2020/06/11/defund-the-police
-joe-biden-cops/.

10 Devon W. Carbado, "Predatory
Policing," *UMKC Law Review* 548
(July 25, 2017), https://papers.ssrn
.com/sol3/papers.cfm?abstract
_id=3008713.

11 Micol Seigel, *Violence Work:
State Power and the Limits of Police*
(Durham, NC: Duke University
Press, 2018).

12 Alice Kim et al., *The Long Term*
(Chicago: Haymarket Books, 2018).

13 Andrea J. Ritchie, *Invisible No More*
(Boston: Beacon, 2017).

14 Kenton Card, "Geographies of Racial

Capitalism with Ruth Wilson Gilmore," *Antipode,* https://antipodeonline.org /geographies-of-racial-capitalism/.

15 Reshaad Shirazi, "It's High Time to Dump the High-Crime Area Factor," *Berkeley Journal of Criminal Law* 21, no.2 (Fall 2016), 76–110, https://www. bjcl.org/articles?v=21.

16 Paul Butler, *Chokehold: Policing Black Men* (New York: New Press, 2018).

17 Kim Moody, "The Roots of Racist Policing," *Spectre Journal,* July 2020, https://spectrejournal.com/the-roots -of-racist-policing/.

18 Richard A. Leo, *Police Interrogation and American Justice* (Cambridge, MA: Harvard University Press, 2009).

19 "Investigation of the Chicago Police Department," US Department of Justice, January 13, 2017, https://www. justice.gov/opa/file/925846/download.

20 Ruth Wilson Gilmore, "The Worrying State of the Anti-Prison Movement," *Social Justice* (February 2015) http:// www.socialjusticejournal.org/the -worrying-state-of-the-anti-prison -movement/.

21 Kimberlé Crenshaw and Andrea Ritchie, *Say Her Name* (New York: African American Policy Forum, 2015), 28.

22 Correia and Wall, 64; Ian Fisher, "Kelly Bans Choke Holds by Officers," *New York Times,* November 24, 1993, https://www.nytimes.com/1993/11/24 /nyregion/kelly-bans-choke-holds-by -officers.html.

23 Correia and Wall, *Police,* 64.

24 Charles Wallace, "LAPD Will Drop One Choke Hold: Bar-Arm Control Grip Cuts Off Air Supply to Lungs," *Los Angeles Times,* May 7, 1982.

25 Correia and Wall, *Police,* 64.

26 Richard Winton, "How the Rodney King Beating 'Banished' the Baton from the LAPD," *Los Angeles Times,* March 3, 2016, https://www.latimes.com /local/california/la-me-rodney

-king-baton-20160303-story.html.

27 Associated Press, "Los Angeles Police Reconsider Using Choke Hold," *New York Times,* September 3, 1991, https:// www.nytimes.com/1991/09/03/us /los-angeles-police-reconsider-using -choke-hold.html.

28 Winton, "How the Rodney King Beating 'Banished' the Baton."

29 Kimberlé Crenshaw, "'You Promised You Wouldn't Kill Me': Atatiana Jefferson, Natasha McKenna, and the Other Black Women We Forget," *New York Times,* October 28, 2019, https://www .nytimes.com/2019/10/28/opinion /police-black-women-racism.html.

30 Scott Sweetow and George Belsky, "A Letter to the American Public: Are Police Reform Proposals Real Solutions or Chimera?," *Police1,* July 27, 2020, https://www.policeone.com /police-reform/articles/a-letter-to -the-american-public-are-police -reform-proposals-real-solutions-or -chimera-1HukkX6Z90Fm6vK8/.

31 Mariame Kaba, *We Do This 'Til We Free Us* (Chicago: Haymarket Books, 2021).

Putting a Black Face on Police Agendas

1 Madison J. Gray, "Right Wing Group Defends Pro-Police Billboards Where BLM Demonstrations Against Police Brutality Occurred," BET, September 18, 2020, https://www.bet.com/news /national/2020/09/18/billboards -police-right-wing-heritage-new-york -atlanta-dallas.html.

2 Richard Pérez-Peña, "Six Baltimore Officers Indicted in Death of Freddie Gray," *New York Times,* May 21, 2015, https://www.nytimes.com/2015/05 /22/us/six-baltimore-officers-indicted -in-death-of-freddie-gray.html.

3 The Tribe CLT, "#KeepItDown Confederate Flag Takedown," YouTube video, 3:02, June 27, 2015, https://youtu.be/gr-mt1P94cQ.

4 Nicholas Casey, "'The Cop Was the Hero in One Viral Video. Another Told a Different Story," *New York Times,* August 15, 2020, https://www .nytimes.com/2020/08/15/us/politics /basketball-cop-gainesville-police.html.

5 Paul Butler, "Why the Fraternal Order of Police Must Go," The Marshall Project, October 10, 2017, https://www .themarshallproject.org/2017/10/11 /why-the-fraternal-order-of-police -must-go.

6 Thomas Mullen, "Black in Blue: Atlanta's First African American Police Officers Were Vanguards of the Civil Rights Movement," *Atlanta Magazine,* September 21, 2016, https://www .atlantamagazine.com/great-reads /black-blue-atlantas-first-african -american-police-officers-vanguards -civil-rights-movement/.

7 Olivia B. Waxman, "How the U.S. Got Its Police Force," *Time,* May 18, 2017, https://time.com/4779112/police -history-origins/.

8 Elizabeth King, "Why a History of the Police's Relationship to the Working Class Is Being Re-Released Now," *Pacific Standard,* November 10, 2017, https://psmag.com/social-justice/ policing-a-class-society.

9 Adam Malka, "Why Law Enforcement Has a Blind Spot for White Male Violence," *Washington Post,* August 12, 2019, https://www.washingtonpost .com/outlook/2019/08/12/why-law -enforcement-has-blind-spot-white -male-violence/.

10 Dylan Matthews, "How Police Unions Became So Powerful—and How They Can Be Tamed," *Vox,* June 24, 2020, https://www.vox.com/policy-and -politics/21290981/police-union -contracts-minneapolis-reform.

11 "Bailiffs, Correctional Officers, & Jailers," Data USA, https://datausa.io /profile/soc/bailiffs-correctional -officers-jailers.

12 Katie Shepherd, "'Putting Dozens of Lives at Risk over $2.75': NYPD Slammed for Pulling Guns on Fare-Looping Teen," *Washington Post,* October 28, 2019, https://www.washingtonpost.com /nation/2019/10/28/nypd-video-guns -pointed-subway-train-unarmed -fare-hopper/.

13 "Black Codes and Pig Laws," *Slavery by Another Name,* PBS, https://www.pbs.org/tpt/slavery-by -another-name/themes/black-codes/.

The New Jim Code

1 Saray Brayne, "Big Data Surveillance: The Case of Policing," *American Sociological Review* 82, no. 5, August 29, 2017, https://doi.org /10.1177/0003122417725865.

2 Julia Angwin et al., "Machine Bias," *Pro Publica,* May 23, 2016, https://www.propublica.org/article /machine-bias-risk-assessments-in -criminal-sentencing.

3 Michelle Alexander, "The Newest Jim Crow," *New York Times,* November 8, 2018, https://www.nytimes .com/2018/11/08/opinion/sunday /criminal-justice-reforms-race -technology.html.

4 Andrea Armstrong, "A Letter to Jay-Z: Don't Keep This Promise," *The Appeal,* April 10, 2018, https://theappeal .org/a-letter-to-jay-z-dont-keep-this -promise-93bee11e20bd/.

5 John Burnett, "As Asylum Seekers Swap Prison Beds for Ankle Bracelets, Same Firm Profits," NPR, November 13, 2015, https://www.npr.org/2015/11/13 /455790454/as-asylum-seekers -swap-prison-beds-for-ankle -bracelets-same-firm-profits.

6 Critical Resistance, http://criticalresistance.org/.

7 Jake Bittle, "The Fight For Fair-Chance Housing Ordinances," *Curbed,* June 12, 2019, https://archive.curbed

.com/2019/6/12/18661475/housing
-renting-felony-convictions.

8 Brian Clifton et al., "White Collar
Crime Risk Zones," The New Inquiry,
https://whitecollar.thenewinquiry.com/.

9 Brian Clifton et al., "Predicting
Financial Crime: Augmenting the
Predictive Policing Arsenal," *The New
Inquiry,* vol. 59, *Abolish,* March 2017,
https://arxiv.org/ftp/arxiv/papers
/1704/1704.07826.pdf.

10 Tristan Greene, "Stop Calling It Bias.
AI Is Racist," TNW News, June 24,
2020, https://thenextweb.com/news
/stop-calling-it-bias-ai-is-racist.

11 Ruha Benjamin, *Race After Technology:
Abolitionist Tools for the New Jim Code*
(Boston: Polity Press, 2019).

Abolition Now

Change from the Roots

1 Dustin Guastella, "To End Police
Violence Fund Public Goods and Raise
Wages," *Non Site,* July 9, 2020,
https://nonsite.org/policing
-symposium/.

2 "Vision for Black Lives," M4BL, https://
m4bl.org/policy-platforms/.

3 Arthur J. Reynolds et al., "Long-
term Effects of an Early Childhood
Intervention on Educational
Achievement and Juvenile Arrest: A 15-
Year Follow-Up of Low-income Children
in Public Schools," *JAMA,* May 9, 2001,
doi:10.1001/jama.285.18.2339.

4 Jann Ingmire, "Chicago Summer Jobs
Program for High School Students
Dramatically Reduces Youth Violence,"
UChicago News, December 4, 2014,
https://news.uchicago.edu/story
/chicago-summer-jobs-program-high
-school-students-dramatically
-reduces-youth-violence.

5 Mike Maciag, "Where Police Don't
Mirror Communities and Why It
Matters," *Governing,* August 19, 2015,
https://www.governing.com/archive
/gov-police-department-diversity.html.

6 Bree Newsome Bass, "Black Cops Don't
Make Policing Any Less Anti-Black,"
Level, Medium, October 22, 2020,
https://level.medium.com/black-cops
-dont-make-policing-any-less-anti
-black-4baf78c2ab29.

7 Jessica Lee, "How Co-Responder
Teams Are Changing the Way
Minneapolis Police Deal with Mental
Health Calls," *Minneapolis Post,*
January 2, 2019, https://www
.minnpost.com/metro/2019/01/how
-co-responder-teams-are-changing
-the-way-minneapolis-police-deal
-with-mental-health-calls/.

8 Libor Jany, "Minneapolis Police
Reveal Changes to Use-Of-Force
Policy," *Star Tribune,* August 9,
2016, https://www.startribune.com/
minneapolis
-police-reveal-changes-to-use-of-force
-policy/389509371/.

9 Libor Jany, "Minneapolis Police
Teaching Officers to Be More
Compassionate," *Star Tribune,*
November 23, 2017, https://www
.startribune.com/minneapolis-police
-teaching-officers-to-be-more
-compassionate/459641903/.

10 Black Organizing Project,
http://blackorganizingproject.org/.

11 "Community Rights Campaign Releases
'Black, Brown, and Over-Policed in
L.A. Schools,'" Fight for the Soul of the
Cities, October 30, 2014,
https://fightforthesoulofthecities.com
/community-rights-campaign
-releasees-new-report-black-brown
-and-over-policed-in-l-a-schools/.

12 Hands Up United,
http://www.handsupunited.org/.

13 A World Without Police,
"A World Without Police," 2016,
http://aworldwithoutpolice.org
/wp-content/uploads/2016/09
/AWorldWithoutPolice_Color.pdf.

14 A World Without Police, https://aworldwithoutpolice.org/.

15 Christopher F. Petrella, "Resurrecting the Radical Pedagogy of the Black Panther Party," *Black Perspectives,* July 3, 2017, https://www.aaihs.org/resurrecting-the-radical-pedagogy-of-the-black-panther-party/.

16 Black Panther Party, "Revolutionary Peoples' Constitutional Convention September 1970, Philadelphia Workshop Reports," *About Place Journal,* https://aboutplacejournal.org/wp-content/uploads/2014/02/RPCC-WORKSHOP-REPORTS1.pdf.

17 Matthew Fleischer, "50 Years Ago Raided Teams Have Been Targeting Communities Ever Since," *Los Angeles Times,* December 8, 2019, https://www.latimes.com/opinion/story/2019-12-08/50-years-swat-black-panthers-militarized-policinglos-angeles.

18 Branko Marcetic, "The FBI's Secret War," *Jacobin,* August 31, 2016, https://www.jacobinmag.com/2016/08/fbi-cointelpro-new-left-panthers-muslim-surveillance.

19 "The Assassination of Fred Hampton: 47 Years Later," People's Law Office, December 4, 2016, https://peopleslawoffice.com/the-assassination-of-fred-hampton-47-years-later/.

20 #SayHerName, https://www.aapf.org/sayhername.

21 Black Women's Blueprint, "Invisible Betrayal: Police Violence and the Rapes of Black Women in the United States," UN Treaty Body Database, September 22, 2014, https://tbinternet.ohchr.org/Treaties/CAT/Shared%20Documents/USA/INT_CAT_CSS_USA_18555_E.pdf.

22 "Daniel Holtzclaw," The Marshall Project, May 4, 2020, https://www.themarshallproject.org/records/2268-daniel-holtzclaw.

23 Victoria Law, "Against Carceral Feminism," *Jacobin,* October 17, 2014, https://jacobinmag.com/2014/10/against-carceral-feminism/.

24 Angela Davis, "Abolition Feminism: Theories and Practices," MR online, January 15, 2018, https://mronline.org/2018/01/15/abolition-feminism-theories-practices/.

25 "Statement on Gender Violence and the Prison Industrial Complex," INCITE!, 2001, https://incite-national.org/incite-critical-resistance-statement/.

26 Nicole A. Burrowes, "Building the World We Want to See: A Herstory of Sista II Sista and the Struggle Against State and Interpersonal Violence," *Souls,* 20, no. 4 (2018), https://doi.org/10.1080/10999949.2018.1607059.

27 "Law Enforcement Violence Against Women of Color & Trans People of Color," INCITE! 2008, https://incite-national.org/wp-content/uploads/2018/08/TOOLKIT-FINAL.pdf.

Casting Off the Shadows of Slavery

1 "Full Text: Abraham Lincoln's Cooper Union Address," *New York Times,* May 2, 2004, https://www.nytimes.com/2004/05/02/nyregion/full-text-abraham-lincolns-cooper-union-address.html.

2 Frederick Douglass, *Frederick Douglass: Selected Speeches and Writing* (Chicago: Chicago Review Press, 2000).

3 Loic Wacquant, "Class, Race and Hyperincarceration in Revanchist America," *Socialism and Democracy,* 2014, 35–56, https://doi.org/10.1080/08854300.2014.954926.

Survivors at the Forefront of the Abolitionist Movement

1 "Statement on Gender Violence and the Prison Industrial Complex," INCITE!, 2001, https://incite-national.org/incite-critical-resistance-statement/.

2   Critical Resistance, http://criticalresistance.org/.

3   INCITE!, https://incite-national.org/.

4   Haunani-Kay Trask, "Hawaiians Remember," *American Experience,* https://www.pbs.org/wgbh /americanexperience/features/island -murder-hawaiians-remember -haunani-kay-trask/.

5   "Statement on Gender Violence," INCITE!

6   Mariame Kaba, "Being MK," http://mariamekaba.com/.

7   "Racial Justice and Abolition Democracy Curriculum Project Established at Columbia University," Giving to Columbia, Columbia University, 2021, https://giving.columbia.edu/racial -justice-and-abolition-democracy -curriculum-project-established -columbia-university.

8   Reframe Health and Justice Consulting, https://www.reframehealthandjustice .com/.

9   Erin Fitzgerald et al., "Meaningful Work: Transgender Experience in the Sex Trade," National Center for Transgender Equality, December 2015, https:// transequality.org/sites/default/files /Meaningful%20Work-Full%20Report _FINAL_3.pdf.

10 "Policing Sex Work," INCITE!, https://incite-national.org/policing -sex-work/.

11 "The Impact of Criminalisation on Sex Workers' Vulnerability to HIV and Violence," NSWP, Global Network of Sex Work Projects, https://www.nswp .org/sites/nswp.org/files/impact_of _criminalisation_pb_prf01.pdf.

12 Jasmine Sankofa, "From Margin to Center: Sex Work Decriminalization Is a Racial Justice Issue," *Amnesty International,* December 12, 2016, https://www.amnestyusa.org /from-margin-to-center-sex-work -decriminalization-is-a-racial -justice-issue/.

13 DecrimNY, https://www.decrimny.org/.

14 Natalie Shure, "Sex Workers' Rights Are Workers' Rights," *Jacobin,* May 1, 2019, https://www.jacobinmag .com/2019/05/sex-workers-rights -are-workers-rights.

15 Julia Naftulin, "Strippers, Dominatrixes, and Sex Workers Are Being Left Out of a Major US Coronavirus Relief Package," *Insider,* April 2, 2020, https://www.insider.com/sex-workers -are-ineligible-for-us-coronavirus-relief -package-2020-4.

16 Victoria Law, "Woman Faces Deportation to a Country She's Never Been To," *Vice,* August 10, 2017, https:// www.vice.com/en/article/599z95 /after-abuse-and-prison-a-woman -faces-deportation-to-a-country-shes -never-been-to.

17 "Ny Nourn Granted Pardon!!!," Survived & Punished, June 27, 2020, https://survivedandpunished .org/2020/06/27/breaking-ny-nourn -granted-pardon/.

18 "Dreams Detained, in Her Words," National Asian Pacific American Women's Forum and Southeast Asia Resource Action Center, September 25, 2018, https://www.searac.org /wp-content/uploads/2018/09 /dreams_detained_in_her_words _report-2.pdf.

19 #ReleaseMN8, https://releasemn8.org/.

20 "Fact Sheet on Domestic Violence and the Criminalization of Survival," Free Marissa Now, https://www.freemarissanow.org /fact-sheet-on-domestic-violence --criminalization.html.

21 "Police Violence and Domestic Violence," INCITE!, 2018, https://incite-national.org/wp -content/uploads/2018/08/toolkitrev -domesticviolence.pdf.

22 "Addressing Harm, Accountability and Healing," Critical Resistance, 2021, http://criticalresistance.org/resources

/addressing-harm-accountability-and -healing/.

Who Is Being Healed?

1 Stephanie Flanders, "Man Found Guilty in Killings at Muffin Shop in Manhattan," *New York Times,* July 7, 2001, https://www.nytimes.com/2001/07/07/nyregion/man -found-guilty-in-killings-at-muffin -shop-in-manhattan.html.

2 *How to Get Away with Murder,* ABC, https://abc.com/shows/how-to-get -away-with-murder.

3 "CR Structure & Background," Critical Resistance, http://criticalresistance.org/.

4 Rex A. Skidmore, "Penological Pioneering in the Walnut Street Jail, 1789–1799," *Journal of Criminal Law and Criminology,* 39, no. 2 (1948), https://scholarlycommons.law .northwestern.edu/cgi/viewcontent .cgi?referer=https://www.google.com /&httpsredir=1&article=3569& context=jclc.

5 Gary Potter, "The History of Policing in the United States, Part 1," Eastern Kentucky University Police Studies Online, June 25, 2013, https://plsonline .eku.edu/insidelook/history-policing -united-states-part-1.

6 David M. Shapiro, "Solitary Confinement in the Young Republic," *Harvard Law Review* 133, no. 2 (December 20, 2019), https://harvardlawreview.org/wp -content/uploads/2019/12/542-598 _Online.pdf.

7 Kevin D. Williamson, "Appalachia: The Big White Ghetto," *The Week,* January 25, 2014, https://theweek .com/articles/452321/appalachia-big -white-ghetto.

8 Francis X. Clines, "Ex-Inmates Urge Return to Areas of Crime to Help," *New York Times,* December 3, 1992, https:// www.nytimes.com/1992/12/23 /nyregion/ex-inmates-urge-return-to -areas-of-crime-to-help.html.

9 "Prison Prisoner Abuse Books," Goodreads, https://www.goodreads .com/shelf/show/prison-prisoner-abuse.

10 "Investigation of Alabama's State Prisons for Men," US Department of Justice, April 2, 2019, https://www.justice.gov/crt/case -document/file/1149971/download.

11 Eloy Bleifuss Prados, "Green Haven Reunion Honors Mamiya's Accomplishments," *The Miscellany News,* April 9, 2014, https:// miscellanynews.org/2014/04/09 /features/green-haven-reunion -honors-mamiyas-accomplishments/.

12 Nadia Lopez, "Why Open a School? To Close a Prison," TED Talks Live video, 7:01, November 2015, https://www.ted.com/talks/nadia_lopez _why_open_a_school_to_close_a_prison /up-next.

13 Tom Barnes, "The Lyrics from Tupac's 'Changes' are Even More Haunting 20 Years after His Death," *Mic,* June 16, 2016, https://www.mic.com /articles/146351/these-lyrics-from -tupac-s-changes-are-even-more -haunting-20-years-after-his-death.

14 Laura Santhanam, "There's a New Global Ranking of Gun Deaths. Here's Where the U.S. Stands," PBS, August 28, 2018, https://www.pbs.org /newshour/health/theres-a-new-global -ranking-of-gun-deaths-heres-where -the-u-s-stands.

Ending the War on Black Women

1 David Williams, "Oprah's O Magazine Puts Up Billboards All Over Louisville Demanding Action in the Breonna Taylor Case," CNN, August 19, 2020, https://www.cnn.com/2020/08/07/us /oprah-breonna-taylor-billboards-trnd /index.html.

2 Skyla Langley, "Popular Magazines Pay Tribute to Breonna Taylor," The Student Printz, September 14, 2020, https://www.studentprintz.com/

popular-magazines-pay-tribute-to-breonna-taylor/.

3   Leah Asmelash, "WNBA Players Dedicate Season to Breonna Taylor and Say Her Name Campaign," CNN, July 25, 2020, https://www.cnn.com/2020/07/25/us/wnba-season-start-breonna-taylor-cnn/index.html.

4   Andrea J. Ritchie, *Invisible No More: Police Violence Against Black Women and Women of Color* (Boston: Beacon Press, 2017).

5   Gerry Everding, "Police Kill Unarmed Blacks More Often, Especially When They Are Women, Study Finds," *The Source* (Washington University in St. Louis), February 9, 2021, https://source.wustl.edu/2018/02/police-kill-unarmed-blacks-often-especially-women-study-finds/.

6   "Policing Women: Race and Gender Disparities in Police Stops, Searches, and Use of Force," Prison Policy Initiative, May 14, 2019, https://www.prisonpolicy.org/blog/2019/05/14/policingwomen/.

7   "What Is Driving Mass Criminalization of Women and LGBTQ People?," Interrupting Criminalization, 2019, http://bcrw.barnard.edu/wp-content/uploads/2019/12/InterruptingCriminalization_FINAL.pdf.

8   Ritchie, *Invisible No More*.

9   "End the War on Black Women," M4BL, June 24, 2020, https://m4bl.org/policy-platforms/end-the-war-black-women/.

10 Ritchie, *Invisible No More*. Also, see Shrouded in Silence, Interrupting Criminalization, https://static1.squarespace.com/static/5ee39ec764dbd7179cf1243c/t/609b0bb8fc3271012c4a93c5/1620773852750/Shrouded+in+Silence.pdf.

11 Mariame Kaba and Andrea J. Ritchie, "We Want More Justice for Breonna Taylor Than the System That Killed Her

Can Deliver," *Essence,* July 16, 2020, https://www.essence.com/feature/breonna-taylor-justice-abolition/.

12 Rachel Herzing and Isaac Ontiveros, "Responding to Police Killing: Questions and Challenges for Abolitionists," Centre for Crime and Justice Studies, November 30, 2010, https://www.crimeandjustice.org.uk/sites/crimeandjustice.org.uk/files/09627251.2010.525940.pdf.

13 Kay Jones and Leah Asmelash, "Louisiana Supreme Court Upholds Black Man's Life Sentence for Stealing Hedge Clippers More than 20 Years Ago," CNN, August 6, 2020, https://www.cnn.com/2020/08/06/us/louisiana-supreme-court-trnd/index.html.

14 Sam Levine, "A Black Woman Faces Prison for a Voting Mistake. Prosecutors Just Doubled the Charges," *Guardian,* July 21, 2020, https://www.theguardian.com/us-news/2020/jul/21/voting-arrest-racist-law-north-carolina-lanisha-brachter.

15 survivedandpunished.org.

16 Andrea J. Ritchie, "The Demand Is Still Defund the Police, Fund the People, Defend Black Lives," Interrupting Criminalization, January 2021, https://www.interruptingcriminalization.com/defundpolice-update.

17 Mariame Kaba, "What's Next? Safer and More Just Communties Without Policing," Interrupting Criminalization, September 2020, https://static1.squarespace.com/static/5ee39ec764dbd7179cf1243c/t/5f85c390635cac03f35913d5/1602601934251/What%27s+Next+Report+.pdf. See also millionexperiments.com and transformharm.org.

18 Simone John, "Elegy for Dead Black Women #1," *S&F Online* 15, no. 3 (2019), http://sfonline.barnard.edu/unraveling-criminalizing-webs-building-police-free-futures/elegy-for-dead-black-women-1/. See also *Invisible No*

More and invisiblenomorebook.com /database.

19 Amina Elahi, "LMPD Releases Nearly Blank Report from the Night of Breonna Taylor's Killing," NPR, June 11, 2020, https://www.npr.org/2020/06 /11/875311065/lmpd-releases-nearly -blank-report-from-the-night-of -breonna-taylors-killing.

20 Richard A. Oppel, Derrick Bryson Taylor, and Nicholas Bogel-Burroughs, "What to Know About Breonna Taylor's Death," *New York Times,* May 30, 2020, https://www.nytimes.com/article /breonna-taylor-police.html.

21 Invest/Divest Louisville, April 27, 2021, https://www.investdivest.org /#carouselPoliceBudget.

22 Eva Lewis, "Remembering Breonna Taylor's Greatness," *Teen Vogue,* June 5, 2020, https://www.teenvogue.com /story/breonna-taylor-family-friends -remember-her-greatness.

23 Andrea J. Ritchie, "A Warrant to Search Your Vagina," *New York Times,* July 21, 2017, https://www.nytimes.com/2017 /07/21/opinion/sunday/black-women -police-brutality.html.

24 Brenda Goodman, "Police Kill Woman, 92, in Shootout at Her Home," *New York Times,* November 23, 2006, https:// www.nytimes.com/2006/11/23 /us/23atlanta.html.

25 William K. Rashbaum, "Woman Dies After Police Mistakenly Raid Her Apartment," *New York Times,* May 17, 2003, https://www.nytimes.com /2003/05/17/nyregion/woman-dies -after-police-mistakenly-raid-her -apartment.html.

26 "Treasure: From Tragedy to Trans Justice; Mapping a Detroit Story" (trailer), Vimeo video, 2:17, 2015, https://vimeo.com/126086558.

27 Andrea J. Ritchie, "Perspective | How Some Cops Use the Badge to Commit Sex Crimes," *Washington Post,* January 12, 2018, https://www

.washingtonpost.com/outlook/how -some-cops-use-the-badge-to-commit -sex-crimes/2018/01/11/5606fb26 -eff3-11e7-b390-a36dc3fa2842 _story.html. See also https://static1 .squarespace.com/static /5ee39ec764dbd7179cf1243c/t /609b0bb8fc3271012c4a9 3c5/1620773852750/Shrouded+in +Silence.pdf.

28 Ritchie, *Invisible No More.*

29 Chelsey Sanchez, "Cop Involved in the Killing of Breonna Taylor Investigated for Sexual Assault," *Harper's Bazaar,* June 15, 2020, https://www .harpersbazaar.com/culture/politics /a32812898/breonna-taylor-cop -sexual-assault-allegations/.

30 Ritchie, "A Warrant to Search Your Vagina."

31 Susan Ferriss, "In Horrifying Detail, Women Accuse U.S. Customs Officers of Invasive Body Searches," *Washington Post,* August 20, 2018, https://www. washingtonpost .com/world/national-security/in -horrifying-detail-women-accuse -us-customs-officers-of-invasive -body-searches/2018/08/18 /ad7b7d82-9b38-11e8-8d5 e-c6c594024954_story.html.

32 "The Breathe Act," M4BL, February 1, 2021, https://breatheact.org/.

33 Andrea J. Ritchie, Mariame Kaba, and Woods Ervin, "#DefundPolice #FundThePeople #DefendBlackLives," Interrupting Criminalization, June 2020, https://static1.squarespace.com /static/5ee39ec764dbd7179cf1243c /t/5f85c35e177b56179c78495c /1602601833821/Defund+Toolkit.pdf.

34 Andrea J. Ritchie, "The Demand is Still Defund the Police, Fund the People, Defend Black Lives," Interrupting Criminalization, January 2021.

34 Ritchie, Kaba, and Woods, "#DefundPolice."

35 Project NIA, "Defund Police," YouTube

video, 3:59, October 13, 2020, https://youtu.be/bTOYpOmk8NA. See also BYP100, Center for Popular Democracy and Law for Black Lives, Freedom to Thrive: Reimagining Safety and Security in Our Communities, https://static1.squarespace.com/static/5500a55ae4b05a69b3350e23/t/595cf69b1b631b031e0542a5/1499264677929/Freedom+to+Thrive+Web.pdf.

36 Andrea J. Ritchie et al., "Reparations Now Toolkit," M4BL, 2019, https://m4bl.org/wp-content/uploads/2020/05/Reparations-Now-Toolkit-FINAL.pdf.

37 "Reparations," Chicago Torture Justice Memorials, August 21, 2020, https://chicagotorture.org/reparations/.

38 Andrea J. Ritchie, "Communities Need to Reduce Violence Against Women of Color Without Police" (2017), Transform Harm, March 1, 2021, https://transformharm.org/communities-need-to-reduce-violence-against-women-of-color-without-police/.

39 Andrea J. Ritchie, "Say Her Name: What It Means to Center Black Women's Experiences of Police Violence," Truthout, September 18, 2015, https://truthout.org/articles/say-her-name-what-it-means-to-center-black-women-s-experiences-of-police-violence/.

40 David Lohr, "Transgender Woman Killed by Police Was 'Harassed and Executed,' Relative Says," HuffPost, September 7, 2017, https://www.huffpost.com/entry/transgender-woman-police-killing-stlouis_n_599df3f7e4b05710aa599d34.

41 Drew Smith, David Change, and Ruby Chinchilla, "Philly Man Charged With Murder of Transgender Woman," NBC 10 Philadelphia, October 1, 2020, https://www.nbcphiladelphia.com/news/local/philly-man-charged-with-murder-of-transgender-woman/2547906/.

42 Rachel E. Morgan and Barbara A. Oudekerk, "Criminal Victimization, 2018," Bureau of Justice Statistics, US Department of Justice, September 2019, https://www.bjs.gov/content/pub/pdf/cv18.pdf.

43 Ibid.

44 Ibid. https://static1.squarespace.com/static/5ee39ec764dbd7179cf1243c/t/5f9c405569362b211c3bcc8d/1604075605257/DEFUND+%26+DVAM.pdf.

45 Andrea J. Ritchie, "Expanding Our Frame," National Black Women's Justice Institute, February 2019, https://950b1543-bc84-4d80-ae48-656238060c23.filesusr.com/ugd/0c71ee_0430993a393840f7af620d34b8e4624e.pdf.

46 Sandy E. James, Carter Brown, and Isaiah Wilson, "2015 U.S. Transgender Survey: Report on the Experiences of Black Respondents," National Center for Transgender Equality, Black Trans Advocacy, and National Black Justice Coalition, November 2017, https://transequality.org/sites/default/files/docs/usts/USTSBlackRespondentsReport-Nov17.pdf.

47 Donna Coker et al., "Responses from the Field: Sexual Assault, Domestic Violence, and Policing," ACLU, October 2015, https://www.aclu.org/sites/default/files/field_document/2015.10.20_report_-_responses_from_the_field.pdf.

48 Naomi Murakawa. "Why Police Reform Is Actually a Bailout for Cops," Level, Medium, October 22, 2020, https://level.medium.com/why-police-reform-is-actually-a-bailout-for-cops-ecf2dd7b8833.

49 Ritchie, Invisible No More.

50 Ibid.

51 Ibid.

52 "End the War on Black Women," M4BL.

53 Invest/Divest Louisville.

54 Invest/Divest Louisville.

55 Andrea J. Ritchie, "The Demand is Still Defund the Police, Fund the People, Defend Black Lives," Interrupting Criminalization, January 2021.

55 Ritchie, Kaba, and Woods, "#DefundPolice."

56 Associated Press, "Deputy Who Tossed a S.C. High School Student Won't Be Charged," *New York Times,* September 3, 2016, https://www.nytimes.com/2016/09/03/afternoonupdate/deputy-who-tossed-a-sc-high-school-student-wont-be-charged.html.

57 Andrea J. Ritchie, "How Black Women's Bodies Are Violated as Soon as They Enter School," *Guardian,* August 16, 2017, https://www.theguardian.com/us-news/2017/aug/16/black-women-violated-us-policing-racial-profiling.

58 Andrea J. Ritchie, "We're Dying Too," *Colorlines,* June 10, 2015, https://www.colorlines.com/articles/were-dying-too.

59 https://sfbayview.com/2016/05/long-live-jessica-williams-nelson/.

60 https://static1.squarespace.com/static/5ee39ec764dbd7179cf1243c/t/60ca7e7399f1b5306c8226c3/1623883385572/Crisis+Response+Guide.pdf.

61 Dominic Bradley and Sarah Katz, "Sandra Bland, Eric Garner, Freddie Gray: The Toll of Police Violence on Disabled Americans," *Guardian,* June 9, 2020, https://www.theguardian.com/commentisfree/2020/jun/09/sandra-bland-eric-garner-freddie-gray-the-toll-of-police-violence-on-disabled-americans.

62 Justice 4 Kayla Moore, December 7, 2019, https://justiceforkaylamoore.wordpress.com/.

63 Jaimee Swift, "Full Decriminalization Is Full Freedom: Tamika Spellman on Belonging and Towards Black Sex Worker Liberation," Black Women Radicals, May 13, 2020, https://www.blackwomenradicals.com/blog-feed/full-decriminalization-is-full-freedom-tamika-spellman-on-belonging-and-towards-black-sex-worker-liberation.

64 "Law Enforcement Violence Against Women of Color and Trans People of Color," INCITE! https://incite-national.org/wp-content/uploads/2018/08/TOOLKIT-FINAL.pdf.

65 Mia, MIngus, "Medical Industrial Complex Visual," *Leaving Evidence* (blog), September 12, 2018, https://leavingevidence.wordpress.com/2015/02/06/medical-industrial-complex-visual/. See also interruptingcriminalization.com/cops-out-of-care.

66 Interrupting Criminalization, https://www.interruptingcriminalization.com..

67 Sensitive Visual, "6Ds Until She's Free," YouTube video, 9:52, July 29, 2020, https://www.youtube.com/watch?v=qwwJ3iH_ULM.

68 "Creative Interventions Toolkit: A Guide to Stop Interpersonal Violence," Creative Interventions, 2012, https://www.creative-interventions.org/toolkit.

69 Rachel Herzing, "Standing Up for Our Communities: Why We Need a Police-Free Future," *Truthout,* July 10, 2020, https://truthout.org/articles/standing-up-for-our-communities-why-we-need-a-police-free-future/.

Bankrolling the Carceral State

1 Naomi Murakawa, "Mass Incarceration Is Dead, Long Live the Carceral State!," Tulsa Law Review 55, no. 2 (Winter 2020), https://digitalcommons.law.utulsa.edu/cgi/viewcontent.cgi?article=3196&context=tlr&fbclid=IwAR3450Ixg090VNMLE07M4nzu1Mc_SPEbJ4hkRMdjA8VD-LrQyf3HtICU6iO.

2 "Here's How Two Federal Programs Helped Expand Police Funding by over 200% since 1980," https://www.cnbc.com/2020/06/25/two-federal-programs-helped-expand-police-funding-by-over-200percent.htm.

3   Richard C. Auxier, " What Police Spending Data Can (and Cannot) Explain amid Calls to Defund the Police," Urban Wire, Urban Institute, June 9, 2020, https://www.urban.org/urban-wire/what-police-spending-data-can-and-cannot-explain-amid-calls-defund-police.

4   "Here's How Two Federal Programs Helped Expand Police Funding."

5   Muzaffar Chishti and Jessica Bolter, "As #DefundThePolice Movement Gains Steam, Immigration Enforcement Spending and Practices Attract Scrutiny," Migration Information Source, Migration Policy Institute, June 25, 2020, https://www.migrationpolicy.org/article/defundthepolice-movement-gains-steam-immigration-enforcement-spending-and-practices-attract.

6   "Budget in Brief: Fiscal Year 2005," US Department of Homeland Security, https://www.dhs.gov/sites/default/files/publications/FY_2005_BIB_4.pdf.

7   "Hearing on 'A Review of the FY 2020 Budget Request for U.S. Customs and Border Protection, U.S. Immigration and Customs Enforcement, and U.S. Citizenship and Immigration Services' on May 9, 2019," US Citizenship and Immigration Services, https://www.uscis.gov/tools/resources-for-congress/testimonies/hearing-on-a-review-of-the-fy-2020-budget-request-for-us-customs-and-border-protection-us#:~:text=USCIS%20is%20nearly%2097%20percent,be%20funded%20with%20discretionary%20appropriations; and "FY 2020 Budget in Brief," US Department of Homeland Security, https://www.dhs.gov/sites/default/files/publications/fy_2020_dhs_bib.pdf, p. 60.

8   Patrick Liu, Ryan Nunn, and Jay Shambaugh, "Nine Facts about Monetary Sanctions in the Criminal Justice System," Brookings Institution, March 15, 2019, https://www.brookings.edu/research/nine-facts-about-monetary-sanctions-in-the-criminal-justice-system/.

9   Taylor Miller Thomas and Beatrice Jin, "As US Crime Rates Dropped, Local Police Spending Soared," *Politico*, 2020, https://www.politico.com/interactives/2020/police-budget-spending-george-floyd-defund/.

10   Carrie Sloan and Johnaé Strong, "Chicago Has Spent Half a Billion Dollars on Police Brutality Cases—And It's Impoverishing the Victims' Communities," *The Nation*, March 11, 2016, https://www.thenation.com/article/archive/chicago-has-spent-half-a-billion-dollars-on-police-brutality-cases-and-its-impoverishing-the-victims-communities/.

What Is & What Could Be

1   David Stein, "Why Coretta Scott King Fought for a Job Guarantee," *Boston Review,* July 16, 2018, https://bostonreview.net/class-inequality-race/david-stein-why-coretta-scott-king-fought-job-guarantee.

2   Barbara Ransby, "Elle Taught Me: Shattering the Myth of the Leaderless Movement," *Colorlines,* April 13, 2017, https://www.colorlines.com/articles/ella-taught-me-shattering-myth-leaderless-movement.

3   YAKI, James Yaki Sayles, http://www.brothermalcolm.net/TRANSFORMED/YAKI.htm.

4   Bill Fletcher Jr. and Jamala Rogers, "Creating a Viable Black Left: Sixteen Lessons Learned in Building the Black Radical Congress," *Black Commentator,* April, 4, 2013, https://blackcommentator.com/511/511_cover_brc_fletcher_rogers_share.html.

5   Orisanmi Burton, "Eddie Ellis and the Struggle for Black Freedom," CounterPunch, August 8, 2014, https://www.counterpunch.org/2014

/08/08/eddie-ellis-and-the-struggle-for-black-freedom/.

6   adrienne maree brown, "An Interview with Activists at the Prison Moratorium Project," Grist, June 22, 2005, https://grist.org/article/brown-prison/.

7   Free Them All for Public Health, https://freethemall4publichealth.org/.

8   Dan Berger, Ryan Fatica, and Duncan Tarr, "As the Coronavirus Spreads, Prisoners Are Rising Up for Their Health," The Appeal, April 27, 2020, https://theappeal.org/prisoners-protest-coronavirus-health/.

9   Toussaint Losier, "Make the Nation Look at Our Demands: The 2018 National Prison Strike and the Crises of Mass Incarceration," EuropeNow, November 8, 2018, https://www.europenowjournal.org/2018/11/07/make-the-nation-look-at-our-demands-the-2018-national-prison-strike-and-the-crises-of-mass-incarceration/.

10   Stuart Schrader, "When Police Play Soldier, Everybody Loses," Level, Medium, October 7, 2020, https://level.medium.com/when-police-play-soldier-everybody-loses-dd48392ba592.

11   Naomi Murakawa, "Police Reform Works—For the Police," Level, Medium, October 21, 2020, https://level.medium.com/why-police-reform-is-actually-a-bailout-for-cops-ecf2dd7b8833.

12   Dan Berger, "'Thinking Black' Against the Carceral State: Angela Davis and Prisoner Defense Campaigns," Black Perspectives, June 3, 2017, https://www.aaihs.org/thinking-black-against-the-carceral-state-angela-davis-and-prisoner-defense-campaigns/.

13   Fay Honey Knopp et al., "Moratorium on Prison/Jail Construction," in Instead of Prisons: A Handbook for Abolitionists, ed. Mark Morris (New York: Faculty Press, 1976), https://www.prisonpolicy.org/scans/instead_of_prisons/chapter4.shtml.

14   Jack Norton, "Little Siberia, Star of the North: The Political Economy of Prison Dreams in the Adirondacks," in Historical Geographies of Prisons, ed. Karen M. Morin and Dominique Moran (New York: Routledge, 2015), https://www.academia.edu/29400505/Little_Siberia_Star_of_the_North_The_Political_Economy_of_Prison_Dreams_in_the_Adirondacks.

15   Docs Populi, https://www.docspopuli.org/.

16   Grace Abels, "'The Genie Is Out': Joe Ingle on 50 Years of Working for Change in Southern Prisons," Facing South, June 26, 2020, https://www.facingsouth.org/tags/southern-coalition-jails-and-prisons.

17   Committee to End the Marion Lockdown, Freedom Archives, https://freedomarchives.org/tag/committee-to-end-the-marion-lockdown/.

18   Ruth Wilson Gilmore, Golden Gulag: Prisons, Surplus, Crisis, and Opposition in Globalizing California, ed. Earl Lewis et al. (Berkeley: University of California Press, 2007).

19   "State Advocacy News: Reform Reponse to Covid-19," The Sentencing Project, April 6, 2020, https://www.sentencingproject.org/news/state-advocacy-news-reform-responses-covid-19/.

20   Anna Bauman, "California Prison Population Drops Below 100,000 for First Time in 30 Years," San Francisco Chronicle, July 30, 2020, https://www.sfchronicle.com/crime/article/California-prison-population-drops-below-100-000-15448043.php.

21   Angela Davis, Abolition Democracy: Beyond Empire, Prisons, and Torture (New York: Seven Stories Press, 2005).

22   Robert W. Williams, "Primary Sources," WEB Du Bois.org, November 1, 2019,

http://www.webdubois.org/wdb
-BlackReconst.html.

23 Clement Petitjean, "Prisons and Class
Warfare: An Interview with Ruth Wilson
Gilmore," *Verso,* August 2, 2018,
https://www.versobooks
.com/blogs/3954-prisons-and-class
-warfare-an-interview-with-ruth
-wilson-gilmore.

24 "What Is the Green New Deal?,"
Sunrise Movement, https://www
.sunrisemovement.org/green-new-deal
/?ms=WhatistheGreenNewDeal%3F.

25 Nick Estes, "A Red Deal," *Jacobin,*
August 6, 2019, https://www
.jacobinmag.com/2019/08/red
-deal-green-new-deal-ecosocialism
-decolonization-indigenous-resistance
-environment.

26 Stephanie Kelton, *The Deficit Myth*
(New York: PublicAffairs, 2020).

27 Peter Wagner and Bernadette Rabuy,
"Following the Money of Mass
Incarceration," *Prison Policy Initiative,*
January 25, 2017, https://www
.prisonpolicy.org/reports/money.html.

28 Stephanie Kelton, "Learn to Love
Trillion-Dollar Deficits," *New York
Times,* June 9, 2020, https://www
.nytimes.com/2020/06/09/opinion
/us-deficit-coronavirus.html.

29 Julilly Kohler-Hausmann, *Getting
Tough: Welfare and Imprisonment
in 1970s America* (Princeton, NJ:
Princeton University Press, 2017).

30 David McNally, *Global Slump:
The Economics and Politics of Crisis
and Resistance* (Oakland, CA: PM
Press, 2011).

31 Hannah Appel, "Reparative Public
Goods and the Future of Finance:
A Fantasy in Three Parts," American
Ethnological Society, August 25, 2020,
https://americanethnologist.org
/features/pandemic-diaries/post
-covid-fantasies/reparative-public
-goods-and-the-future-of-finance
-a-fantasy-in-three-parts.

32 Ruha Benjamin, "The Shiny, High-Tech
Wolf in Sheep's Clothing," *Level,*
Medium, October 23, 2020, https://
level.medium.com/the-shiny
-high-tech-wolf-in-sheeps-clothing
-17d8db219b6d.

33 Sarah Holder, Fola Akinnibi, and
Christopher Cannon, "'We Have Not
Defunded Anything': Big Cities Boost
Police Budgets," *Bloomberg CityLab,*
September 22, 2020, https://www
.bloomberg.com/graphics/2020
-city-budget-police-defunding
/?sref=OIejgNtz.

34 Chris Uggen et al., "Locked Out 2020:
Estimates of People Denied Voting
Rights Due to a Felony Conviction," The
Sentencing Project, October 20, 2020,
https://www.sentencingproject
.org/publications/locked-out-2020
-estimates-of-people-denied-voting
-rights-due-to-a-felony-conviction/.

35 Rosa Luxemburg, *Reform or Revolution*
(London: Militant Publications, 1986).

36 Kaissa Karhu, "Transcript: In
Conversation with Ruth Wilson
Gilmore," *UCL,* June 7, 2020, https://
www.ucl.ac.uk/racism-racialisation
/transcript-conversation-ruth
-wilson-gilmore.

37 Mariame Kaba and John Duda,
"Towards the Horizon of Abolition:
A Conversation with Mariame Kaba,"
The Next System Project, November 9,
2017, https://thenextsystem.org/learn
/stories/towards-horizon-abolition
-conversation-mariame-kaba.

The Journey Continues

1 Naomi Klein, "A Message from the
Future II: The Years of Repair," *The
Intercept,* October 1, 2020, https://
theintercept.com/2020/10/01
/naomi-klein-message-from-future
-covid/?fbclid=IwAROHubJA9jb
_UaSAIHixp4uQOCb3OiXdaf7A
HOv7HOoOnPmDxlMRSRBzP1s.

2 Stokely Carmichael, "From Black
Power to Pan-Africanism," speech,

Whittier College, March 22, 1971, http://
americanradioworks.publicradio.org
/features/blackspeech/scarmichael
-2.html.

3   Penumbra Theatre, "Junauda Petrus
Reads Her Poem: Give the Police
Departments to the Grandmothers,"
Vimeo, video, 6:22, June 2020,
https://vimeo.com/426276718.

4   Mariame Kaba, "To Stop Police
Violence, We Need Better Questions—
and Bigger Demands," *GEN,* Medium,
September 25, 2020, https://gen
.medium.com/to-stop-police-violence
-we-need-better-questions-and-bigger
-demands-23132fc38e8a.

5   "The Growth of Incarceration in
the United States: Exploring Causes
and Consequences," National Institute
of Corrections, US Department of
Justice, 2014, https://nicic.gov
/growth-incarceration-united-states
-exploring-causes-and-consequences.

6   Pooja Gupta, "How Unemployment
Affects Serious Property Crime:
A National Case-Control Study," *The
Journalist's Resource,* February 14,
2016, https://journalistsresource.org
/economics/unemployment-property
-crime-burglary/.

7   Micah Herskind, "Some Reflections on
Prison Abolition," Medium, December 7,
2019, https://micahherskind.medium
.com/some-reflections-on-prison
-abolition-after-mumi-5197a4c3cf98.

8   Transform Harm,
https://transformharm.org
/transformative-justice/.

9   "The Abolitionist Map," The Digital
Abolitionist, https://www
.thedigitalabolitionist.com/the
-abolitionist-map.

10 Paula X. Rojas, "Are the Cops in Our
Heads and Hearts?," *S&F Online 13,*
no. 2 (2016), https://sfonline.barnard
.edu/navigating-neoliberalism-in-the
-academy-nonprofits-and-beyond
/paula-rojas-are-the-cops-in-our
-heads-and-hearts/.

11 Dan Berger et al., "What Abolitionists
Do," *Jacobin,* August 24, 2017, https://
www.jacobinmag.com/2017/08/prison
-abolition-reform-mass-incarceration.

12 Ruth Wilson Gilmore, *Change
Everything: Racial Capitalism and
the Case for Abolition* (Chicago:
Haymarket Books, 2021).

Abolition for the People

Resource Guide

Here's a non-exhaustive resource guide packed with articles, books, art, interviews, organizations, and campaigns that can provide you with further opportunities to extend your understanding of abolition and contribute to the movement for a future without policing and prisons. Abolition now. Abolition for the people. —The Editors

Police & Policing

Invisible No More: Police Violence Against Black Women and Women of Color by Andrea Ritchie (Boston: Beacon Press, 2017)

States of Confinement: Policing, Detention, and Prisons edited by Joy James (New York: Palgrave, 2002)

Slave Patrols: Law and Violence in Virginia and the Carolinas by Sally E. Hadden (Cambridge, MA: Harvard University Press, 2003)

Policing the Planet: Why the Policing Crisis Led to Black Lives Matter by Jordan T. Camp (New York: Verso, 2016)

Slavery by Another Name: The Re-Enslavement of Black Americans from the Civil War to World War II by Douglas A. Blackmon (New York: Anchor Books, 2009)

MIGRA! A History of the U.S. Border Patrol by Kelly Lytle Hernandez (Berkeley: University of California Press, 2010)

Dark Matters: On the Surveillance of Blackness by Simone Browne (Durham, NC: Duke University Press, 2015)

Badges without Borders: How Global Counterinsurgency Transformed American Policing by Stuart Schrader (Durham, NC: Duke University Press, 2015)

Rise of the Warrior Cop: The Militarization of America's Police Forces by Radley Balko (New York: Public Affairs, 2013)

"How Police Unions Enable and Conceal Abuses of Power" by Steven Greenhouse, New York Times, June 2020, https://www.newyorker.com /news/news-desk/how-police-union -power-helped-increase-abuses

"Community Compilation on Police Abolition" by Sarah-Ji and Monica Trinidad Hacking/Hustling Collective, ISSUU, Oct 2016, https://issuu.com /ftpzines/docs/gbnf_zine_all

Prisons & Carcerality

Arrested Justice: Black Women, Violence, and America's Prison Nation by Beth E. Ritchie (New York: NYU Press, 2012)

Captive Genders: Trans Embodiment and the Prison Industrial Complex edited by Eric Stanley and Nat Smith (Oakland: AK Press, 2015)

The New Abolitionists: (Neo)Slave Narratives and Contemporary Prison Writings edited by Joy James (New York: State University of New York Press, 2005)

Forced Passages: Imprisoned Radical Intellectuals and the U.S. Prison Regime by Dylan Rodríguez (Minneapolis: University of Minnesota Press, 2006)

Soledad Brother: The Prison Writings of George Jackson by George Jackson (New York: Lawrence Hill Books, 1970)

Assata: An Autobiography by Assata Shakur (New York: Lawrence Hill Books, 1999)

Jailhouse Lawyers: Prisoners Defending v. the USA by Mumia Abu-Jamal (San Francisco: City Lights Books, 2009)

First Strike: Educational Enclosures in Black Los Angeles by Damien M. Sojoyner (Minneapolis: University of Minnesota Press, 2016)

Are Prisons Obsolete? by Angela Y. Davis (New York: Seven Stories Press, 2003)

Right to be Hostile: Schools, Prisons, and the Making of Public Enemies by Erica R.

Meiners (New York: Routledge, 2007)
*Compulsory: Education and the
Dispossession of Youth in a Prison
School* by Sabina E. Vaught
(Minneapolis: University
of Minnesota Press, 2017)
*Texas Tough: The Rise of America's Prison
Empire* by Robert Perkinson
(NY: Metropolitan Books, 2010)
Live from Death Row by Mumia Abu-
Jamal (New York: Perennial, 2002)
Prison Culture Blog by Mariame Kaba,
Prison Culture, April 2020
Rustbelt Abolition Radio: Interview with
Nick Estes, *Rustbelt Abolition Radio,*
July 2018.
"Against Captivity: Black Girls and
School Discipline Policies in
the Afterlife of Slavery," Connie Wun,
Sage Journals, November 2015
"#MeToo Behind Bars: When the
Sexual Assaulter Holds the Keys to
Your Cell" by Victoria Law,
Truthout, March 2018

Fuck Reform

"Reformist Reforms vs. Abolitionist
Steps in Policing"
by Critical Resistance,
https://static1.squarespace.com
/static/59ead8f9692ebee25b72f17f/t
/5b65cd58758d46d34254f2
2c/1533398363539/CR_NoCops
_reform_vs_abolition_CRside.pdf
The End of Policing by Alex S. Vitale
(New York: Verso Books, 2017)
"Police Reform Won't Fix a System That
Was Built to Abuse Power" by Stuart
Schrader *The Nation,* June 2020
*The First Civil Right: How Liberals Built
Prison America* by Naomi Murakawa

(Oxford: Oxford University Press, 2014)
*Prison by Any Other Name: The Harmful
Consequences of Popular Reforms*
by Maya Schenwar and Victoria Law
(New York: The New Press, 2020)
"'Mass Incarceration' Reform as Police
Endorsement," Dylan Rodríguez
Black Agenda Report, February 2018

Abolition Now

We Do This 'Til We Free Us by
Mariame Kaba (Chicago: Haymarket
Books, 2021)
What is the Prison Industrial Complex
(PIC)? What is Abolition?
by Critical Resistance,
http://criticalresistance.org/cr
_abolish-policing-toolkit_2020
Our Communities, Our Solutions:
An Organizers' Toolkit to Abolish
Policing (2020) by Critical
Resistance, http://criticalresistance
.org/cr_abolish-policing
-toolkit_2020
"The Worrying State of the Anti-Prison
Movement" by Ruth Wilson Gilmore
Social Justice, February 2015,
http://www.socialjusticejournal
.org/the-worrying-state-of-the-anti
-prison-movement
"The Case for Prison Abolition: Ruth
Wilson Gilmore on COVID-19,
Racial Capitalism & Decarceration,"
Democracy Now! May 2020, https://
youtu.be/1HWqYANmWLY
"Yes, We Mean Literally Abolish the
Police" by Mariame Kaba
New York Times, June 2020,
https://www.nytimes
.com/2020/06/12/opinion/sunday
/floyd-abolish-defund-police.html

"Reclaiming Our Lineage: Organized Queer, Gender-Noncomforming, and Transgender Resistance to Police Violence" by Che Gossett, Tourmaline, and AJ Lewis, *S&F Online*, 2012, http://sfonline.barnard.edu/a-new-queer-agenda/reclaiming-our-lineage-organized-queer-gender-nonconforming-and-transgender-resistance-to-police-violence

Decarcerating Disability: Deinstitutionalization and Prison Abolition by Liat Ben-Moshe (Minneapolis: University of Minnesota Press, 2020)

"Prison Abolition Requires Decriminalizing Sex Work," *Rewire News Group*, July 2020, https://rewirenewsgroup.com/article/2020/07/24/prison-abolition-requires-decriminalizing-sex-work

"Towards the Horizon of Abolition: A Conversation with Mariame Kaba," *The Next System Project*, November 2017, https://thenextsystem.org/learn/stories/towards-horizon-abolition-conversation-mariame-kaba

"What Abolitionists Do" by Mariame Kaba, David Stein, Dan Berger, *Jacobin*, August 2017, https://www.jacobinmag.com/2017/08/prison-abolition-reform-mass-incarceration

"Social Movements and Mass Incarceration: What is to be Done?," Dan Berger, *Taylor & Francis Online*, July 2013

Transformative Justice: A Curriculum Guide by Project NIA 2013, https://transformharm.org/wp-content/uploads/2018/12/tjcurriculum_design_small-finalrev.pdf

Fumbling Towards Repair: A Workbook for Community Accountability Practitioners, Mariame Kaba and Shira Hassan, Just Practice, 2019, https://just-practice.org/fumbling-towards-repair

Building Accountable Communities Web-Series Barnard Center for Research on Women, http://bcrw.barnard.edu/building-accountable-communities

Resource Hubs/Networks/Toolkits/Organizations/Projects/Campaigns

Transform Harm Resource Hub: transformharm.org

Creative Interventions: creative-interventions.org

INCITE!: incite-national.org

Asian Prisoner Support Committee: asianprisonersupport.com

Black Alliance for Just Immigration: baji.org

California Coalition for Women Prisoners: womenprisoners.org

Survived & Punished: survivedandpunished.org

Interrupting Criminalization: interruptingcriminalization.com

Micah Bazant Artwork: micahbazant.com

National Jericho Movement: thejerichomovement.com

Mamas Activating Movements for Abolition and Solidarity: motheringisradical.com

Toolkit for the Movement by Center for
  Constitutional Rights:
  ccrjustice.org/toolkit-for-the
  -movement
Marsha P. Johnson Institute:
  marshap.org/about-mpji
Transgender Gender-Variant & Intersex
  Justice Project (TGIJP):
  tgijp.org
Center for Political Education:
  politicaleducation.org
Young Women's Freedom Center:
  youngwomenfree.org
National Bailout:
  nationalbailout.org

Glossary

Police & Policing

Abolition: The formal elimination of police, policing, and systems of surveillance and punishment. Abolition calls for investing in systems focused on the public good, including community-based accountability, mutual aid, health care for all, and equitable access to education and housing.

Carceral state: A term often used to refer to institutions of confinement and surveillance like jails, detention centers, and prisons. Its reach, however, is not limited to the criminal legal system and includes things like child protective services, schools, and health care— all of which are disproportionately used to monitor and police low-income, Black, and Indigenous people and communities of color.

Copaganda: The reproduction and circulation in mainstream media of propaganda that portrays the police as generally fair and hard-working and portrays Black and Indigenous people and communities of color as criminal and deserving of the brutal treatment they receive. Such cultural framing not only perpetuates the criminalization of these communities but has been critical to legitimizing and reinforcing the need for a more expansive criminal legal system that fuels mass incarceration.

Community accountability: A strategy to address harm that rejects the involvement of police and prisons and instead calls on the community to help right the wrongs that transpired. It prioritizes healing over punishment.

Defund the police: To divest funds from police departments and reallocate resources to non-policing forms of public safety and community support, such as social services, youth services, housing, education, health care, and other community resources. Defunding the police is a strategy for reimagining and creating systems of accountability and transformation.

Prison industrial complex: The prison industrial complex (PIC) is a term used to describe the overlapping interests of government and industry that use surveillance, policing, and imprisonment as solutions to economic, social, and political problems. (Source: Critical Resistance)

Restorative justice: A humanizing approach to community-building and problem-solving rooted in Indigenous practices that does not rely on punishment for the harms that have been caused but instead seeks to restore the bond that was broken between community members and the community at large. This is done often in a small group through direct communication between the victim and the offender as well as representatives from the community.

Transformative justice: An abolitionist framework for responding to harm and violence that does not rely on the state and does not reinforce or perpetuate violence. This approach understands that state institutions such as police, prisons, and Immigration and Customs Enforcement (ICE) were created to be violent in order to maintain social control. Transformative justice works to alter the conditions that cause harm through cultivating violence prevention measures like healing, connection, and accountability. It prioritizes seeking safety for those harmed, changing the behaviors of those who caused harm, and a transformation of the conditions that allowed the harm to occur. (Sources: Mia Mingus and #DefundPolice Toolkit)

Prisons & Carcerality

Social control: When norms, rules, laws, and structures of society are weaponized against groups of people to marginalize them by depriving them of their liberties and human agency, and to punish them. Social control is also about power—delineating between those who have the power to police and punish and those who remain vulnerable to surveillance and control. (Source: Marilyn Buck)

Colonialism: The violent takeover of a territory or nation through war and ongoing destruction of entire societies, including their culture and religion, for the purpose of exploitation and extraction of resources. Colonialism includes characterizing Indigenous and/or Native inhabitants of land as uncivilized, criminal, and savage, and colonizers as symbols of progress, civilization, and normality. These characterizations serve to justify violence against Native and Indigenous populations.

Settler colonialism: A particular form of colonialism that seeks to replace the original population of the colonized territory with a new society of settlers, often through forced imprisonment,

slavery, or genocide. As with all forms of colonialism, it is based on domination from an outside party that is typically organized or supported by an imperial authority. Beyond the use of military occupation and terror, it also establishes institutions, policies, and practices as a means to legitimize occupation and invalidate Indigenous populations, their cultures, and their customs. (Source: Tate LeFevre)

Crime: A socially and politically constructed category whose contours encompass not only morally condemnable acts such as murder and rape but also many acts that are criminalized to justify surveillance and punishment and reinforce prevailing racial, social, and economic hierarchies.

Carceral class: Persons of African descent who are systematically stigmatized as unfit for freedom and deserving of the dehumanization that comes with being incarcerated. The idea of the carceral class is the product of an anti-Black framework that represents Black people as the locus of crime and Blackness as synonymous with criminality. As a classification, the carceral class denotes that your freedom can be stripped from you at any given moment. (Source: Dr. Ameer Hasan Loggins)

Respectability politics: A set of beliefs holding that conformity to prescribed mainstream standards of appearance and behavior is more valuable and will protect a person who is part of a marginalized group from the carceral state, prejudices, and systemic injustices.

Decolonization: An ongoing practice to resist and remedy the violence of colonization through direct action, and by drawing focus to the liberation of colonized communities. It often employs Indigenous knowledge and practices, such as restorative justice and land trusts, as well as self-defense, to transform the cultural, political, and economic practices established by colonizers.

School-to-prison pipeline: A term used to describe the phenomenon by which the educational system, through a nexus of disciplinary policies and practices, disproportionately funnels children and young adults from Black, Indigenous, and communities of color directly into the criminal legal system.

Fuck Reform

Exoneration: When the conviction for a crime is removed, either through demonstration of innocence, a flaw in the conviction, or otherwise. However, exoneration rarely clears a "criminal record" and punishment can linger long after, despite proof of innocence. (Source: The Innocence Project)

Pro se litigants: Parties representing themselves in court without the assistance of an attorney. This phenomenon has been on the rise, with the increasing cost of legal representation and mistrust in lawyers and the legal system at large being cited as significant factors.

The 13th Amendment: "Neither slavery nor involuntary servitude, except as a punishment for crime whereof the party shall have been duly convicted, shall exist within the United States, or any place subject to their jurisdiction." While the 1865 amendment purportedly abolished slavery, the statement's conditions allowed for and created the premise by which slavery was permitted through incarceration.

The 1994 crime bill: Extolled and signed into law by President Bill Clinton, the passage of this bill, which was the largest crime bill in US history, led to an increase in incarceration rates, lengthier prison sentences, more draconian sentencing laws, and the construction of more prisons. It imposed mandatory life sentences and authorized prosecutors, in some cases, to charge youth for adult crimes. The bill is notorious for criminalizing and punishing communities of color, while also institutionally rendering them susceptible to—and victims of— state-sanctioned "premature death."

New Jim Code: Ruha Benjamin's term for how technology and automation have the potential to disguise and exacerbate discrimination. This can be further perpetuated by tools such as predictive policing programs, criminal risk assessment tools, and electronic ankle monitors.

Reformism: The ideological and political position that fixates on reform as the primary (if not exclusive) driver of social change/justice. Reformism avoids and even criminalizes people's efforts to catalyze fundamental change, instead employing simplistic mandates of "nonviolence," incrementalism, and compliance with the law as the only legitimate ways to protest or seek to undo unjust systems.

Abolition Now

The Reconstruction Era: The post–Civil War years between 1865 and 1877 during which Black people in Congress and the community organized a multipronged, national movement that didn't just dream of freedom, but implemented it—in both policy and society. However, it was also marked by the development of convict leasing and sharecropping, the birth of the KKK, and lynchings. The Reconstruction Era ended due to the Compromise of 1877, which ushered in the restrictive and oppressive Black Codes. (Source: Equal Justice Initiative & Mumia Abu-Jamal)

Electoral justice: As defined by Jessica Byrd, co-founder of the Electoral Justice Project of the Movement for Black Lives, "the process of making change—in politics, policies, and social practices." Electing representatives and officials like judges, district attorneys (DAs), mayors, senators, and others who not only have experiences in common with their communities, but are delegates from their communities that understand the need for a system overhaul. (Source: Rukia Lumumba)

Mutual aid: Mutual aid is work that directly addresses the conditions the movement seeks to address, such as by providing housing, food, health care, or transportation in a way that draws

attention to the politics creating need and vulnerability, such as the Black Panther Party's Free Breakfast Program. (Source: Dean Spade & Robin D. G. Kelley)

Decarceration: To release and free incarcerated communities while providing them with access to support and resources, including but not limited to: healing trauma, restoration of civil rights, and ending the suffering the carceral system has imposed on families and communities. (Source: Rukia Lumumba)

Clemency: The process by which a governor, president, or administrative board may reduce a defendant's sentence or grant a pardon. Mass clemency campaigns are part of an abolitionist strategy to reduce prison populations and deconstruct the carceral state.

Abolition democracy: Coined by W. E. B. Du Bois in his 1935 study, *Black Reconstruction in America,* abolition democracy refers to the political struggle led by formerly enslaved people in the wake of the Civil War to construct new institutions while also eradicating violent ones. (Source: Berger & Stein)

Reparative public goods: Policies and measures that center redress and reparations, rather than exclusion and exception. Examples include social housing, education for all, and health care for all. (Source: Hannah Appel)

About the
Contributors

Mumia Abu-Jamal is an internationally celebrated writer, radio journalist, and organizer who has authored six books and hundreds of columns and articles. Abu-Jamal is a former member of the Black Panther Party and supporter of Philadelphia's radical MOVE organization. He has spent the last thirty years in prison, almost all of it in confinement on Pennsylvania's Death Row.

Bree Newsome Bass is an award-winning writer, filmmaker, and grassroots community organizer most widely known for her act of civil disobedience in 2015, when she scaled a thirty-foot flagpole at the South Carolina capitol and lowered the Confederate flag in protest following the racist murders of nine Black parishioners during a prayer meeting at Emanuel AME in Charleston. Her actions, in collaboration with a team of other activists, led to the permanent removal of the flag two weeks later and inspired similar efforts to remove racist symbology around the nation. Bass remains a vocal critic of modern structural racism, giving lectures on the topic while promoting the importance of local organizing and the role of art, media, and communications in movement building.

Ruha Benjamin is Professor of African American Studies at Princeton University, Founding Director of the Ida B. Wells Just Data Lab, and author of the award-winning book *Race After Technology: Abolitionist Tools for the New Jim Code,* among many other publications. Her work investigates the social dimensions of science, medicine, and technology with a focus on the relationship between innovation and inequity, health and justice, knowledge and power. Benjamin is the recipient of numerous awards and fellowships including from the American Council of Learned Societies, the National Science Foundation, the Institute for Advanced Study, and the President's Award for Distinguished Teaching at Princeton. For more info visit www.ruhabenjamin.com.

Dan Berger teaches at the University of Washington, Bothell, coordinates the Washington Prison History Project, wrote *Captive Nation: Black Prison Organizing in the Civil Rights Era,* and co-edited *Remaking Radicalism: A Grassroots Documentary Reader of the United States, 1973–2001.*

Simone Browne is Associate Professor at the University of Texas at Austin. She is also Research Director of Critical Surveillance Inquiry (CSI) with Good Systems. CSI works with scholars, organizations, and communities to curate conversations, exhibitions, and research that examine the social and ethical implications of surveillance, both AI-enabled and not. Focusing on algorithmic harms, CSI continually questions "What's good?" in order to better understand the development and impact of AI.

Browne's book, *Dark Matters: On the Surveillance of Blackness,* examines surveillance with a focus on transatlantic slavery, biometrics, airports, and creative texts. She is writing her second book, *Like the Mixture of Charcoal and Darkness,* which examines the interventions made by artists whose works grapple with the surveillance of Black life, from policing and the FBI's COINTELPRO to encryption, electronic waste, and AI.

Kimberlé Crenshaw is the Co-Founder and Executive Director of the African American Policy Forum, and the Founder and Executive Director of the Center for Intersectionality and Social Policy Studies. She is the Promise Institute Professor at UCLA Law School, the Isidor and Seville Sulzbacher Professor at Columbia Law School, and is popularly known for projects that she has named, such as "intersectionality," "critical race theory," and the #SayHerName Campaign. She is the host of the podcast *Intersectionality Matters!*, the moderator of the impactful webinar series *Under the Blacklight: The Intersectional Vulnerabilities That the Twin Pandemics Lay Bare*, and a columnist for *The New Republic.* Kimberlé is one of the most cited scholars in the history of the law and was named *Ms. Magazine*'s "No. 1 Most Inspiring Feminist," honored as one of the ten most important thinkers in the world by *Prospect Magazine,* and included in *Ebony*'s "Power 100" issue. In early 2021, she received the Ruth Bader Ginsburg Lifetime Achievement Award from the Association of American Law Schools. She received her JD from Harvard, her LLM from the University of Wisconsin, and her BA from Cornell University, and sits on the boards of Sundance, VDay, and the Algorithmic Justice League.

Angela Y. Davis is a scholar, activist, writer, and Distinguished Professor Emerita of History of Consciousness and Feminist Studies at UC Santa Cruz. Her work as an educator—both at the university level and in the larger public sphere—has always emphasized the importance of building communities of struggle for economic, racial, and gender justice. She is the author of ten books, including *Women, Race and Class*; *Blues Legacies and Black Feminism: Gertrude "Ma" Rainey, Bessie Smith, and Billie Holiday*; *Are Prisons Obsolete?*; *The Meaning of Freedom: And Other Difficult Dialogues*; and, most recently, *Freedom Is a Constant Struggle: Ferguson, Palestine and the Foundations of a Movement.* Having helped to popularize the notion of a "prison industrial complex," she now urges her audiences to think seriously about the future possibility of a world without prisons and to help forge a twenty-first-century abolitionist movement.

Kenyon Farrow is a writer, editor, and strategist. Farrow has coordinated campaigns large and small, local, national, and global on issues related to public health, criminalization/mass imprisonment, homelessness, LGBT rights, and racial justice. He is a sought-after speaker, editor, and group facilitator for social justice organizations and campaigns. He's worked with organizations such as PrEP4All, Partners for Dignity & Rights, Treatment Action Group, and Housing Works. He serves on the board of the LGBT Center of Greater Cleveland, the New York Transgender Advocacy Group, and Global Black Gay Men Connect.

Morning Star Gali is a member of the Ajumawi band of the Pit River Tribe located in northeastern California. She serves as Project Director for Restoring Justice for Indigenous Peoples (RJIP) and as the California Tribal and Community Liaison for the International Indian Treaty Council. She's also the Tribal water/policy organizer for Save

California Salmon. Dedicated to raising awareness and visibility within the unique climate of California's urban and rural Native communities, Gali coordinates support of Indigenous-led organizing efforts. Gali continues to lead large-scale actions while coordinating Native cultural, spiritual, scholarly, and political gatherings throughout California.

She is deeply committed to advocating for Indigenous sovereignty issues such as missing and murdered Indigenous women (MMIW), climate justice, gender justice, and sacred sites protection on behalf of the tribal and intertribal communities in which she was raised. Prior to returning to her ancestral homelands and working for her Tribe, she served as a volunteer and advocate on behalf of incarcerated and formerly incarcerated Indigenous peoples in California, working with a number of Indigenous-led grassroots organizations in the Bay Area for over two decades.

Cynthia Garcia is an out, queer, undocumented womxn living in Oklahoma City. She serves as the national campaigns manager for community protection at United We Dream, where she runs a nationwide hotline of support for immigrants whose family members have been abducted by ICE agents and teaches them how to organize and fight back. Garcia is herself protected from deportation because of the Deferred Action for Childhood Arrivals (DACA) program.

Derrick Hamilton is the co-founder of Friends and Family of the Wrongfully Convicted. He spent twenty-one years in prison for a murder he did not commit. Once released on parole in 2011, he convinced the *New York Times* to investigate cases of former detective Louis Scarcella, the detective who framed him. Based on the investigation, Brooklyn prosecutors agreed to look into all of Scarcella's cases. To date, sixteen people have been exonerated, including Hamilton. He works as an advocate for the wrongfully convicted and spends most of his time seeking to level the playing field in the criminal justice system for Blacks and Hispanics, who are systematically discriminated against by the system.

Mariame Kaba is an organizer, educator, curator, and prison industrial complex (PIC) abolitionist who is active in movements for racial, gender, and transformative justice. Kaba is the founder and director of Project NIA, a grassroots abolitionist organization with a vision to end youth incarceration. Kaba is currently a researcher at Interrupting Criminalization: Research in Action at the Barnard Center for Research on Women, a project she cofounded with Andrea Ritchie in 2018. Kaba has cofounded multiple other organizations and projects over the years, including We Charge Genocide, the Chicago Freedom School, the Chicago Taskforce on Violence against Girls and Young Women, Love & Protect, the Just Practice Collaborative, and Survived & Punished. She is a member of the Movement for Black Lives Policy Table. Kaba is a current Lannan Foundation Cultural Freedom Fellow. Kaba's leadership, organizing, and influence extend widely as she offers a radical analysis that influences how people think and respond to how violence, prisons, and policing affect the lives of people of color. Kaba is the author of *Missing Daddy* (Haymarket, 2019). Her current book, *We Do This 'Til We Free Us: Abolitionist Organizing and Transforming Justice*, a *New York Times* bestseller, was published by Haymarket Press in February 2021.

Colin Kaepernick holds the all-time NFL record for most rushing yards in a game by a quarterback. The Super Bowl QB took a knee during the playing of "The Star-Spangled Banner" in 2016 to bring attention to systemic oppressions, specifically police terrorism against Black and Brown people. For his stance, he has been denied employment by the league. Since 2016, he has founded and helped to fund three organizations— Know Your Rights Camp, Ra Vision Media, and Kaepernick Publishing— that together advance the liberation of Black and Brown people through storytelling, systems change, and political education. Kaepernick sits on Medium's board and is the winner of numerous prestigious honors including Amnesty International's Ambassador of Conscience Award, the Robert F. Kennedy Human Rights Ripple of Hope honor, GQ magazine's Citizen of the Year, the NFL's Len Eshmont Award, the *Sports Illustrated* Muhammad Ali Legacy Award, the ACLU's Eason Monroe Courageous Advocate Award, and the Puffin/Nation Institute's Prize for Creative Citizenship. In 2019, Kaepernick helped Nike win an Emmy for its "Dream Crazy" commercial.

Robin D. G. Kelley is the Gary B. Nash Endowed Chair in US History at UCLA. His books include *Thelonious Monk: The Life and Times of an American Original* (2009); *Africa Speaks, America Answers: Modern Jazz in Revolutionary Times* (2012); *Freedom Dreams: The Black Radical Imagination* (2002); *Race Rebels: Culture Politics and the Black Working Class* (1994); *Yo' Mama's DisFunktional!: Fighting the Culture Wars in Urban America* (1997); and *Hammer and Hoe: Alabama Communists During the Great Depression* (1990). He is currently completing two books, *Black Bodies Swinging: An American Postmortem* and *The Education of Ms. Grace Halsell: An Intimate History of the American Century* (both forthcoming from Metropolitan Books). His essays have appeared in several anthologies and publications, including *The Nation, Monthly Review, The New York Times, Counterpunch, Souls, Black Music Research Journal, Callaloo, Black Renaissance/Renaissance Noir, Social Text, Metropolis, American Visions, Fashion Theory, American Historical Review, Metropolis, Frieze: Contemporary Art and Culture,* and *The Boston Review,* for which he also serves as Contributing Editor.

James Kilgore is a Media Fellow at MediaJustice, where he directs the Challenging E-Carceration Project. He is the author of five books, four of which he drafted during his six and a half years in prison. His 2015 volume, *Understanding Mass Incarceration* won a National Book Social Justice Award. He lives in Urbana, Illinois, with his partner, Terri Barnes, and codirects the FirstFollowers Reentry Program.

Kiese Laymon is a Black southern writer from Jackson, Mississippi. He is the author of *Long Division*; *How to Slowly Kill Yourself and Others in America*; and *Heavy: An American Memoir*.

Talila A. Lewis is an abolitionist organizer-educator-attorney who works to unite communities and struggles by grounding all social justice movements in disability justice. Lewis's current efforts primarily focus on abolishing the medical-prison industrial complex and helping people understand the inextricable links between ableism, racism, classism, and all forms of systemic and structural oppression and inequity. Lewis created the only national database of deaf/blind imprisoned people in the US and works to correct and prevent deaf wrongful convictions as the volunteer director of HEARD (@behearddc). Lewis also serves as a consultant for dozens of social justice organizations on various topics including racial, economic, gender, reproductive, healing, and disability justice and as an expert on cases involving multiple-marginalized disabled people. A founding member of the Harriet Tubman Collective and cocreator of the Disability Solidarity praxis, Lewis has taught at Rochester Institute of Technology and Northeastern University School of Law.

Ameer Hasan Loggins, PhD, is a graduate of UC Berkeley's African American Studies doctoral program and is currently a postdoctoral fellow at Stanford University. Loggins aided in the development of Colin Kaepernick's Know Your Rights Camp and served as the camp's lead speaker. His work has been featured in *The Guardian, Washington Post, ESPN,* and *New York Magazine*. Most recently, Loggins co-edited and contributed to Kaepernick Publishing and Medium's Abolition for the People project

Rukia Lumumba, a legal professional and transformative justice strategist, is founding executive director of the People's Advocacy Institute and codirector of the Electoral Justice Project of the Movement for Black Lives. Lumumba works at the intersections of criminal and electoral justice defending the human rights of those behind prison walls, engaging communities in community-led governance efforts, community-led public safety, and an intentional grassroots process for cultivating ideas and developing solutions to violence, punitive legal systems, and social injustice facing far too many communities. Her work is centered on the belief that community agency is what architects robust systems change and is what is needed to build new institutional power that paves the way for a more just system rooted in restoration, resilience, and self-determination.

Erica R. Meiners is a writer, educator, and organizer whose current work includes *For the Children? Protecting Innocence in a Carceral State* (University of Minnesota, 2016), a co-edited anthology *The Long Term: Resisting Life Sentences, Working Towards Freedom* (Haymarket Press, 2018), and the co-authored *Feminist and the Sex Offender: Confronting Sexual Harm, Ending State Violence* (Verso, 2020). The Bernard J. Brommel Distinguished Research Professor at Northeastern Illinois

University, Meiners is a member of her labor union, University Professionals of Illinois, and she teaches classes in justice studies, education, and gender and sexuality studies. Most important, Meiners has collaboratively started and works alongside a range of ongoing mobilizations for liberation, particularly movements that involve access to free public education for all, including people during and after incarceration, and other queer abolitionist struggles. A member of Critical Resistance, the Illinois Death in Custody Project, the Prison+Neighborhood Arts/Education Project, and the Education for Liberation Network, she is a sci-fi fan, an avid runner, and a lover of bees and cats.

Cristina Jiménez Moreta is a community organizer, strategist, and freedom fighter who is a co-founder of United We Dream (UWD). Moreta migrated to Queens, New York, from Ecuador with her family at the age of 13, seeking a better life, and grew up undocumented. She is the former executive director of UWD. Under her leadership, UWD grew into a powerful grassroots network of 800,000 members across twenty-eight states.

Naomi Murakawa is an associate professor in the Department of African American Studies at Princeton University. She studies the reproduction of inequality in twentieth- and twenty-first-century American politics, with a focus on racial criminalization and the politics of carceral expansion. She is the author of *The First Civil Right: How Liberals Built Prison America*

(Oxford University Press), which won the Michael Harrington Book Award from the American Political Science Association. Her research has been supported by Columbia Law School's Center for the Study of Law and Culture, the Robert Wood Johnson Foundation's Health Policy Research Program, and CUNY Graduate Center's Advanced Research Collaborative. She is the *Abolitionist Papers* series editor at Haymarket Books.

Mark Anthony Neal is James B. Duke Professor of African & African American Studies and Professor of English, and Chair of the Department of African and African American Studies at Duke University. Neal is the author of six books, including *What the Music Said: Black Popular Music and Black Public Culture; Soul Babies: Black Popular Culture and the Post-Soul Aesthetic; Looking for Leroy: Illegible Black Masculinities;* and the forthcoming *Black Ephemera: The Crisis and Challenge of the Black Musical Archive.* Neal also directs the Center for Arts, Digital Culture and Entrepreneurship (CADCE), which produces original digital content, including the weekly video podcast *Left of Black* (now in its eleventh season), produced in collaboration with the Franklin Humanities Institute. Neal is a three-time graduate of SUNY institutions, earning BA and MA degrees in English from Fredonia, and a PhD in American Studies from the University of Buffalo.

Tamara K. Nopper researched and wrote the data stories visualized throughout this book. Nopper is a sociologist, writer, editor, and data artist whose research and publications focus on Black-Asian relations, the racial and gender wealth gap, financialization, criminalization, punishment, and the social impact of technology. A Fellow at Data for Progress and an Affiliate of the Center for Critical Race and Digital Studies, Nopper's scholarship and writing have appeared in numerous academic publications as well as in *The New Inquiry, Jacobin, Truthout*, and *Verso Books Blog*. She is the editor of *We Do This 'Til We Free Us: Abolitionist Organizing and Transforming Justice*, a book of Mariame Kaba's writings and interviews (Haymarket Books).

Marlon Peterson is a writervist. Since his decade of incarceration, he has written, created programming, lectured, organized, and advocated alongside the formerly incarcerated, victims of gun violence, womxn, immigrants, and young people. Peterson is the author of *Bird Uncaged: An Abolitionist's Freedom Song*, host of the *DEcarcerated* podcast, and owner of his own social impact endeavor, the Precedential Group Social Enterprises, and its nonprofit arm, Be Precedential, Inc. His TED talk, "Am I Not Human? A Call for Criminal Justice Reform," has amassed more than 1.2 million views.

As a Soros Fellow, Senior Atlantic Fellow, and Aspen Civil Society Fellow, Peterson has used his activism and pen to advocate for safer communities, to eliminate the footprint of law enforcement, and to amplify the work of individuals and grassroots organizations across the globe. Peterson's writervism and *DEcarcerated* podcast have allowed him to lecture and conduct workshops throughout the US, Trinidad and Tobago, South Africa, and Oxford, London.

Peterson's bylines have appeared in *USA Today, The Nation, Ebony, Essence, Gawker, The Marshall Project, The Root, Cassius.com,* and *Mic.com*. His essays have also been published in *How to Slowly Kill Yourself and Others* by Kiese Laymon; *How We Fight White Supremacy* by Kenrya Rankin and Akiba Solomon; and Colin Kaepernick's *Medium Series: Abolition for the People*. Peterson is a soca and steelpan lover, and a Brooklyn representer.

Christopher Petrella is a historian of nineteenth- and twentieth-century racialization in the United States and serves as a writer, editor, researcher, and strategist for Kaepernick Publishing, Know Your Rights Camp, and Ra Vision Media. Petrella's writing and public scholarship examines intellectual histories of race and resistance in the US and has been featured in *The New York Times* and on NPR and CNN. He is a regular contributor to *The Washington Post* and is currently writing his first book with Haymarket, provisionally titled *Real White: Histories of White Supremacy in New England*. *Real White* challenges New England's self-presentation as an imagined community of white racial piety and antiracist mythmaking over and against the US South. For more information, please see christopherfrancispetrella.net.

Derecka Purnell is a human rights lawyer, writer, and organizer. She works to end police and prison violence by providing legal assistance, research, and trainings to community-based organizations through an abolitionist framework. Purnell received her JD from Harvard Law School, her BA from the

University of Missouri–Kansas City, and studied public policy and economics at the University of California, Berkeley, as a Public Policy and International Affairs Law Fellow. Her writing has been published in *The New York Times, The Atlantic, The Guardian, Cosmopolitan, Harper's Bazaar, Teen Vogue, The Appeal, Truthout, Slate, Boston Review, Huffington Post, Vox,* and *In These Times.*

Andrea J. Ritchie is a Black lesbian immigrant survivor who has been documenting, organizing, advocating, and agitating around policing and criminalization of Black women and girls and trans and gender-nonconforming people for the past three decades.

She is the author of *Invisible No More: Police Violence Against Black Women and Women of Color* (Beacon Press 2017) and coauthor of the African American Policy Forum report *Say Her Name: Resisting Police Brutality Against Black Women*, and *Queer (In)Justice: The Criminalization of LGBT People in the United States* (Beacon Press 2011). She was a member of the national organizing collective of INCITE! Feminists of Color Against Violence, and an editor and contributor to the *Color of Violence: The INCITE! Anthology* (South End Press, 2006; Duke Press, 2012) and the *Law Enforcement Violence Against Women of Color and Trans People of Color* Organizer's Toolkit, released in 2008.

She cofounded the Interrupting Criminalization initiative with Mariame Kaba, with whom she is coauthoring the forthcoming *No More Police: A Case for Abolition* (New Press, 2022). She also cofounded In Our Names Network, a network of more than twenty organizations working to end police violence against Black women and girls and trans and gender-nonconforming people. She is a member of the Movement for Black Lives Policy Table, where she contributed to drafting the Vision for Black Lives, the Reparations Now Toolkit, and the BREATHE Act. In these capacities and through the Community Resource Hub, she works with dozens of groups across the country organizing to divest from policing and secure deep investments in community-based safety strategies that will produce genuine and lasting public safety.

Dylan Rodríguez is an abolitionist teacher, writer, and scholarly activist. He was named to the inaugural class of Freedom Scholars in 2020 and is President of the American Studies Association (2020–2021). He has worked as a Professor at the University of California, Riverside, since 2001, and recently served as the faculty-elected Chair of the UCR Division of the Academic Senate (2016–2020) and Chair of Ethnic Studies (2009–2016).

Rodríguez's work attempts to address the normalized proliferation of logics of anti-Blackness and racial-colonial violence in everyday state, cultural, and social formations. He conceptualizes abolitionist and other forms of movement as part of the historical, collective genius of rebellion, survival, abolition, and radical futurity.

He is the author of three books, most recently *White Reconstruction: Domestic Warfare and the Logic of Racial Genocide* (Fordham University Press, 2021), and is coeditor of *Critical Ethnic Studies: A Reader* (Duke University Press, 2016). Rodríguez can be reached by email at dylanrodriguez73@gmail.com as well as on Twitter (@dylanrodriguez), Instagram (dylanrodriguez73), and Facebook (www.facebook.com/dylanrodriguez73).

kihana miraya ross is originally from the Bay Area. She received her doctorate from UC Berkeley in 2016 and is currently an assistant professor of African American Studies at Northwestern University. Her program of research examines the multiplicity of ways that anti-Blackness is lived by Black students and the ways Black educators and students engage in educational fugitivity to refuse and resist. ross's most recent articles include "Call It What It Is: Anti-Blackness," published in *The New York Times* and "Anti-Blackness in Education and the Possibilities of Redress: Toward Educational Reparations," to be published in *Amerikastudien/American Studies: A Quarterly.* Her forthcoming book-length manuscript explores both the ways Black girls experience anti-Blackness in their larger school and also the numerous ways their production of Black Girl Space facilitates a reimagining of a Black girl identity and a radical Black subjectivity. Her current research project explores the city of Evanston's bold and unprecedented legislative decision organized around the concept of race-based reparations. ross is particularly compelled to understand how the intersection of increased attention to anti-Blackness in education specifically and the injection of new energy into the fight for reparations is informing and inspiring radical dreams and seeding new possibilities and visions of educational justice for Black children.

Stuart Schrader is the author of *Badges Without Borders: How Global Counterinsurgency Transformed American Policing* (University of California Press, 2019). He teaches courses on policing and incarceration, Black internationalism, and social theory at Johns Hopkins University, where he is the Associate Director of the Program in Racism, Immigration, and Citizenship. His writing has also appeared in *The Baffler, N+1, The Nation, The New Republic, The Washington Post, Viewpoint Magazine,* and other venues.

Russell Shoatz III was born on May 7, 1967, to Thelma Christian and Russell Shoatz Jr. He is well-versed in a multitude of healing modalities and restorative justice best practices. Shoatz has lived a life of unique complexities that are the sum total of resilience. He is an administrator, artist, healer, feminist, legal beagle, visionary, carpenter, four-star chef, devoted father, and the list goes on.

His father, a Black Panther, BLA General, and founder of Philadelphia's Black Unity Council, has been imprisoned since 1971. Shoatz championed the campaign to free his father from twenty-five years of solitary confinement by ingeniously acquiring the services of the Abolitionist Law Center and corporate powerhouse Reed Smith. After settlement, Shoatz and his father created programming centered around healthy integration of returning neighbors and creation of Massive Online Open Courses (MOOCS).

He has facilitated and spoken at conferences, festivals, museums, memorials, public schools, and universities, including Yale and Harvard. He has also presented for UNESCO on Internal Truth and Reconciliation (his very own thesis on self-healing). Shoatz is the creator of the multimedia juggernaut *Blu* magazine, which the *New York Times* referred to as "the most informative reading since the *Panther Paper.*" Shoatz curated the 10th annual Oscar Grant Vigil and helped lobbied BART for station name change, mural, and vigil restorative production rights.

Dean Spade has been working to build queer and trans liberation based in racial and economic justice for the past two decades. He's the author of *Normal Life: Administrative Violence, Critical Trans Politics, and the Limits of Law,* the director of the documentary *Pinkwashing Exposed: Seattle Fights Back!* and the creator of the mutual aid toolkit at BigDoorBrigade.com. His latest book, *Mutual Aid: Building Solidarity During This Crisis (and the Next)*, was published by Verso Press in October 2020.

David Stein is a UC President's Postdoctoral Fellow in the department of African American studies at the University of California, Los Angeles. His book, *Fearing Inflation, Inflating Fears: The Civil Rights Struggle for Full Employment and the Rise of the Carceral State, 1929–1986*, is forthcoming from the University of North Carolina Press.

Connie Wun, PhD, is a co-founder of AAPI Women Lead. She also leads national research projects on race, gender, and violence. Dr. Wun is a 2020 Soros Justice Fellow and has received numerous awards, including a National Science Foundation fellowship. Her research has been published in academic journals, anthologies, and online platforms. She is also a former high

school teacher, college educator, and sexual assault counselor.

Acknowledgments

This book is dedicated to all past and present freedom fighters, political prisoners, and radical Black and Brown liberation organizations across the globe that envision a better future—a future free of the white supremacist and anti-Black violence of policing and prisons—and work every day to organize and build better ways of being together in the world.

Like most projects worth undertaking, there are countless people whose quiet yet fierce labor made *Abolition for the People* possible. I am grateful to everyone at Kaepernick Publishing, Ra Vision Media, and Know Your Rights Camp for their fearless dedication to realizing a future where everyone can thrive.

I am equally appreciative of the talented editors at Medium who were instrumental in bringing to fruition the first iteration of this collection in October 2020, as well as Melcher Media and Ingram, our publishing and distribution partners, respectively, for their care and commitment to shepherding this project to completion.

And finally, I'd like to offer special thanks to all writers, editors, and artists who contributed to this project. Without them, what you see before you today would not have been possible.

Colin Kaepernick

Copyright © 2021 by Kaepernick Publishing

www.kaepernickpublishing.com
Printed in the United States of America
ISBN: 978-1-59591-116-2
Library of Congress Cataloguing-in-Publication data is available for this title.

10 9 8 7 6 5 4 3 2 1

Cover art by Emory Douglas
Illustration treatment by Gluekit
Book produced by Melcher Media
Distributed by Two Rivers Distribution
Book adapted from the Abolition for the People digital series on Medium